The Theory of Organisations

The Theory of Organisations

A Sociological Framework

David Silverman
Senior Lecturer in Sociology
University of London Goldsmiths' College

BASIC BOOKS, INC., PUBLISHERS
New York

301.1832
Si3t
77697
Feb. 1972

First American edition: 1971
© 1970 by David Silverman
Library of Congress Catalog Card Number: 72-150812
SBN 465-08438-9
Printed in the United States of America

For Gillie

Preface

I WOULD like to thank Professor Burns of the University of Edinburgh for his extensive comments on an earlier draft and for many suggestions which I have attempted to incorporate into the present text. I am also most grateful to Keith Thurley, Donald MacRae, Stephen Hill, and to Michael Phillipson and David Walsh (both of whom are colleagues at Goldsmiths') for their encouragement and help. The suggestions made by Duncan Gallie helped greatly in my attempt to present ideas with clarity. I owe a special debt of gratitude to my publisher, Alan Hill.

A diagram used in Chapter Seven first appeared in a paper of mine in the *British Journal of Sociology*, with whose permission it is reproduced. The University of London, Central Research Fund provided financial support for some research and I gratefully acknowledge their help.

Contents

Introduction

ALL PUBLISHED works represent in some way the intellectual biographies of their authors. This book is no exception. Several years of teaching courses in Industrial Sociology and Formal Organisations, both in England and the United States, have given me an abiding interest in the complexities of social life in organisations. At the same time, a concern with the potentialities and limitations of general sociological theories has remained with me, nurtured by the insights and questions of colleagues and students. Expressed very simply, by binding one interest to another, this work is an attempt to examine what may be gained by relating a sociological perspective to the study of organisations.

Perhaps to a greater extent than is true in many other areas, the study of organisations has been of interest to members of a wide range of disciplines with rather different perspectives. It is, therefore, unfortunate but hardly surprising that the present state of the field should bear little resemblance to an ordered collection of knowledge. Such attempts at systematisation as have been made have frequently been accompanied by exaggerated claims for the all-inclusiveness of the particular synthesis being presented and have at once been resisted by those committed to alternative theoretical schemes. At an entirely different level, the practice of abstracted empiricism (sometimes explicitly prescriptive in purpose) has made a very strong impression on organisational analysis.

The present work attempts to bring to this situation a reasoned argument deriving from a self-consciously sociological perspective. The nature of this argument may be stated in four propositions: first, that the development of the study of organisations can be shown to have a certain pattern; secondly, that one of the directions in which it now appears to be leading has rather serious limitations; thirdly, that at this stage a statement of an alternative approach making use of certain parts of the literature will prove more fruitful than another attempt at synthesis; and, finally, that such an approach may

I

be usefully derived from an emerging sociological frame of reference. Each of these propositions is implicit in the subsequent analysis and will be briefly examined below.

1. The Pattern

The view that students of organisations have grown more sophisticated over the years in terms both of the questions they ask and the methods that they use to provide answers is hardly surprising or contentious. This view is implicit rather than explicit in the subsequent analysis. It may be useful, therefore, to summarise here some of the more significant areas of advance in the study of organisations:

(a) Organisation analysis in the first few decades of this century began from the questions asked by those in positions of authority, to whom it sought to offer effective and preferably cheap 'solutions' to troubling problems. I think it may safely be claimed that contemporary writers are concerned rather less with 'techniques' and rather more with knowledge; that they have moved away from an over-riding concern with prescription to an attempt to apply the insights of a wide range of disciplines and conceptual schemes in order to gain an understanding of organisational life; and that, consequently, they have asked a broader range of questions and attained more significant answers than was the case in earlier work.

(b) Early work tends to be one-sided in the sense of giving a great deal of emphasis to one aspect of an organisation and tending to ignore its other features. A good example of this is, on the one hand, Taylor's (1913) concentration on formal organisational structure and, on the other hand, Roethlisberger and Dickson's (1939) emphasis on informal social relationships. Once again, later studies have adopted a broader outlook which has illustrated the inter-relatedness of one aspect of an organisation with another and, in so doing, has sought to question the conventional categories used to distinguish various aspects of organisational life.[1]

(c) A concern with limited prescriptive interests can be associated with a failure to grasp the wider social context in which the members of organisations interact. The larger range of interests of contemporary writers has led to a new focus upon the manner in which organisation and environment are related.

(d) The two earlier works already referred to are devoted to studies of industrial organisations. As more sophisticated concepts and methods of study have developed, students of organisations have broadened their range of interest to include the comparative analysis of all organisations, industrial or otherwise. By so doing, they have been able to discard old myths and to introduce fresh insights into an important area of social life.[2]

2. Some Limitations

Enough has probably been said to indicate the areas in which the study of organisations has advanced in the last thirty or forty years. It does not require a determinist view of the course of history, however, to understand that any advance will be associated with the generation of new problems and uncertainties. Paradoxically, such problems have arisen in organisation analysis largely because one comprehensive and sophisticated conceptual scheme has appeared to offer a satisfactory way out of the dead-end towards which earlier work seemed to be leading.

The scheme referred to is the Systems frame of reference. Drawing on the resources of inter-disciplinary General Systems Theory and sociological Structural-Functionalism, this approach begins from the assumption of the inter-relatedness of apparently isolated phenomena which underlay the critique of early organisation theory. It then goes on to examine the needs for survival and adjustment of all systems and to specify the self-regulating mechanisms which systems use to satisfy these needs.

The Systems approach has led to some important theoretical work (cf. Parsons, 1964, and Etzioni, 1961a) and to significant empirical analyses of organisations (cf. Gouldner, 1965). It also has severe logical difficulties. These are discussed in detail in Chapters Two and Three and it will only be necessary to present one example here. To use the concepts of organisational needs and of a system's self-regulating activities in any way other than as a heuristic device is inadmissible since it implies that the power of thought and action may reside in social constructs—this is sometimes known as the problem of reification. On the other hand, it is doubtful whether systems theorists can offer any explanation of social change without resorting to reifications. If my focus is at the level of the system, I am directly drawn to an emphasis in my explanations of change upon the purposive actions of the system which, recognising threats to its existence, seeks to adapt in an adjustive manner.[3]

3. Synthesis or Alternative?

Given the difficulty just discussed (and other difficulties to be presented later), the student of organisations who is interested in placing his work within a broad theoretical context is faced with a choice; he can make use of a revised and logically more satisfactory Systems approach or he can look around for the elements of an alternative theoretical scheme. Important writers, notably Gouldner (1959 and 1967), have argued the case for the former choice. Their argument is impressive and the path which they suggest has the advantage of being relatively well-trodden.

In this book, however, I seek to argue that the time is right for the presentation of a clear-cut alternative to what is fast becoming a Systems orthodoxy. I believe that my argument is strengthened by a recent work on the history of science by Thomas Kuhn (1962). Kuhn rejects the view that science has advanced by the careful accumulation of data leading to an ever more refined picture of the way things are. Instead of this 'cumulative' view, Kuhn argues for the central importance in the history of science of the emergence of new 'paradigms' which define the nature of the reality being considered in original ways. The history of science then becomes the history of competition between different paradigms referring to the universe of entities that do or do not exist, the nature of admissible problems, and the standards by which a problem-solution should be judged adequate. One paradigm succeeds another as it becomes clear that one is incapable of explaining a novel problem.[4]

4. The Alternative

At one time it seemed that the alternative to Systems theory and its sociological offshoot Structural-Functionalism should centre around their alleged concentration on consensus and order and their apparent incapacity to explain conflict situations. European sociologists, notably Dahrendorf (1958) and Rex (1961), aided by one or two American colleagues (cf. Horton, 1964), led the attack on functionalism which they sought to replace with what was termed a conflict model of social structures. In organisation theory, this critique was reflected largely in empirical studies, for instance those by Dalton (1959) and Scott et al. (1963), and only occasionally did it appear in theoretical work, e.g. Krupp (1961). As it became clear, however, that functionalism could handle social conflict (Coser, 1965) and that an analysis of social order is fundamental to any sociological perspective (Cohen, 1968), the conflict/consensus non-debate slowly but surely ground to a halt.

I will argue in this book that the most important area of difference between contemporary sociological theories arises over what is perhaps the most fundamental issue of all: namely, the nature of the social order that sociologists study and of the major characteristics of social reality thereby implied. Following Berger and Luckmann (1966), I will seek to draw out the implications for study and for theory-building of a view of social reality as socially constructed, socially sustained and socially changed. This view is clearly too complex to develop within the confines of a brief introduction and I would suggest that the reader who is mainly interested in the general sociological theory underlying my analysis should turn at once to Chapter Six. I feel obliged, nevertheless, to give one illustration of what this view implies.

As I write this, I have before me a learned journal containing a paper seeking to establish a way to define the goals of an organisation (Gross, 1969). This has been a perennial problem for sociologists, especially since studies have revealed that the original goal of the founder often tends to get displaced (cf. Blau, 1955, and Sills, 1958). So far as I know, however, nobody has considered seriously in what sense organisations have goals or, to put it rather differently, how it is that members of organisations are able to perceive organisational goals towards which they orient their actions. To answer this question one might examine how organisational goals arise as symbols to legitimate the actions of certain actors in the eyes of others. Viewed in this light, then, goals may be placed in the category of cultural objects which members use to make their actions accountable.

For our present purpose, however, the answer to the question is less significant than that the question should be asked at all. I would argue that it only arises within a frame of reference which recognises that the bases of everyday life are problematic: I call this an 'Action' frame of reference. While social action presents a *routine* character, it is in fact socially *accomplished*, i.e. dependent on a series of unstated assumptions, accepted and rejected courses of action. As Goffman (1959) has so clearly shown, definitions of reality are the accomplishments of actors engaged in a co-operative task. Yet the work of many sociologists reflects the everyday picture of the social world, accepting its non-problematic nature and being prepared to use the same sort of explanations that are accepted on the commonsense level (i.e. 'what-everybody-knows', as Garfinkel, 1967, puts it).

The reflexive character of many contemporary accounts of organisations is illustrated in their unstated assumptions that organisational goals and rules are, as it were, 'out there' (i.e. exist separately from the actors' definition of the situation), and that it is possible to explain actions by reference to a goal or rule without examining the social process whereby such symbols develop and lose legitimating significance, i.e. the process whereby they are made accountable to members.[5] Considerations of this nature provide the *raison d'être* for this book.

The Structure of the Text

There is practical difficulty involved in combining an historical summary of the development of a subject with the presentation of an original theoretical position. Since summaries of the literature on organisations may be found elsewhere, this work concentrates on outlining what was described earlier as 'a reasoned argument'. As an almost inevitable outcome of this, the choice of material has been highly selective. If important theorists have been omitted, this is because their arguments are not entirely relevant to the point of view expressed here.

The book begins with an examination of some of the problems involved in defining 'organisation' and in distinguishing one 'type' of organisation from another. This is followed by a discussion of the Systems approach, which, as I have just argued, is one of the major conceptual schemes available to the student of organisations. Chapters Two to Five are variations around a Systems theme: Chapter Two looks at some of the broad assumptions of the approach, while the next three chapters deal respectively with Structural-Functionalism, Organisational Psychology and Socio-Technical Systems—the most important representatives of this approach in organisational analysis.

Chapter Six provides the logical contrast with Chapter Two by setting out the central assumptions of what I have called an Action frame of reference. Once again, the next three chapters are used to expound the approach: Chapter Seven examines its implications for the study of organisations and Chapters Eight and Nine review some of the literature which has revealed the potentialities of the approach in organisational analysis. The concluding chapter, Chapter Ten, reviews some of the earlier arguments and takes up some of the methodological implications of an action analysis.

REFERENCES

1. The formal/informal dichotomy is now largely discredited among contemporary organisation theorists; see Gouldner (1959) and Etzioni (1960).
2. Despite their different avowed aims, for instance, it may well be that mental hospitals, prisons, and army barracks have important characteristics in common; cf. Goffman (1968).
3. Cohen (1968) stresses that the least convincing aspect of the Systems approach lies in its inability to explain change as it arises not from system needs but from the interaction of motivated actors.
4. On the question whether the approach that I suggest is an alternative to Systems theory or complements it, see the concluding section of Chapter Six.
5. For a discussion of the literature on organisations in these terms, see Chapters Eight and Nine.

1

Organisations: Problems of Definition

IT IS a basic tenet of sociology that an organised pattern can be discerned in all social life. Further, sociologists of many theoretical persuasions would be inclined to agree that a certain order in any social relationship is necessary so that the participants themselves may make sense of each other's actions.[1] Language provides a key to the order which we perceive to exist in the everyday social world. Through language we have a predefined set of categories to use in comprehending the commonsense world. Through language we are able to define ourselves and to direct our actions towards the comprehensible acts of other men, i.e. we are able to think and to act *socially*.

Sociologists are concerned with the organisation (or structure) of forms of language and their relationship to social life.[2] In addition, they consider such problems as the organisation of families, communities and political systems. Yet the theory of *organisations* is traditionally concerned only with certain types of organised social life.

Partly for convenience and partly on the basis of empirical observation, it has become normal practice to distinguish *formal* (or complex) organisations from what is called *social* organisation.[3] Formal organisations, in the words of a recent text, have 'been established for the explicit purpose of achieving certain goals', and possess both rules (designed to anticipate, and to shape, behaviour in the direction of these goals) and 'a formal status structure with clearly marked lines of communication and authority'.[4] Where social life is carried on without a framework of explicit goals or rules which define a formal status structure, it is usually thought more appropriate to use the term 'social organisation'.[5] Armies, business enterprises and churches are, therefore, quite different from families,

8

friendship groups and communities.[6] We shall now examine briefly the arguments supporting this assertion.

The Problems with a Definition in Terms of Goals

The attribution of goals to certain types of organisation occurs in everyday speech and is reflected in the dictionary definition of organisation as, among other things, a 'systematic arrangement for a definite purpose'.[7] Much sociological analysis has followed this lead, suggesting that formal organisations have 'objectives which are explicit, limited and announced' (Udy, 1965, p. 678), and are structured so as to attain 'a particular type of goal' (Parsons, 1964) or 'a recognised, limited goal' (Firth, 1964). The advantage of considering organisations in this manner lies not so much in its appeal to commonsense (indeed the commonsense view of the nature of the goal of a particular organisation is often rejected by such writers) but in the way in which it provides a referent by which to judge the 'health' of the system in comparison to others. The reasons why any one organisation is or is not attaining its goal may then be explained and organisational structures classified according to their degree of success.

The first difficulty with this argument is that to say that an organisation has a 'goal' may be to involve oneself in some of the difficulties associated with reification—that is, with the attribution of concrete reality, particularly the power of thought and action, to social constructs. We can ask an individual about his goals or purposes but it is difficult to approach an organisation in the same way. It seems doubtful whether it is legitimate to conceive of an organisation as having a goal except where there is an ongoing consensus between the members of the organisation about the purposes of their interaction.[8]

This problem will become clearer as we examine the attempts that have been made to identify the goal(s) of particular organisations. Four principal methods have been used:

1. The *original* stated goal of the organisation has been employed. This has the advantage that when an organisation is established there is normally some formal written statement made about its intended purposes. Thus a radical

political party may make some reference in its charter to the goal of 'changing society'. Sometimes such a goal may be achieved.[9] More commonly, the desire to obtain power may make the leadership falter in its attachment to social change. When a means used to obtain a goal becomes more important than the goal itself, a concentration of attention on an organisational charter may be misleading. Moreover, this phenomenon of the displacement of goals is by no means confined to political organisations.[10]

2. In order to overcome this difficulty, it has been suggested that the *current* goals of the leadership of an organisation might be established. Thus Etzioni (1961b) maintains that 'the legitimate primary orientation' of an organisation can be ascertained from the people currently in positions of authority. This assumes, however, an identity between what top people tell us and the goals that are actually being pursued within an organisation. It overlooks the interest which men may have in concealing their activities from an outside observer and directs our attention away from 'non-legitimate' primary and secondary orientations. At best, this method would tell us something about the goals of a certain group; it would hardly define for us the goal(s) of the organisation.

3. Miller and Rice (1967) argue that the leaders of an enterprise may define its goal in an inappropriate way. It is far better for the observer to '*infer*' what they call the 'primary task' of an organisation through an examination of the behaviour of its various parts. In particular, one should concentrate upon the relationship between an organisation and its environment. Organisations must obtain resources from the wider society, seek to convert these in certain ways, and obtain some sort of market for their 'output'. By observing the input–output process, one can establish the goal of an organisation, or rather the needs it must satisfy in order to survive and to adapt successfully.[11] However, since such needs are often hidden from the members of the organisation themselves, such an approach lays itself open to the charge of reification. The method is further complicated by the possibility that, because there is no certainty over the nature of survival or death as used to refer to social inter-

action, different observers may infer different goals, needs, or primary tasks.

4. Simon (1964), while accepting many of these criticisms, believes that organisational goals may be established through an ingenious if complex method. Men usually define and judge actions by referring to a set of requirements or constraints rather than to a single goal. Simon gives the example of bricklayers who, when asked what they are doing, might equally well say 'laying bricks', 'building a wall', or 'helping to build a cathedral'. When dealing with men in organisations it is useful to view the constraints which are experienced by the organisational decision-maker as the goal(s) of the organisation. Simon warns us, however, that he is referring here only to those constraints that arise within an organisational *role* and not to the constraints generated by the *personal* motivations of the decision-maker. It is not normally an obligation of an employee to seek promotion but he is usually required to produce a given amount or to give a certain service to a client. When the series of role-requirements that govern the behaviour of organisational members is established, we may speak of the organisational goal. However, as Simon himself recognises, the distinction between personal and organisational goals is difficult to maintain in practice. In many ways it reminds one of earlier attempts to distinguish between formal and informal behaviour in organisations. As has been largely true in the latter case, later researchers may find it more useful to drop such distinctions altogether.

Problems with a Definition in Terms of Formality of Social Relations

The difficulties involved in ascertaining the goals of organisations have led some writers to concentrate upon the supposedly high formality of their internal social relationships. Following on Weber's (1964) characterisation of the ideal-typical features of bureaucracies (a clearly defined hierarchy where office-holders have very specific functions and apply universalistic rules in a spirit of formalistic impersonality), they have stressed the consciously organised pattern of relations within formal organisations. Among many others, this is true of Blau and

Scott (1963), whose definition of formal organisation was given at the beginning of this discussion, Firth (1964), for whom '. . . organisation implies a systematic ordering of positions and duties which defines a chain of command' (p. 60), and March and Simon (1958), who refer to explicit, stable roles which make for a high degree of predictability and co-ordination in organisational behaviour (p. 89 *passim*). However, as all post-Weberian studies have demonstrated, many organisations have no clear hierarchy of authority (Burns and Stalker, 1961); officials can have very diffuse functions (Gouldner, 1954) and act in a far from impersonal manner (Crozier, 1964).[12]

It is true, nevertheless, that families and friendship groups possess very few of these characteristics; even if there is an authority hierarchy in the family it is qualitatively different. The problem can perhaps be resolved by dropping the simple formal/social dichotomy and replacing it by a continuum with formal organisations tending to cluster on one side and social organisation on the other.

Bates: Definition by Type of Integration

A further attempt to establish the defining features of formal organisations is to be found in a paper by Bates (1960). He argues that social systems may be distinguished from one another in terms of their relative internal specialisation and goal-consensus. This will, in turn, influence the type of relationships that come to predominate within them and thereby the process through which they are integrated or unified. Communities, which are non-specialised and in which actors are oriented towards different goals, are unified primarily by *conjunctive* relationships. By this is meant that their members find that, in order to attain their private goals, they must act in conjunction with others. The system is held together by the process of bargaining between individuals wanting to pursue different goals. Formal organisations, on the other hand, are more specialised and their members may be thought to pursue the same general goals. They are integrated mainly by *reciprocal* relationships in which the action of one person implies and requires a certain action by the other.[13]

The neatness of Bates's solution contains within it, unfortunately, the seeds of further difficulties. His conjunctive and reciprocal relationships bear a very strong resemblance to Durkheim's much earlier concepts: organic and mechanical solidarity. But, while the goal-consensus implied in the latter may not be too much of a distortion of the nature of the simple societies to which it was meant to apply, it is at least problematic whether the same assumption may be made about prisons, factories, hospitals and so on. Integration through reciprocal relationships may not be a particularly useful distinguishing characteristic of such organisations. Indeed, Selznick's (1949) study of the process of co-optation of elements opposed to the interests of certain members of an organisation, and Cyert and March's (1963) work on the 'quasi-resolution of conflict' within an 'organisational coalition', suggests that conjunctive, rather than reciprocal, relationships may be the more typical. One final point: Bates's argument rests on the assumptions of the specificity of goals and the formality of relations within organisations. As pointed out earlier, these are problematic.

Synthesis: the Distinguishing Characteristics of Organisations

This might appear to suggest that each supposedly unique characteristic of formal organisations presents a misleading picture of their nature. Nevertheless, one ought not to dismiss the commonsense use of language which distinguishes quite clearly between 'organisations' (I.C.I., the police) and 'family', 'friends', etc. There is a powerful argument that boundaries of this type, which delineate one type of social form from another, must be drawn if we are to advance in the direction of those 'theories of the middle-range' that Merton (1949) believes to be fundamental to contemporary sociological analysis. Moreover, to the extent that people orient themselves differently towards organisations and so behave in a distinct manner within them, then it is useful to distinguish organisations from other social institutions.

It seems to me that an ideal type of formal organisation (which I shall now refer to simply as 'organisation') should stress at least three distinguishing features. These incorporate the elements of truth in the previous discussions.

1. Organisations, unlike other social arrangements, arise at

an ascertainable point in time. They are easier to perceive as artefacts, consciously established to serve certain purposes which are generally stated at the time. Their founder(s) further provide them with a set of rules which generally lay down clear lines of authority and communication with the intention of ensuring that these purposes may most readily be attained (this fits in with the views of Blau and Scott, 1963, and Stinchcombe, 1965).[14] The displacement of goals through time, which often takes the form of a rule designed to attain an end becoming for certain members the end in itself (Michels, 1949; Merton, 1949; Blau, 1955), means that the original purpose of an organisation has limited value in explaining the current goals of its members or the nature of their interaction. It is likely to be of most importance as a legitimating symbol to which lip-service is paid as a means of simulating a consensus when pursuing a sectional end. Thus an attempt is made to forestall potential opposition by maintaining that a particular action is 'for the good of the organisation' (Burns, 1961; Simon, 1957; Biddle, 1964).[15]

2. As artefacts, organisations will be characterised by a patterning of relationships which is less taken-for-granted by the participants who seek to co-ordinate and to control.

3. It follows that a relatively great amount of attention will be paid in organisations to the discussion and execution of planned changes in social relations, and in the 'rules of the game' upon which they are based. There may be, it is true, discussion about the 'best' structure of the family in contemporary societies. It is more likely, however, that this matter will be raised as a general issue of social policy and of ethical standards rather than as a regular topic of conversation in the family circle.

Typologies of Organisations

It has been argued that the dividing line between many organisations and other social institutions is less than clear. If there is not to be a simple dichotomy between formal and social organisation, it becomes particularly necessary to distinguish various types of formal organisation.

Moreover, it is clear that most significant statements about organisations (or, indeed, about any phenomenon) presume comparative study. What happens at a plant of Ford Motor Company may be put into perspective if we contrast it with British Leyland Motors, while entirely new vistas may emerge if both are compared with what we know about social life in, say, a charitable association or a prison. To make this possible, it is necessary first to devise an analytical framework by means of which a study of one organisation may be related to that of another. One procedure is the construction of what Burns (1967) calls 'a comprehensive classificatory scheme'. This involves the development of a system of categories into which research data from different organisations may be fitted. While such a scheme needs to be logical, its most important characteristic should be comprehensiveness. Burns argues one must reject attempts to build exhaustive catalogues of variables from research findings or from what amounts to commonsense opinion. They tend to be unwieldy and fail to distinguish analytically separable processes. Instead, he offers a comprehensive scheme of his own which moves from higher to lower levels of generality, from the relationship of the organisation as a whole to the environment down to the involvement of individuals in the organisation and their behaviour.[16] According to this method: 'The objects for classification are not organisations or parts or attributes of organisations but analytical concepts and frames of reference within which methodological procedures can be designed and comparative studies usefully made' (p. 127).

The most immediate purpose of such schemes is descriptive. Typologies of organisations, on the other hand, are less modest and much more directly concerned with explanation and prediction. Often based on a variable which, to the writer concerned, seems to characterise organisations (e.g. technology, authority structure or specific function), a typology is developed which distinguishes different organisations in terms of their relation to this variable. Implicit in this is the hypothesis that organisations with, for instance, Technology A, Authority Structure B or Function C will differ (in predictable ways) from those with Technology X, Authority Structure Y or Function Z.

The range of variables used to construct typologies has been very large. Nevertheless, it is possible to detect a certain pattern among the different analyses. Some typologies concentrate on one aspect of the social relationships *within* organisations and use this to explain the other features of the organisation and sometimes also the nature of its relations to the outside world. Others make use of the relationship of the organisation as a whole to its *environment* and seek to explain through it the typical processes and problems that arise in the organisation itself. This type may be further distinguished by whether the independent variable used is the influence of the environment on the organisation (input) or the organisation's contribution to the environment (output). These distinctions are hardly clear-cut or all-embracing. Their advantage is that they reveal, as will be seen, the nature of the theoretical models which underlie the construction of typologies and thus allow more systematic discussion of their relative uses and limitations.

We shall now turn to some examples of each variety of typology.

1. *Environment-Input Typologies.* In another paper, Burns (1966) has distinguished between typologies which stress technology and those which stress the rate of environmental change. Both, however, fit into the environment-input category, since they use external pressures to explain organisational form.

Woodward (1958 and 1965) has distinguished production systems along a continuum of technical complexity. Unit (or small batch), mass and process production are each associated with an appropriate form of organisational structure: mass production produces a highly bureaucratic organisation, while the other two tend to have less clearly defined role-systems and make greater use of expert knowledge in meeting problems. The relationship is explained on the basis of the 'situational demands' generated by different technologies which make themselves felt on informal relationships as much as on the formal structure.[17] Knowledge of these demands makes it possible to predict not only organisational form but the behaviour of managers and workers and even the state of industrial relations.

The rate of environmental change has been used as a basis for a typology by both Burns and Stalker (1961) and Emery and Trist (1965). According to the former, the technical and market situation of an organisation may be relatively stable, or it may change in a relatively predictable or unpredictable manner. Mechanistic structures, characterised by a hierarchy of positions with highly defined functions, tend to emerge in a stable environment. In a changing or unstable environment, the prevailing organisational form involves a continual re-definition of roles and co-ordination is achieved by continual meetings between managers and a great deal of lateral com-munication. This form is called organic. Emery and Trist reach much the same conclusion but distinguish between four types of environment ('placid randomised', 'placid clustered', 'disturbed reactive' and 'turbulent' fields) in terms of their rate of change and whether its direction is predictable. Finally, Hage (1965) has suggested that organisations which face frequent threats to their continued existence, for instance military organisations, are likely to respond to their environment by means of a highly mechanistic, centralised structure.

2. *Environment-Output Typologies.* One of the concerns of struc-tural functional analysis is to analyse the unintended conse-quences of action for the rest of society. It is hardly surprising, therefore, that a typology in terms of the functions of organisa-tions should be appealing. The form of the organisation is seen as determined by the part it plays for the social system as a whole, rather than by the goals of its members. If the need of the system which it satisfies (adaptation, goal-attainment, integration or pattern-maintenance) can be established, it becomes possible to predict the organisational response—although a full analysis would require knowledge of the relationship of the organisation to its own lower-level systems. An environment-output typology of this nature has been used by Parsons (1965) and Katz and Kahn (1966) and applied to 'integrative' organisations by Scott (1959). Katz and Kahn's typology, for instance, dis-tinguishes organisations by whether they are most important for their productive, maintenance, adaptive or managerial-political functions.

Environment-output typologies are not only used within an explicitly functionalist frame of reference. Blau and Scott's (1964) 'who benefits' typology is specifically concerned with the nature of the output from an organisation. Four types of organisation are distinguished, each with a different 'prime beneficiary': 'mutual-benefit associations' (where the prime beneficiary is the membership), 'business concerns' (owners), 'service organisations' (clients), and 'commonweal associations' (the general public).

The general difficulty in employing environment-output typologies lies in establishing the precise nature of the output of any organisation when the output is more abstract than, say, the production of goods and the provision of services. This comes to light most clearly in Blau and Scott's formulation. They see no difficulty in establishing the prime beneficiary of any organisation because its purposes, and the groups that it exists to serve, will be clearly defined. But this assumes that its goals are 'explicit, stable and coherent' and tends to 'forget that organisational goals are often, indeed usually, in dispute' (Burns, 1967, pp. 122–3). Once this is realised, the definition of the prime beneficiary becomes problematic. Indeed, there are at least five possible ways of determining who he is: who is perceived by the members of an organisation to benefit most in practice; who they think should legitimately benefit; who is perceived by the general public as benefiting/deserving to benefit; and who may be said by an observer to benefit most.

A limitation of all the attempts so far considered to distinguish organisations by the nature of their relationship with the environment is that the environment is seen primarily as a source of resources and problems for the organisation taken as a whole. Blau and Scott, for instance, use their typology in order to suggest that 'special problems are associated with each type (of organisation)', p. 43. These problems have to be met by specific organisational forms and by what Thompson and McEwen (1958) call 'procedures for gaining support from the organisational environment'—according to them these include competition with other organisations, bargaining, co-optation and coalition. The concern is, therefore, with efficiency; the analysis centres on the degree of 'fit' between organisational requirements and environmental characteristics. Such an approach arises from within the Systems Model. It also, although this is incidental, identifies the interests of sociology with those of management, which is very much concerned with the efficient running of organisations in relationship to changing markets and so on. The 'happy coincidence', as Lawrence and Lorsch (1967) put it, between the concerns of the sociologist and the executive is thus historically highly specific.

Much research on organisations concentrates then on the problems of efficiency and effectiveness. Price (1968), in a summary of the literature, reports, for instance, that they are 'classical' problems, 'highly researched' and 'commonly implied' in the literature (p. 3). The argument against this concentration of interest is simply that these are generally not very interesting sociological problems, at least as usually conceived. While it may be possible to explain the degree to which an organisation is 'efficient', this will not help in understanding why its structure is as it is, unless we make the teleological assumption that organisations take the form that they do as a response to their needs, one of which is presumably 'efficiency'.[18] From this viewpoint, they are only prevented from attaining full efficiency by a recalcitrant environment and personnel.

It is possible, nevertheless, to view the environment as a source of meanings for the members of organisations. The problem is then not efficiency but the manner in which the 'stock of knowledge' (Schutz, 1964) in a society impinges on organisational behaviour and is modified by it. Different meaning-structures may then be identified as a means of explaining and predicting the prevailing expectations within an organisation. The work of Bendix (1959) has already been referred to in this respect. Stinchcombe (1965) has also shown how organisations which are created at different periods tend to have certain common characteristics, while the way in which authority is legitimated within them may influence class relations in the wider society. The most obvious example of this type of study is, however, to be found in the work of Weber (1948 and 1964). His ideal-types of traditional, charismatic and rational-legal types of authority show the ways in which organisational behaviour derives from meaning-structures typical of certain societies, and prepare the ground for systematic historical study of different organisational forms.

3. *Typologies Based on Intra-Organisational Factors.* As has already been noted, it is possible to distinguish organisations by factors

operating within the organisation itself rather than in terms of the relationship between organisation and environment. Environment-input typologies have been mainly concerned with identifying the problems to which organisations must adapt if they are to survive and flourish. Typologies based on intra-organisational factors have not been associated to the same extent with this System model. They have not involved the positivist assumption that the objective attributes of factors outside the organisation determine the behaviour of its participants, and have been less immediately concerned with the problems of the system. However, it would be foolish to suggest that any one variety of typology is *necessarily* more associated with the System or Action model. The environment can be shown as the source of meanings through which members of organisations define their actions, just as an analysis in terms of intra-organisational factors can seek fruitfully to establish the patterns of interaction which are associated with particular types of meaning-structure specific to the organisation. On the other hand, the pattern of interaction can be considered as the outcome of impersonal organisational forces which directly affect the behaviour of those concerned. The manner in which Etzioni (1961a) handles his typology in terms of compliance provides an example of this last case.

The members of organisations, according to Etzioni, may be involved in different ways. Calculative involvement implies a commitment of low intensity to the formal goals of the organisation and an emphasis on the material rewards deriving from the association with it. People who are committed to these goals are morally involved, while those with a negative commitment of high intensity have an alienative involvement. All three types of involvement reflect different forms of compliance with the power exercised by a superordinate person or group. Power, in turn, is found in three forms: coercive, resting on the threat or application of physical sanctions, remunerative, based on control over the allocation of material resources in the form of material rewards, and normative which arises from the allocation and use of symbolic rewards and deprivations. Each type of involvement can co-exist, Etzioni suggests, with the exercise of each form of power. Nevertheless, three types of power and involvement are congruent: coercive-alienative, remunerative-calculative and normative-moral. This is because these forms of compliance-structure are more 'effective' than non-congruent types. This produces a 'strain' in organisations towards such congruence.

Etzioni's analysis is highly suggestive and appears to encompass many important differences in the way in which individuals may define their situation within an organisation and interpret the behaviour of a superior or subordinate. However, by explaining congruence in terms of a supposed dynamic towards greater efficiency, he retreats towards a positivist, System form of explanation. By not answering the question, as Burns (1967) puts it, of 'for whom and for what are organisations to be reckoned effective?' (p. 121), he makes us suspect that his analysis is in terms of an unquestioned system goal. This reliance on explanations in terms of impersonal processes and 'given' goals puts him into still further difficulties if we take up the problem of how organisations become incongruent in the first place. It is hardly surprising, therefore, that Burns is able to accuse Etzioni of an 'exercise in higher tautology' (ibid.).

Analysis which focuses on compliance-structures is not very far removed from the Barnard (1938) and Simon (1957) conception of an inducement-contribution balance. This seeks to explain the contribution that members of an organisation make in terms of the inducements that they are offered. These inducements, in turn, derive from the contributions of others. This has been taken up by Clark and Wilson (1961) who have constructed a typology of organisation in terms of the major incentive which is offered to members and hence the rewards that they derive from their involvement. Utilitarian organisations offer primarily material incentives, solidary organisations provide intangible rewards (such as the opportunity to associate with like-minded people), while purposive organisations offer their members the satisfaction that is to be gained in the attainment of the organisation's stated end.

While Clark and Wilson are inclined to think in terms of organisations themselves taking actions, their analysis has something to offer from an Action perspective. It is clear, for instance, that the behaviour of members of an organisation towards each other will be influenced by the nature of their involvement. Thus the action of a trade union leader will be interpreted in different terms than will apply, say, to a manager, while each will legitimate his behaviour by means of a separate set of symbols. Again, as Clark and Wilson hint, incentive systems become modified if the original meaning of involvement changes or if expectations are no longer validated. At times which are seen as crises affecting everyone, people, especially those with a moral involvement, may become more concerned with satisfactions to be derived from the attainment of the formal end of the organisation.

The work of Goffman (1968) represents the most fruitful attempt so far to apply an Action perspective to the development of a typology based on intra-organisational factors. Goffman establishes the category of 'total institution' to distinguish organisations in which the prevailing definitions of the situation derive from within the organisation itself. Other meanings are consciously excluded by those in authority, if they are not already limited by the inmates' isolation from the outside world. He then goes on to show how the pattern of interaction within such institutions has certain recurring features peculiar to them. Members are cleansed of their outside identities by having to undergo a mortifying process during which their personal possessions are almost entirely removed, they are made to wear a uniform or to answer only to a number. They often react to this situation by intransigence or withdrawal, both of which are interpreted, at least in hospitals or prisons, as signs of the disease or criminality of those concerned. Long periods of stay, however, are more likely to generate the adaptations of colonisation (establishing an identity within the organisation which is more important than previous identities in society) or conversion (appearing to accept the staff view about oneself). Both these adaptations allow the inmate to 'make-do' by working the system to his advantage and, thereby, increasing his power and status relative to other inmates and even to staff members.

Goffman's study reveals the insights that may be derived by linking the behaviour of members of organisations to the sets of meanings which operate in certain social contexts. It is these, rather than the demands made upon organisations by their environment or upon men by machines, which provide a satisfactory explanation of human action. Had Goffman sought to distinguish organisations by means of the more conventional categories, it is unlikely that he would have produced the insights he gains by a classification which groups together organisations which apparently perform very different functions and have (at least according to Blau and Scott) entirely separate prime beneficiaries.[19] But Goffman's scheme only allows us, at present, to make use of the categories of 'total' and, presumably, 'non-total' institutions. What is clearly required now is an analysis of the range of meaning-structures arising within both types of institution.

Conclusions

In this chapter I have attempted to point out some of the difficulties that arise in establishing 'organisations' as a legitimate area for special study. I went on to consider some of the issues that arise when one seeks to develop organisational 'types' and to compare one with another.

Since the view of the defining characteristics of an organisation which was offered was not totally different from that presented in other discussions, it might have seemed that the first part of the chapter was merely of formal value—in the sense that any academic debate begins by defining its terms. However, the intention behind it was rather broader. By clarifying the status of the term 'organisation', certain important issues involved in the construction of a theory become more apparent. First, by illustrating the tenuous nature of the distinction between organisations and other social arrangements, it suggests that the former may not be cut off from society and viewed as 'closed' systems. Any theory of organisations must specify the nature of their relationships with the wider society. Secondly, if similar processes may arise both in organisations and in other social institutions, then this suggests the inseparability of theories of organisations from theories of society and the need to pay attention to the theoretical orientations available from the study of the latter.

One such orientation stresses the way in which social relations are shaped by the needs of social systems. Such a Systems perspective is becoming increasingly important in organisational analysis and will be examined in Chapter Two.

REFERENCES

1. A problem may seem to arise with collective behaviour which is often defined by its unstructured character. Nevertheless even in such a case men will be subjectively aware of a degree of order in the actions of other men.

2. See especially Duncan (1968) for an examination of the links between language and social order.

3. Both Udy (1965) and Simon (1957) move from wider to more limited definitions of an organisation. Simon begins by noting that: 'In the pages of this book, the term organisation refers to the complex pattern of communications and other relations in a group of human beings. . . . The sociologist calls this pattern a "role system" ' (p. 72), but a little later he is defining administrative organisations as 'systems of co-operative behaviour' (ibid.).

4. Blau and Scott (1963), pp. 1 and 14.

5. Firth (1964) distinguishes social structure from social organisation which is the process rather than the form of social action. It consists of: '. . . the working arrangements of society' and reflects 'the processes of ordering of action and of relations in reference to given social ends . . .' (p. 45).

6. An additional argument to support this distinction, by Bates (1960), is discussed below.

7. S.O.E.D.

8. Etzioni (1960) has used this type of argument to support the analysis of organisations in terms of a 'System' rather than 'Goal' Model—see Chapter One. A clever defence of the attribution of goals and actions to organisations by Haworth (1959) is considered in the same chapter.

9. Sills (1958) examines the consequences of goal-attainment for the future behaviour of the members of a charitable organisation.

10. Cf. Blau (1955) who pointed out how agents in an employment agency displaced the goal of the agency when their security was threatened.

11. This is very similar to the views of Parsons (1964), Katz and Kahn (1966) and Gross (1969). The open-systems perspective which they share is discussed in Chapter Two.

12. This, of course, does not detract from the validity of the ideal-type as a tool of investigation. The concentration of organisation theorists upon specificity of role-expectations within formal organisations has been criticised by Hickson (1966).

13. Bates also discusses institutions which he considers as socio-

logical constructs; the 'correlative' relationships within them reflect the separate and unrelated actions of the parts which, nevertheless, may be regarded as serving the same purpose and/or related to the same functional requisite, e.g. 'culture'.

14. According to Stinchcombe, organisations are characterised by a 'set of stable social relations deliberately created, with the explicit intention of continuously accomplishing some specific goals or purposes' (p. 142).

15. Biddle suggests that the *purpose* of an organisation refers to 'a task for the organisation in terms of which other tasks are justified' (p. 163) and argues that the term *goal* should be reserved for the intentions of the actors themselves and for the intentions they attribute to others; again, Simon points out that members of an organisation are expected to 'orient their behaviour with respect to certain goals that are taken as "organisational objectives" ' (pp. 72–3).

16. His 'list of analytic categories' comprises: '1) Relationships between the organisation and its environment; 2) Definitions of tasks and division of labour; 3) Communication system; 4) Authority structure; 5) Systems of engagement and rewards; 6) Involvement (responsibility); 7) Definition of individual social identities in organisation settings' (1967, pp. 130–1).

17. '. . . although "situational demands" did not determine formal organisation', she notes, 'they appeared to have considerable influence on spontaneous or informal development. In a number of firms formal organisation did not satisfy "situational demands" adequately, while informal organisation did' (Woodward, 1958, p. 38).

18. 'Propositions involving efficiency as a dependent variable', Mayntz argues, 'can explain why a certain organisation is or is not efficient but hardly why its structure and internal processes are as they are' (1964, p. 112).

19. According to Blau and Scott (1963), hospitals, as 'service organisations', have different problems from prisons, which are to be regarded as 'commonweal associations' (pp. 43–58).

2

Organisations as Systems

THE QUESTIONS that are first asked about a certain aspect of
social life usually reflect the concerns of those who are directly
involved with it. Almost without exception, such people are in
positions of authority. Early studies of, say, poverty or crime,
thus tend to concentrate on immediate causes and to look for
possible solutions. As social scientists bring to bear on such
areas a more complex conceptual apparatus, they often perceive
that 'solutions' are not readily available and that problems
themselves can be defined in rather different terms.[1] The study
of economic organisations provides a good example of this type
of process.

One of the earliest attempts to examine business enterprises,
at the beginning of the twentieth century, took 'efficiency' as
its problem and concentrated on explaining why organisations
were or were not satisfying their goals. The content of its advice
to managers centred around areas which were readily comprehensible to them—the formal organisational structure and the
utilisation of human and mechanical resources.[2] At about the
same period, Max Weber's sociological ideal (or pure) type
of bureaucracy stressed the contribution to efficiency of the
rational, formally instituted aspects of organisation. Although
Weber was more concerned to offer a clear-cut tool for analysis
than to deny the empirical importance of informal behaviour,
later social scientists grew dissatisfied with what appeared to be
a concentration upon formal structures and organisational
goals—the Rational or Goal model of organisations.[3] Influenced by the discovery of the unconscious (Freud) and of non-
rational motives (Pareto), the Human Relationists proposed
that Man's social needs were rarely satisfied by formal structures. Man's major allegiance was to the primary groups of
friends or family. It followed that most attention should be

paid to informal activities and to the factors influencing the formation and character of workgroups.

To later students of organisation, it seemed illogical, however, to replace one distorted emphasis with another. Neither the formal nor the informal aspects of organisations appeared to demand prior attention. A dilemma about the future course of research was eventually resolved by referring to two parallel tendencies in social thought. First, functionalism, an increasingly important perspective in sociology, stressed the similarities between biological and social structures. Social institutions, in much the same way as organisms, have needs of survival and adaptation to their environment which they satisfy by means of a particular pattern of interdependence between their parts. Viewed as Natural Systems, organisations are composed of an inter-related series of processes: it is the inter-relationship and the process, rather than one or another separate aspect, which should constitute the object of study.[4] Secondly, General Systems Theory emphasised the similarity of the processes occurring in many different types of relationship. Whether one is dealing with a machine, an organism or an organisation, it is fruitful to use the idea of a supply of resources ('input'), a conversion process ('throughput'), and the production of an object or objects ('output'). Once again, the way in which the parts are shaped by the process as a whole is emphasised.

Organisations as Systems: Assumptions

It will now be useful to examine some of the main assumptions underlying the view of organisations as systems. These are that organisations are composed of a set of interdependent parts; organisations have needs for survival; and organisations, as systems, behave and take actions.

1. *A set of interdependent parts.* Each part of an organisation contributes and receives something from the whole. The process through which the parts are related should be the main area of study. In this process, both resources and problems are exchanged.[5] This will become clearer if we take a hypothetical example—the relations between a Personnel and a Production

Department in an industrial enterprise. Of course in actual systems analysis one may often examine relationships between analytically separable parts of the organisation, rather than parts defined by the organisation itself.

Let us assume that a strike threatens at our enterprise. By offering an acceptable wage-increase, the Personnel Department is able to avoid the strike. By so doing, it has provided a resource for the Production Department—a contented work-force, for at least the time being. Its output is the input of another department. At the same time, the Personnel Department, through its generosity, may have created a problem for the Sales Department, who now find it difficult to market a product whose price will have to be increased. It may now be necessary to lay off a number of workers. Thus, in turn, the action of the Sales Department constitutes an input into the Personnel Department—a problem which it will have to resolve.

By settling the strike in a particular manner, the action of the Personnel Department has a consequence for the functioning of the organisation as a whole; for other enterprises who share the same market and for the local community who must cope with unemployment. At the same time, in making its decision the Personnel Department will be influenced by these and other institutions to which it is related.

2. *System needs.* Organisations, as social systems, are governed by a series of needs which they must satisfy if they are to survive. Only one of these needs is goal-attainment. Etzioni (1960) has criticised the concentration on an organisation's goals on the grounds that the formal goals of an organisation, to be found in its charter, may never be taken seriously by its members, while informal goals may vary and are difficult to establish. To consider an organisation merely in terms of goal-attainment is to confuse objects that are not on the same level of analysis. An organisation is a social system (a 'real' state, as he puts it), while a goal is a cultural entity (a symbol).[6] This being so, it is far more satisfactory to view an organisation as a system with needs and to examine the extent to which it uses its resources for optimum need-satisfaction.

Etzioni argues that such a perspective is relatively sophisticated for it recognises that goal-attainment is only one of many needs—by being goal-oriented an organisation may fail to meet other functional requirements such as securing the support of its membership. It also allows for the fact that these needs may be met in multiple ways. For Etzioni, moreover, the System Model, by focusing on needs (a property of the organisation itself) rather than upon goals (a property of individuals or groups), avoids the difficulty of viewing organisations from the position of one particular group, usually an elite.[7]

3. *System behaviour.* System theorists believe that it is useful to follow the commonsense practice of attributing actions to organisations themselves as well as to the members of organisations.[8] If systems have needs, then they may also take action to satisfy those needs. If one talks in terms of organisations behaving, however, one runs the risk of attributing human characteristics to social constructs. The most developed defence of the system position against such criticism is to be found in a short paper by Haworth (1959) called, appropriately enough, 'Do Organisations Act?'

Haworth considers what he calls the 'reductionist' assertion that statements about organisational acts are merely groupings of single statements about individual acts. He himself argues that statements about organisational acts ought, at certain times, to be taken literally and that to reduce them in every instance would be to trivialise them. Organisations are sometimes responsible for an act in the sense that it derives from a certain set of social relationships which appear to be independent of the personal qualities of those concerned. This is clearest when an act is repeated many times even though the personnel have changed. One should only attempt to reduce statements about organisations when the personal characteristics of individuals are more important in explaining their behaviour than their formal status. When this is not so, it is meaningful and indeed necessary to talk of 'the organisation' taking the action.

Organisations as Systems: Questions Raised

The different types of statement that are made about organisations often derive from the use of varying perspectives or models. Different models suggest different questions. Three questions seem to predominate in the work of system theorists: the nature of the inter-relation of systems; the contribution that this network of inter-relations makes to the survival or effectiveness of the whole; and the nature of system dynamics.

1. *System relations.* The first task of the system theorist is to determine the nature of the relationships between the assortment of systems and sub-systems that he chooses to distinguish. The concepts of input, throughput and output can be used to trace the flow of tangible and intangible objects (e.g. economic resources and levels of motivation) within the organisation and also between it, other organisations, and the wider society.

2. *System effectiveness.* The system theorist asks how satisfactory any given pattern of relationships is in terms of the needs of the organisation as a whole. Certain processes may, for instance, encourage or inhibit the adaptation of the system to its environment.

Etzioni (1960) suggests that there are two types of System Model that have been used to deal with this question. The Survival Model is concerned with the processes which are necessary for an organisation merely to survive, while the Effectiveness Model also deals with conditions associated with the optimum use of resources. The latter is more useful, he argues, because it encourages consideration of functional alternatives to existing patterns instead of the static, if not tautological, analysis of the Survival Model which comes near to saying that if everything is to be as it is, then everything *has* to be as it is.

3. *System dynamics.* System theorists are divided over the forces which make organisations change and which influence the direction which change takes. According to the more traditional view, the needs of the system as a whole, especially the need for survival, shape the actions of system parts. This is supposed to occur through a 'hidden hand'; as Thompson (1967) puts it, 'spontaneously or naturally' (p. 6). Change occurs from two sources. The system is presumed to evolve as a whole in the direction of greater internal consistency, and to have a spontaneous tendency towards homeostasis—or self-

stabilisation in the face of outside threats to its survival.[9] While parts of the system may not serve the goal (i.e. may be 'dysfunctional'), these will in the long run become modified so as to serve the system or will 'disengage' themselves from it. If neither event occurs the system will 'degenerate'.

Other system theorists, notably Gouldner and Etzioni, have been wary about explaining organisational behaviour in terms of overall system needs. Gouldner (1967), in an important paper, has pointed out how certain parts of systems may be relatively more autonomous than others; the part, therefore, may sometimes determine the whole. Again, the evolutionary assumptions underlying the traditional explanations of system change would be questioned by some system theorists who doubt whether organisations have an inbuilt tendency towards integration and self-maintenance. It may, therefore, be necessary to drop the analogy between an organisation and an organism: organisations may be systems but not necessarily *natural* systems.[10]

Of course if systems are not shaped by their needs and have no internal dynamic, then it becomes difficult to offer a system theory of change. It is hardly surprising, therefore, that so many system theorists should concentrate on the consequences rather than upon the causes of action.[11]

Environment and System

It has already been stated that organisations interact with other social systems. System theorists, however, have paid varying amounts of attention to the environment and have viewed its relationship to organisational behaviour in many ways. Before pointing out, in a concluding section, the nature of an alternative to the systems perspective, it will be necessary to consider the organisational environment in relation to system theory.

In complex industrial societies, where institutions tend to have highly specialised meanings, the expectations attaching to different roles vary considerably and the potential for conflict between them is relatively great. The members of an organisation, for instance, are not defined purely by their organisational roles. The worker is not merely a worker but a father, friend, trade union member, and so on. Any attempt to explain why organisations are as they are must therefore take into account the environment in which they are located. Or, to put it another way, any attempt to understand the pattern of interaction within one role-system must pay attention to the other role-systems in which its members are involved.

An acknowledgment of the importance of the environment could lead to the proposition that, since everything is related to everything else, nothing may be understood without firstly comprehending the whole of which it is a part. As knowledge of the whole presumes certain knowledge of the parts this argument is self-defeating. What is obviously required is to specify the level with which a particular study is concerned and to take factors at a different level as given. (They should be treated as important variables which must be taken into account but not explained.) In practice, guided by their theoretical orientations or by their methodological predispositions, students of organisations have given varying amounts of attention to extra-organisational factors and explained their influence in somewhat different ways. It is possible to distinguish three types of approach which view organisations as closed, partially-open and open systems. Each of these views will now be discussed and their limitations pointed out.

1. *Closed systems*. Extra-organisational factors may, in effect, be ignored by arguing that the hypotheses being tested derive from certain sociological and/or psychological laws which, because they are general in their application (e.g. 'the need to belong to a primary group'), are unaffected by factors external to the organisation. As Wilensky (1957) and Landsberger (1958) have pointed out, this is often the approach favoured in human relations studies which concentrate on the workgroup and treat 'technology' as an external variable (Whyte, 1959).

It is also the rationale behind certain types of 'laboratory' studies which seek consciously to exclude external factors by randomly assigning roles in a fake organisation to a group of available individuals, usually students. Behaviour is then explained as the outcome of psychological forces (e.g. a favourable reaction to being encouraged by a supervisor) which compel those concerned to act in a certain way.[12]

This approach is clearly deficient from a Systems perspective, which is concerned with spelling out the relationships between higher and lower level systems which interact both within and across organisational boundaries. It might be argued, however, that it adds to an understanding of the factors influencing group interaction and thus has a certain usefulness in terms of the Action approach. This argument seems to me to be based on a false premise.

Underlying the closed system view is the positivist assumption that objective factors, detected by the observation of the scientist, exert a direct influence upon human behaviour. Thus what is defined by the observer as expressive supervision or high reward is used to explain the action and motivations of those who are exposed to them. The characteristic feature of social action, however, is that it is motivated. It assigns meanings to situations and to the acts of others and thus the individual reacts to his definition of the situation and not to the observer's. Since it is reasonable to assume that these definitions arise in the course of both intra- *and* extra-organisational interaction, it is generally inadmissible to exclude factors outside the organisation.

2. *Partially-open systems.*[13] This view, while recognising the influence of the environment, argues that it is sometimes best to give prior attention to organisational variables in order to limit the scope of the study. In this case, external factors (e.g. the social background of those concerned, the cultural traditions of the host community) are used only as 'controls' to explain *ex post facto* complexities in the data, while hypotheses derive entirely from internal factors (e.g. technology, organisational rewards).

The research strategy embodied in partially-open systems has the appeal of sophistication—because it considers the environment; and of simplicity—because it deals with it only at the final stage of analysis. It has also been suggested that, because the boundary lines of organisations are quite clearly drawn, it is far easier to exclude external variables until a relatively later stage than would be the case in an analysis of, say, a community or a friendship group.[14] The majority of empirical studies of organisations appear to have followed this analytical framework.

To view an organisation in this way, however, involves a fairly obvious difficulty. To develop hypotheses solely in terms of internal variables, and then only to introduce external variables as a means of reducing inconsistencies in the data, prevents rather than assists an understanding of the processes through which the two are systematically related. Such an understanding can clearly only come from theories and hypotheses which begin from both. The way in which the partially-open systems approach neglects this difficulty and its effect on research design is clearly illustrated in the work of Turner and Lawrence (1965).

The authors develop what they call a 'requisite task attribute' (RTA) index of the physical nature of various factory jobs. They then hypothesise a direct relationship between RTA and worker satisfaction: thus a high RTA job (e.g. one which involved high-content, non-repetitive work) was predicted to produce a satisfied worker, while workers doing low RTA work would be dissatisfied. However, their evidence suggested very little relationship between RTA and satisfaction, while, for certain groups of workers, there was an inverse relationship between the two. Their first reaction is to defend the method and to suggest that people are seeking to mislead them or are afflicted with false consciousness. 'Some workers', they report, 'see their jobs as having higher attributes than the researchers. . . . Is there a sub-population that is systematically *distorting* their perceptions of their jobs?' (p. 67, my italics). They soon have to admit, however, that it is entirely possible that certain workers are actually attracted to 'low content' work.

Once the argument has reached this point, it is obviously no longer possible to restrict one's explanations to purely organisational variables. So, at this late stage, religious affiliation and place of residence are introduced as the determinants of orientation to work. The Protestant Ethic, they suggest, is strongest among workers from small towns and rural areas; among this group the original hypothesis relating the content of work to job satisfaction is supported. 'City' workers, on the other hand, are predominantly Catholic and interested in maximising their immediate economic rewards in exchange for the least complex task. It is among this group that the unexpected inverse relationship is to be found.

Unless subsequent researchers are willing to incorporate consideration of the nature and sources of the subjective meaning of situations into the early stages of a research design, work of this type will tend to lead only to a number of perhaps interesting but unrelated findings; it will contribute little to the development of systematic theories of organisational behaviour.

3. *Open systems.* Both views already discussed embody certain positivist assumptions. For instance, it is argued that organisational structures or the psychological needs of the participants *determine* behaviour. Little attention is given to the purposes of those concerned and to the meanings that they attach to situations. Yet these meanings are the source of action. They are also sustained or modified by interactions which are not merely confined to the organisation concerned. A conception of 'a fair day's work' will typically reflect certain meanings prevailing within the wider society and will influence the response of both management and unions to claims by workers. The open system approach, however, introduces the environment into analysis in order to relate it to the problems of the system as a whole and the explanation of behaviour which it gives, in terms of the 'demands' of the environment, is as positivist as the other two approaches.

Implicit in the conceptualisation of organisations as systems (with system needs and problems) is a direction of attention towards the environment in which the system is located. For if organisations are systems, then so are the institutions and societies of which they are a part. Since a society is a collection of sub-systems of greater or lesser complexity, the functioning of each (as well as the functioning of the whole) depends upon its inter-relationship with the others. Study then should centre on the boundary-exchange of resources between different social systems. The crucial processes of each system now become, in terms of a cybernetic model, input, throughput and output (Katz and Kahn, 1966).

Organisations can now be seen to be dependent for their survival and efficiency upon an exchange of goods and services with their environment. This provides them with a goal (Parsons, 1961) or a primary task (Miller and Rice, 1967), and with resources to obtain this goal, such as land, labour and capital ('input'). It also provides the individual participant with the appropriate motivations. At the same time, each sub-system of society must react by making efficient use of the resources given it ('throughput') and adapting to the problems created by the nature of these resources. The properties of its environment may, for instance, preclude a 'natural coinci-dence' between the attainment of an organisation's primary task and the satisfaction of the sentiments of its members (Miller and Rice). In such a case, a coincidence between the two must be contrived. In reacting to meet such problems, the organisation is able to provide resources for other sub-systems and also to generate other problems that they must solve ('output'). This will, in turn, produce a changed environment ('feedback') with which it must once more deal. Organisational stability and change can now be explained by positing a tendency towards homeostasis which governs the relationship between sub-systems.

The open system position allows the researcher to focus upon easily ascertainable aspects of the environment of an organisa-tion and to predict their likely effects upon organisational structure. He can then proceed to associate different organisa-tional forms with, for instance, type of technology (Woodward, 1965) or rate of market change (Emery and Trist, 1965; Burns and Stalker, 1961; Lawrence and Lorsch, 1967). What passes between organisations and society is, therefore, clearly defined (resources and problems) and their relationship takes the form it does because both sides are concrete entities with needs to satisfy which are empirically quite distinguishable from the motives of individuals (who are themselves constrained by these needs).

The limitations of this perspective become clear when it is asked why, if organisations 'must' adapt to their environment, they do so, if at all, at such greatly varying rates? The answer that is normally given is that one of the components of the system, in addition to technology and the formal structure, is the predispositions of the members. 'The tools of action' of the organisation (its members) may be 'recalcitrant' and resist taking what would be, from the system's point of view, effective action (Selznick, 1949). Their predispositions derive from the cultural system of the society and are another input into the organisation which must be taken into account.

It may also be argued, however, that the environment, *as perceived by the observer*, never exerts this sort of influence on patterns of interaction within organisations. The explanation of why people act as they do may lie not in a combination of 'objective' and 'subjective' factors, but in a network of meanings which constitute a 'world-taken-for-granted' (Schutz, 1964) by the participants. Indeed, 'objective' factors, such as technology and market structure, are literally meaningful only in terms of the sense that is attached to them by those who are concerned and the end to which they are related. This resolves the question of the differential adaptation of organisations to their environment. Organisations do not react to their environment, their members do. People act in terms of their own and not the observer's definition of the situation. The members of different organisations may attach separate meanings to what has occurred and hence react in different ways. This point has been made most clearly by Weber (1964) and it is worth quoting him at length. 'Every artifact, such as for example a machine,' he writes, 'can be understood only in terms of the meaning which its production and use have had or will have for human action; a meaning which may derive from a relation to exceedingly various purposes. Without reference to this meaning such an object remains wholly unintelligible. That which is intelligible or understandable about it is thus its relation to human action in the role either of means or of end; a relation of which the actor or actors can be said to have been aware and to which their action has been oriented. Only in terms of such categories is it possible to "understand" objects of this kind' (p. 93).

It follows from this argument that the rest of society is related to what happens in organisations in at least two ways. Firstly, as participants in society, the members of organisations import certain common definitions of the situation, as well as separate 'sub-universes of meaning', into their organisational behaviour. To take one example, within a broad agreement about the appropriate authority that management may claim, there may be many different interpretations of each attempt to exercise this authority—what the manager regards as a legitimate exercise of his functions may be interpreted by workers as 'pulling rank'. When organisations are first created, their 'meaning-structures' reflect those generally prevalent in roles of a similar nature in the broader society: Bendix (1959), for instance, has noted how in Anglo-Saxon societies managers usually accept the 'good faith' of their workers who reciprocate by accepting the legitimacy of managerial authority; in pre-1917 Russia, however, management made no such assumption. As interaction continues, these expectations become modified to a certain extent in each organisation, although they are never completely separate from the prevailing meaning-structure of the society (if only in the language in which they are phrased).

Secondly, the participants may see the environment as threatening or as creating an opportunity, and act accordingly. For example, a shop steward may perceive that full employment makes him less liable to be victimised by management and may use more militant methods (McCarthy, 1967). Or the leaders of the Tennessee Valley Authority may informally co-opt local people whom they see as threatening by offering them executive responsibility (Selznick, 1949). In neither case, I suggest, may these actions usefully be regarded as the outcome of the system adapting in order to meet its needs.

The way in which the sociologist treats the relationship between the organisation and the environment follows directly from his decision whether it is better to view social structures as Immanent or Transcendental. The former position holds that this relationship arises out of the meanings which individuals attach to the behaviour of others; the processes that then develop stem from these meanings and are susceptible to change by the persons concerned; they are not separate from and above the individuals. According to the second view, we should be concerned with an impersonal process, reflected in the action of individuals but quite separate from their intentions.

Alternatives to System Theory

The outline of an alternative to what has been presented so far in this chapter can best be discussed by beginning from a work by Sherman Krupp (1961).

In a critical study of organisation theory, Krupp implies that the System Model, just as much as the Goal Model, involves examining an organisation from the point of view of the executive. The environment, for instance, is to be considered only inasmuch as it affects the problems of the organisation, which is to say the problems of those with authority. Moreover, in seeking to explain what actually happens in organisations in terms of a series of impersonal processes (e.g. homeostasis), it directs attention away from purposive human action with intended as well as unintended consequences. For instance, an assumed tendency towards the resolution of conflict (in order to meet organisational goals) need not operate if it does not suit the interests of the participants.[15]

This suggests that it would be more fruitful to analyse organisations in terms of the different ends of their members and of their capacity to impose these ends on others—it suggests an analysis in terms of power and authority. From this perspective, organisational change occurs when the available resources of different groups alter and this affects 'the relative strengths of the rival claimants' ability to alter, in their favour, any given structure of authority' (p. 175). Such a pattern of contested authority implies that it is crucially important to understand the subjective purposes of each act at least as well as its significance for the satisfaction of organisational need. 'Participant acceptance of organisational goals', as he puts it, '. . . may reflect organisational efficiency, but, in broader strokes on a larger canvas, it may be a part of a structure of authority, it may belong to a system of subordination' (p. 183). Moreover, the consequences of interaction are important for those concerned as well as for the system: 'effectiveness in securing goals may appear as organisational efficiency, but to the participants it may mean subordination' (ibid.).

Two apparently opposed ways of viewing organisations have now been suggested—each of which, incidentally, reflects one side of a recent, if by now somewhat inconsequential, debate among sociologists. The Systems approach stresses the way in which the action of the parts is structured by the system's need for stability and goal-consensus, and emphasises the processes of integration and adaptation. The alternative approach argues, as so far presented, that organisations are merely the ever-changing product of the self-interested actions of their members and concentrates on conflict and the role of power. The relative advantages of each approach are readily apparent. They seem merely to stress one side or other of the same coin: 'Society makes Man' (Systems), 'Man makes Society' (Action). Since both sides have an element of truth, so it appears do both approaches.

It is important to note, however, that the assumptions of each approach need not be so limited as they sometimes appear. The Systems approach can incorporate analysis of conflict as Coser (1965) and others have demonstrated. It can also, as in the work of Gouldner (1959, 1967), attempt to come to grips with the ends of the participants (see Chapter Four). Equally, the Action approach would be very limited if it could only concern itself, as Krupp appears to be suggesting, with the problems of power and had to assume the necessity of conflict. However, just as systems theory need not identify members with the formal goals of an organisation, so action analysis does not have to take it for granted that men are purely political animals.

If we concentrate on the game-like qualities of social life, it becomes clear that organisations are made up of not one but a series of games, each with its own meanings and standards of expected behaviour. Following Burns (1966), interaction may be defined in terms of the working organisation and its characteristic norms ('a fair day's work for a fair day's pay'), the political process (where it is expected that people will compete for power) and the status structure (where they compete for prestige). While analytically separate, the playing of each game interacts with another. They may sometimes be in conflict, as when the rules of the political game infringe on expected behaviour in the work or status games. More frequently, one game is manipulated so as to further the interests of the participants in another game. Even in what appears to be entirely a political conflict, each side will normally justify its behaviour by appealing to the norms of the working organisation (e.g. it will say that what it is trying to do is in the best interests of the organisation as a whole).[16]

The Systems approach, in assuming that organisations 'exist as instruments for the attainment of valued future states', has limited itself unnecessarily by tending to play down the political and status concerns of those concerned and by implying that goals and actions are largely conditioned by the problems of the organisation and by role-expectations as defined by the formal structure. Those who would propose an alternative have tended to fall into the other trap of exaggerating the extent to which the members of organisations are concerned with advancing their power and status and have failed to take sufficient account of the possible existence of shared values (to which, at the very least, lip-service will be paid), as well as that of the interdependence of one group's privileges with those of another. The practical consequence of this is that, when analysing interaction, one ought to remember that there is a 'plurality of action systems available to the individual' any one of which may be invoked as the frame of reference for a particular action (Burns, 1966, p. 177).

The real debate is not about whether conflict or consensus is more characteristic of organisations. This can only be settled empirically and is, anyway, in need of reformulation before it can be properly tested. Instead, it is concerned with the relative insights that may be derived by analysing organisations from the transcendental view of the problems of the system as a whole, with human action being regarded as a reflection of system needs, or from the view of interaction that arises as actors attach meanings to their own actions and to the actions of others.[17] The second position does not deny that the social structure of an organisation may be experienced as constraining by its members. However, this constraint depends on meanings, which are the products of human interaction and are both sustained and changed by it.

REFERENCES

1. Berger (1966) uses delinquency as an illustration of this point. To view delinquency as a problem is to accept the perspective of the authorities; to the delinquent gang, on the other hand, attempts to limit its own autonomy constitute the problem. It is better to adopt neither perspective but to attempt to understand both. In the course of doing so, it is likely that everyday categories such as 'delinquency' will become more problematic.

2. I have in mind here the Scientific Management School of F. W. Taylor.

3. This model is criticised in two important papers, Gouldner (1959) and Etzioni (1960).

4. Structural-functionalist studies of organisations are discussed in the next chapter.

5. A recent work on organisation theory states: 'Approached as a natural system, the complex organisation is a set of inter-dependent parts which together make up a whole, because each contributes something and receives something from the whole, which in turn is interdependent with some larger environment' (Thompson, 1967, p. 6).

6. The logical problems involved in conceptualising organisations as 'real states' will become more apparent in Chapter Six.

7. This assumes that the needs of social systems can be empirically established. Even system theorists, such as Merton (1949) and Selznick (1948 and 1949), seem somewhat doubtful about such an assumption; see Chapter Three.

8. 'My focus', Thompson (1967) writes, 'is on the behaviour of organisations; behaviour within organisations is considered only to the extent that it helps us understand organisations in the round' (p. 1).

9. Once again Thompson is useful. In his view of organisations: 'Survival of the system is taken to be the goal and the parts and their relationships *presumably* are determined through evolutionary processes' (ibid., p. 6, my emphasis).

10. Etzioni specifically takes Gouldner up on whether the system they both propose should be regarded as 'natural'. He himself appears to believe that a system is an heuristic device and should not have innate tendencies (such as self-maintenance) attributed to it.

11. This is a major argument in Chapter Three.

12. Explanations of behaviour in terms of psychological forces are by no means always preferred in laboratory studies—see Chapter Ten.

13. Parsons (1961) calls his system 'partially-open'. The term is not used in the same sense here and Parsons' model is discussed in the section on 'open systems' that follows.

14. Blau and Scott (1963) suggest that the study of organisations is 'less complicated' (p. 14) than the study of communities or societies.

15. 'The central question is this,' Krupp writes, 'what if it pays more from the participant point of view to have intra-organisa-

tional conflict than not to have this conflict? Then it will occur' (1961, p. 165). A similar attempt at 'demystification', to use a currently popular word, is made by Mayntz (1964): 'To say that an organisation tends to maintain itself', she argues, 'can be nothing but a short-hand expression for the fact that there are specific persons or groups inside or outside the organisation who wish to maintain it . . .' (p. 114).

16. On the extent to which organisations are not purely political systems, see Crozier (1964), especially Chapters 6–7. The game analogy, as applied to social life in organisations, is discussed in Chapter Nine of the present text.

17. For a discussion of an Immanent and Transcendental view of society, see Horton (1964).

3

Structural-Functionalism

ALL PERSPECTIVES offer insights in exchange for limitations in approach: 'A way of seeing', as Poggi has put it, 'is also a way of not seeing.'[1] This chapter discusses critically some of the assumptions upon which structural-functional analysis is based and the view of organisations which it presents. My purpose, however, is not to deny the value of the approach but, by pointing out its deficiencies, to suggest the need for the sort of alternative which has previously been examined.

The historical origins of the application of this approach to organisations go back to the theoretical critique of the Hawthorne studies of workgroup behaviour. This led in two directions. According to one view, the sources of rationality in the participants' behaviour (which the Hawthorne researchers sought to discount) might instead have been fruitfully analysed in terms of perceived conflicts of interest between actors with different experiences of the organisation and of the wider society. Such an interpretation would require a prior orientation towards the attachment of the actors to the dominant role-system and towards an explanation of the causes, as well as the consequences, of their behaviour. Alternatively, it was possible to argue that the inter-relatedness of phenomena which the studies revealed, together with the often unintended consequences of behaviour, could best be explained by a stress on the resemblances between an organisation and a natural system. Hence what was called for was an analysis of the relationship between the activities of the parts of the system and the system's needs, in order to emphasise the sympathetic adjustments of one to the other (see Figure 3.1 below). The deficiencies of the Hawthorne approach, it could then be argued, derived from its failure to locate the action of isolated men in the context of a fully-defined social system. The nature

44

of the Structural-Functionalist approach which was implicit in the second critique will now be briefly discussed, while the rest of the chapter will be devoted to an examination of the work of four fairly representative theorists.

Functionalism begins with Hobbes' problem of order and proceeds to ask some important and interesting questions. 'How is it', functionalists would ask, 'that society manages to work and to survive continual changes of personnel? How do people with different genetic make-ups and personality types learn to co-exist with one another and even to enter into more

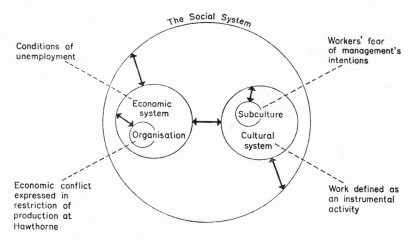

Figure 3.1: Hawthorne—A Systems Analysis

or less stable and predictable forms of relationship?' In answering these questions, functionalists take as their concern the relationship of the parts to the whole in order to show how what appear to be isolated, if not inexplicable, social phenomena may fulfil some wider purpose related to the stability of society. Thus, their perspective, rather than an ideological bias, generates a concern with the causes and consequences of social equilibrium; problems of change and conflict, while they are considered, are treated as subsidiary phenomena. However, it is misleading to attempt to characterise a universal functionalist approach; indeed, the effect of many criticisms of it has been weakened by the attribution of a false degree of uniformity to its proponents. Yet it is true that there are by no means as many functionalisms as there are functionalists. At the cost of over-simplification, we shall consider only what seem to be the two major schools.

Mertonian Functionalism

Not all functionalists make use of the organic analogy implicit in 'natural systems'; neither do they always attempt to develop a view of all the component parts, and their inter-relations, of the system itself. This has been the characteristic position held by Robert Merton; his concern is with 'middle range' theories which can help to explain the consequences of one institutional area for another. To help in their construction he has introduced three concepts; 'latent' or unintended functions as well as 'manifest' functions; 'dysfunctions' as well as functions; and 'functional alternatives' in place of the conservative assumption that because a society, given its present form of organisation, is able to 'work', it could not function just as well or even better with a different pattern of relationships. Using these concepts, and as an illustration of a middle-range theory, he goes on to show how the American phenomenon of 'boss' dominated politics, long thought by liberals to be 'dysfunctional' to society, may play important 'latent' functions, in particular by providing a channel of upward mobility for otherwise depressed groups in the population. From such forms of explanation, Merton (1949) argues that it may be possible to develop a theory of the characteristics of social systems in general, but such a level of generality is best attained as the final step after a long process of lower-level theory testing rather than *a priori* from the armchair.

From the point of view of the student of organisations, Merton's approach can offer some real insights. Behaviour inside organisations, as elsewhere, is by no means always what it seems. The consequences of action may be very different from those intended; what is often thought to be 'bad' for an organisation may, after closer inspection, be seen to perform vital functions. Similarly, a part of its structure which nobody has questioned for several generations may turn out to have 'dysfunctional' consequences or a 'functional alternative' may fill its place much better. Again, conflict can, according to Merton's analysis, have latent functions for a society and for the organisations within it. This has been most clearly indicated by Coser (1965) who has discussed the unintended functiona conse- quences of certain types of conflict. Thus, instead of being necessarily destructive of the order within an organisation, a view which is not uncommon among managers, certain forms of conflict may, through their 'adaptive' or 'safety-valve' functions, play a part in maintaining organisational stability.

Once one tries, however, to apply Merton's concepts to a specific organisation, one runs into the problems of 'dys- functional for whom . . .?', or 'performing a latent function for what . . .?' Since Merton is not really concerned with relating the consequences of behaviour to the stated or observed ends of individuals or groups, it at once becomes apparent that his referent is the assumed needs of systems, whether societies or organisations. Thus, while at this stage he does not want to build his system and, moreover, is particularly troubled by the proper meaning and even the validity of the notion of system 'needs',[2] nevertheless his analysis presupposes the existence of such a model. Indeed, by having committed himself initially to a concern with the functions rather than the consequences of behaviour, he has left himself with little alternative. For 'functions' are not the same as 'consequences': the former con- cept limits concern with action to whether or not it meets ends or needs which are held to prevail and, in Merton's case, these must be the needs of the system. So Merton's middle-range theories are really dependent on the use of a systems frame- work. As such, they are susceptible to the criticisms, to which we shall return, of providing no satisfactory explanation of social change or of the causes, as distinct from the consequences, of action.

General Concerns of the Functionalist Perspective

If functionalist forms of explanation are dependent on a view of society as a system, then it follows that to be satisfactory they must contain an explicit rather than implicit reference to the demands which such a system makes on its component parts. If, therefore, Merton is unhappy about the concept of society's 'needs', then he should be (but is not) unhappy about functionalism as such. Other functionalists have had no such qualms and have set out to examine the consequences of viewing society and the organisations within it as natural systems. In doing so, they have had to explain three things: the boundaries of their system, the relation to it of its component sub-systems and, since theirs is an 'open' system, its relation to other systems. Before considering the major functionalist theorists of organisations, the general reaction of such writers to each of these problems will be presented.

The definition of the system and its boundaries is, it has been suggested, the first stage of functionalist analysis. However, there is no easy answer to this problem: if it is difficult to define society, or the social system, it is just as hard to define an organisation. Most definitions of the latter, for instance Udy's: 'Any group of persons plus the system of roles defining their interaction with one another' (Udy, 1965, p. 678), would include nearly all social life. Thus, in order to distinguish 'formal' or 'complex' organisations from other sorts of structure, most functionalist sociologists have appealed to the supposedly clear-cut goals of the former. The boundaries of the organisation may then be located by assessing the extent to which any object or process is primarily concerned with the survival and goal-attainment of the system in question.

Sub-systems inside organisations, to take the second problem, can now be understood by reference to the functions they perform for the adaptation, goal-attainment and integration of the whole. Thus, to take just one example, Bakke (1966) distinguishes between identification, perpetuation, workflow, control and, finally, homeostatic activities; the last of these serves 'to stabilise and vitalise the organisation as a whole in an evolving state of dynamic equilibrium' (p. xxi). Thus, as with the wider social system, the role of any sub-system is to meet the needs of the system; the nature of any aspect of an organisation is, therefore, *explained* when we have demonstrated the contribution it makes to the whole.

If sub-systems perform functions for one system, then this system in turn meets the needs of higher-level systems, from whose point of view it itself is another sub-system. Functionalists, therefore, have little choice but to operate with an 'open' system model: in doing so, they attempt to establish the ways in which any system meets its needs through other systems (its 'input') and the services which it then goes on to provide for them (its 'output'). Thus, Etzioni (1961b), in arguing for greater attention to be paid to an organisation's environment, suggests the following problems which should be answered: '. . . the relations between organisational behaviour and the biological and physiological capacities and needs of the actors, and . . . the respective adaptations between the organisation and its geographical-physical environment' (p. 136). The environment can provide an organisation both with suitably

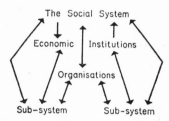

Figure 3.2

motivated members and with raw materials and technical knowledge to help it accomplish its task. Indeed, it is impossible to understand the ways in which an organisation achieves its goal without reference to it: 'In any particular situation', Udy (1965) argues, 'the problem is likely to resolve itself into a question of whether, in view of the constraints of the *social setting*, certain technologically fixed tasks can be organised and/or motivated' (p. 689). In turn, the 'output' of the organisation provides other systems with goods and services. Thus Stinchcombe notes how an organisation's goals or purposes are generally *functions* performed for some larger structure. For example, armies have the goal of winning possible military engagements. 'The fulfilment of this goal is a function performed for the larger political structure, which has functional requirements of defense and conquest' (p. 142). This intermeshing of systems is illustrated in Figure 3.2 above.

An Initial Evaluation

If the motto of Sociology is to be 'Only connect . . .', and it
seems reasonable that it should be, then it might appear that
the open-system model of the functionalists has much to
recommend it. For above all, in its attempts to show the
dependence of one system upon another, it stresses the inter-
relatedness of phenomena and reminds us that just to relate one
narrow variable to another, without taking account of the
social context in which they both function, is not good science
but merely bad sociology. Again, there is clearly some advantage to be gained if, instead of limiting ourselves to the concepts
of the society we are studying, we can move outside of them
and, by so doing, come to grips with the often misunderstood
and nearly always unintended nature of social interaction. Yet
what are benefits from one point of view are handicaps from
another. By moving away from the actors' definition of the
situation and of the choices available to them, we run the risk
of reifying the systems that we construct. By emphasising the
unintended, we minimise the role of intended action in the
shaping of structures. In doing so, it is easy to become primarily
concerned with the consequences rather than the causes of
social action. The function of a particular social pattern for,
say, the stability of an organisation reveals nothing about its
causes: indeed, it is very difficult to make any causal statement
without reference to human motivation. Within a functionalist
framework, as Dore (1961) has noted, one can only move to
'why' questions if one postulates either an immanent tendency
towards the functional integration of the parts of any system or
an evolutionary process whereby the system becomes more
and more adapted to its environment.[3]

The final judgment on any approach must be whether it
raises provoking questions: to some extent, this is something
which each individual has to decide for himself. Nevertheless,
it will be argued in this chapter that the Structural-Functionalist approach, while in many ways it is suggestive, has
sufficient deficiencies to make it necessary to disagree with
Davis's (1959) view that 'we are all functionalists now', and to
propose an alternative. This argument can now be developed
with reference to three functionalist studies of organisations.

Selznick: The Recalcitrance of the Tools of Action

The work of Philip Selznick will first be considered. We shall take as an example of his method a theoretical paper and a much longer empirical study of one organisation (Selznick, 1948 and 1949). His contribution is particularly interesting since it represents the earliest attempt systematically to apply a functionalist perspective to the study of organisations.

Selznick, like many subsequent writers, uses the 'needs' of systems as his basic conceptual tool (these include: 'the need for some continuity of policy and leadership, for a homogeneous outlook, for the achievement of continuous consent and parti-cipation on the part of the ranks', 1949, p. 10).

In attempting to satisfy its needs an organisation is faced by the tendency of its constituent parts to resist actions which do not serve their own purposes. Selznick calls this the problem of *recalcitrance*. People are recalcitrant because they act as whole persons and not simply in terms of their narrowly-defined, formal organisational roles. The institutions and other organi-sations which comprise the environment are recalcitrant be-cause the organisation has to deal with them in terms of general rules which cannot cover every empirical situation or cope with constant change. Thus, in an implied critique of Weber (which has a parallel in the work of Gouldner, 1954), Selznick would argue that an appeal to the sanctity of rules is an inadequate basis for a claim to legitimacy. The issue of legitimacy is re-current and its solution problematic. An organisation, there-fore, must constantly seek to legitimate its activities to its members and to an often hostile environment. Central to its functioning is the nature of its response to problems, threats, or needs which cannot be met in culturally approved ways. Even temporarily successful strategies, such as giving a share of authority to threatening groups or persons in exchange for their co-operation in other fields, only create further problems to which there may be no formally legitimate response.

Selznick's classic study of the Tennessee Valley Authority employs this sort of theoretical perspective. Thus the T.V.A. engages in self-defensive behaviour in order to satisfy its need for stability and goal-attainment. It has to adjust to the environ-ment in which it is located by co-opting threatening outside elements, while, in turn, the environment must adapt to the requirements of the T.V.A. This process of mutual adaptation secures only a temporary equilibrium because it has unintended consequences which are both functional and dysfunctional for the systems concerned. For instance, while the commitment of the T.V.A. to a land-grant college system was a way of coming to terms with the local environment, at the same time it caused difficulties with the federal administration and hence further instability was generated. The pattern is, therefore, one of 'strain' and adaptation, with systems engaged in continual action in order to adjust to one another.

The needs of organisations, he argues, are not necessarily met through the conscious action of men but by the unanticipated consequences of their actions. Functional alternatives will arise, for instance, when needs cannot be met in culturally approved ways. His analysis, therefore, depends upon the impersonal processes through which organisations function rather than upon the motivations of the actors. 'Organisational behaviour', he suggests, must 'be analysed in terms of organisational response to organisational need' (1949, p. 259). Above all, needs are experienced and a response made to them by the System itself: 'The organic, emergent character of the formal organisation considered as a co-operative system must be recognised. This means that the *organisation* reaches decisions, takes action and makes adjustments' (1948, pp. 27–8).

In addressing himself so directly to the problems of the System, Selznick does not ignore totally the motivations of its participants. However, he supposes that these will often reflect the 'needs' of the organisation: 'There are certain needs', he argues, 'generated by the organisation itself, which command the attention and energies of leading participants' (1949, p. 10). Now to explain behaviour in terms of the motivations of individuals is one thing; to attribute these motivations to needs of which they are not necessarily aware (whether they are the personality needs of the psychologists or Selznick's needs of organisation) and whose very existence is based upon the perceptions of the observer, is clearly quite another. Selznick does recognise the difficulties in his position for, in a footnote, he accepts that 'the concept of "basic needs" in organisational analysis may be open to objections similar to those against the concept of instinct', in much the same manner as Merton. However, he hardly resolves the problem by going on to state that we may use the concept of 'basic needs', 'if we understand that it refers to stable systems of variables which, with respect to many changes in organisational structure and behaviour, are independent' (ibid., p. 252). This does little to help him substantiate the validity of the concept and his own view of the nature of organisational needs; for we are all free to have our own value-judgments about what such needs are like. Further, if we analyse organisations in terms of their needs then, except teleologically, we are hardly in a position to consider the causes, as distinct from the consequences, of action; for the basic 'cause' of any act can only be that the needs of the system made it 'necessary'.

This is made clear by the unusual interpretation which Selznick gives to the 'meaning' of action. His approach 'directs our attention to the meaning of events. This leads us away from the problem of origins. The meaning of an act may be spelled out in its consequences, and these are not the same as the factors that called it into being' (1949, p. 253). However, one can agree that causes are not the same as consequences without accepting that the meaning of an act can be clearly understood in terms of its consequences (imputed to it, no doubt, by the observer rather than the actors concerned). This avoidance of the problem of causes is a central weakness of the functionalist approach. In looking for the causes of action, one must pay attention to the actor's 'in-order-to' motive and this, despite Merton's view of the manifest functions of an act, is an area which has been constantly de-emphasised in functionalist analysis.

While Selznick does not ignore what he calls 'the social character of the personnel' and their power commitments, he sees these as essentially subsidiary to the processes whereby the system attains stability. From the point of view of the management of the system, the fact that the 'tools of action' (people) are 'recalcitrant' (unwilling to accept the formal definition of their role) is a constraining factor. But it is the system problems from which the observer must derive his primary frame of reference.

Parsons: The Social System

Talcott Parsons's most significant contribution has been his attempt to construct a model of the working of all the parts of a social system and, in so doing, to synthesise what he regards as the major elements in the works of the classic sociologists (cf. Parsons, 1949). In trying to summarise his work, one runs the risk of grossly over-simplifying: Mills's (1959) two-page summary of *The Social System*, for instance, is rather less than serious. Nevertheless, because Parsons's ideas are so central to any functionalist theory of organisations and because there are certain recurring features of his work, an outline of his approach is presented below.

The concept of function implies a view of the systemic qualities of society and of its component parts including organisations. Parsons's 'social system' sets out to illustrate just this: to show how a network of interlocking systems and sub-systems function and thereby meet the needs of each other. In doing so, Parsons claims that he has solved Hobbes's problem of order by integrating disparate individual motivations into a coherent and ordered society; or, to use his terminology, by the integration of 'personality systems' and the 'cultural system' into the 'social system'. The concept which Parsons uses to make his systems cohere is the 'central value system' or shared orientations towards action which, Parsons claims, is at the basis of any society. By defining the type of role-relationships which can arise, this allows the individual to develop stable expectations about the behaviour of others; conversely it enables others to meet his expectations and to carry out their role-obligations in return for the rights which adhere to their roles. Thus, behaviour is made predictable and society persists even though its members change.[4]

The definition of its value-system, Parsons would argue, is a first priority before we can attribute functions to the parts of a system. Thus, before we can assert that some process, such as social stratification, is functional for society, Parsons would maintain that it is necessary to establish that society's values legitimate the norms upon which the process is based: if we do not do so, then our assessments of functionality will be very misleading.[5] Similarly, since organisations, like societies, are to be seen as systems, our first concern in dealing with them must be to define their values or goals. So predictably Parsons means by an organisation: 'a social system organised for the attainment of a particular type of goal' (1964, p. 56).

Parsons's approach is, therefore, to view organisations as *societies writ small*. He is helped in doing so by the fact that organisations seem to have many of the characteristics of social systems in a much more clear-cut form than is readily visible when dealing with a whole society. Organisations, unlike societies, appear to have relatively obvious goals. The wall-chart of an organisation's hierarchy is usually available but there is no parallel guide to the way in which the component parts of a society are differentiated. The services which organisations perform for other systems are usually readily observable and hence the description of their open-system characteristics is rather easier than when dealing with a society. Finally, problems of adaptation, integration and order arise in a much more visible form than in society and are generally resolved in a much more conscious manner. Thus, as Landsberger (1961) has noted, complex organisations provide 'an excellent test of Parsons' general theory' (p. 214). Or, to put it another way, if Parsons's theory is to be able to claim any explanatory power, it ought to be able to demonstrate it in a setting most favourable to it. Whether it succeeds should become clearer when we see how, after defining the boundaries of his system, Parsons goes on to treat the remaining problems with which functionalist analysis is concerned: the relation of sub-systems to the system, and the way in which the system is integrated with other systems.

The explanation of the integration of individuals and groups into an organisation is to be found ultimately, Parsons maintains, in the value-system of the society as reflected in the goal of the organisation. This structures the way in which roles are defined in such a way as to be appropriate to the expectations which organisational members bring to their work. These expectations are derived from the processes of socialisation and internalisation of norms. Successful role-playing is associated with *psychological* satisfaction (approval, recognition and security) and *instrumental* satisfaction (that is, it can provide a means for the achievement of the 'generalised goals' laid down by the central value system). Instrumental satisfactions are provided by the 'inducements' which, by offering individuals materials and other rewards, motivate them to play their organisational role. In addition, Parsons notes, such motivation may be based on 'coercion' and/or 'therapy'.

However, while Parsons is concerned to explain the relations between a social system and personality and cultural systems, he is also interested in the links between one social system and another.[6] An organisation is tied to society, Parsons maintains, by the value-system which it shares and by its 'functional requirements' which it can only meet through the society and which must be satisfied if it is to 'survive'. These prerequisites for existence consist of the capability to 'adapt', to attain its goals, to 'integrate' its constituent parts and to allow for 'latency' or 'pattern-maintenance' (that is, the maintenance of the dominant value-system and the patterns of interaction it lays down). The first two requirements are factors related to an organisation's efficiency, the last two to stability.

Parsons then goes on to consider the means by which organisations typically meet these needs. In doing this, he uses a cybernetic model considering the input of resources and motivations into an organisation and the output of these for other systems. In particular, in relation to an environment an organisation achieves 'stability' through the processes of 'adaptation' (obtaining resources like land, labour and capital), 'operation' (making use of these resources) and 'co-ordination' (making use of the motivations which individuals bring to their roles in order to serve organisational goals). In return, the organisation's stability and goal-attainment contributes to the stability and goal-attainment of the wider society. There is thus a 'boundary exchange' between higher and lower level systems: what for the organisation is a goal is a function for a higher system.

The scope of Parsons's solution must be measured in relation to the depth of the problem he has set himself. If it is to be considered successful, it must, as Landsberger (1961) notes, show how individuals can attain their ends, while simultaneously furthering the system's end, maintaining stable relations with other parts of the system and remaining integrated with higher and lower level systems. Moreover, the argument must be convincing not only in logical terms but also as an approximation of the way in which organisations do actually function, or at least as a picture which bears some resemblances to what we know about patterns of social interaction.

Now Parsons and the functionalists in general have often, and wrongly, been criticised for not taking account of change and conflict in their explanations. Although they do indeed consider these phenomena, in a perspective designed to explain the persistence of social systems we must expect that they will be treated as essentially subsidiary. Thus, Parsons distinguishes 'equilibrium' analysis, which assumes a system to be given, from 'structural change' analysis, which does not. But he then goes on to argue that change must always be viewed in a wider setting of equilibrium: 'It is almost always necessary', he suggests, 'to assume some structural elements to be *given*, while analysing processes of change in others, particularly changes in the structure of sub-systems to the more extensive system' (Parsons, 1965, p. 31).

Change, according to Parsons, can arise in one of two ways: from the pressures of the environment or from within the organisation. The former is 'exogenous' change; it occurs because the environment changes and the organisation must adapt. The latter, which Parsons calls 'endogenous' change, has its source in 'strains' within the organisation: 'A strain', he notes, 'is a tendency to disequilibrium in the input–output balance between two or more units of the system' (1967, p. 196). It typically arises when too much attention is paid to either efficiency (adaptation and goal-attainment) or to stability (integration and latency). The source of any instability, however, ultimately lies in the environment, in particular the 'central value-system' obtaining in the society: 'The crucial focus of change', as he puts it, 'lies in the stability of the value system' (Parsons, 1967, p. 198). This central value-system, which expresses the moral sentiments as well as the normative expectations of a society, defines the goal of an organisation and is at the source of the exercise of legitimate authority within it.

The reaction of the organisation to strains (either exogenous or endogenous) is to adjust and to adapt in the direction of a new type of stability or a new arrangement for maximum effectiveness. The postulate of the dynamic equilibrium of social systems which this involves is, as Van den Berghe (1963) has pointed out, the fundamental logical cornerstone of functionalist analysis. Even if one accepts the view that Systems may be said to take action, it is by no means clear that the reaction to external or internal forces of change is always adaptive. For instance, where there are perceived conflicts of interest, the set of dominant expectations within an organisation may be contested and any change in them need not necessarily contribute to the stability of the system. Thus change may arise through conflict and contradiction rather than through the institutionalisation of limited patterns of deviance. Moreover, where there are changes in the pattern of interaction, how is one to tell if the system has adapted, become a new type, or died?

Parsons's unsatisfactory treatment of change and conflict arises from his prior orientation, as a functionalist, to the consequences rather than the causes of action: he is primarily interested in tracing the consequences of a change rather than in examining its sources, in the functions rather than the causes of conflict. This is further illustrated in his view of the relation between organisations and society. Calling an organisation a 'partially-open' system, he treats it and the environment as two sets of givens and then goes on to consider the ways in which the former adjusts to the demands of the latter. There is no explanation offered of why particular organisations pursuing certain goals arise at some times and in certain situations: 'We treat an organisation for purposes of analysis', he notes at one point, 'as an already established and going concern' (1964, p. 23). Moreover, it is not immediately apparent why organisations must have a goal which fits within a dominant value-system of the society, nor, if this is not to be a universal phenomena, are we told how deviant organisations arise and operate. It is difficult, for instance, to see how Parsons could explain the origins of a revolutionary organisation except, perhaps, in terms of inconsistencies in the central value-system. Even this runs the risk of being a tautological explanation.

An obvious defence of Parsons's schema is that it involves merely the elaboration of a set of categories which are not meant to be exhaustive but to provide an essential basis for the analysis of the complexities of the real world. The weakness of this argument is that one is never sure what Parsons is trying to do: whether building a model, describing the conditions necessary for stability in any system, or making statements about the relationships between phenomena that he believes actually occur.[7] If the last case, then it is misleading to suggest that organisations, because their parts are interdependent, are normally in a state of equilibrium from which they can only be disturbed by outside forces.[8] As a description of the conditions making for stability, it fails to recognise that organisations may survive and even flourish without a common value-orientation among their members, while even as a model it has all the limitations (and the advantages) of the Systems approach.

Given the doubtful status of the Parsonian theory, it is hardly surprising that empirical studies of organisations appear to have made very little use of it. Scott (1959) has, however, attempted to apply the work of Parsons to some of the literature on organisational behaviour. She follows him in distinguishing organisations in relation to the type of function they perform for society (adaptation, goal-attainment, integration or latency). She goes on to compare mental hospitals and prisons, both of which may be classed as 'Integrative' organisations because they are primarily concerned with the adjustment of members to each other and to the institutionalised expectations of the wider society.

However, while there may well be similarities between such organisations, it seems most likely that these derive not from their 'function' for society but from their character as total institutions: in this case, the pattern of interaction within them might, as Goffman (1968) has noted, resemble what occurs within army barracks or monasteries, both of which it is difficult to class as integrative organisations. The problem of applying Parsons really amounts to this: need something which the sociologist attributes to organisations (namely their function for society) without any reference to the ends actually pursued within them have any bearing on the nature of their internal social relationships?[9] Are prison officials really concerned with their supposed Parsonian function, or is the integrative function of their organisation something which constrains them in practice? The utopian elements which arise in the 'unseen hand' nature of the theory can best be illustrated by

Scott's view of the sources of the power available to such organisations. 'Power is allocated by society to organisations', she suggests, 'in a proportion roughly correlative with the importance of their functions' (1959, p. 389)—for instance, the Mafia?

It is only fair to point out that Parsons is aware that the perspective he offers is somewhat one-sided. In acknowledging that his analysis is from a 'cultural-institutional' (or System) point of view, he suggests that there is an alternative: 'the "group" or "role" point of view which takes sub-organisations and the roles of individuals participating in the functioning of the organisation as its point of departure' (1964, p. 20). However, instead of exploring the potentialities of what could develop into an Action approach, he gives a weak example of what he has in mind (in terms of the sociologist beginning from the role of the actors within the formal organisation) and does not discuss it further. Moreover, he seems to equate such an approach with theories, such as that of Barnard (1938), which are concerned with the efficiency of bureaucracies.[10]

Katz and Kahn: Open-System Theory

Daniel Katz and Robert Kahn (1966) in *The Social Psychology of Organisations* make explicit use of the work of Parsons in their attempts to describe the open-system characteristics of organisations. Writing at the Survey Research Center of the University of Michigan, where many of the early tests on the validity of human relations techniques (especially in regard to styles of supervision) were first carried out, they represent a trend in American Industrial Sociology away from the limited psychological perspective of the Hawthorne researchers and towards the functionalists' System concept.

They begin by pointing out the advantages of 'system' theory for understanding the way in which different organisational structures influence behaviour: 'In our attempts to extend the description and explanation of organisational processes', they remark, 'we have *shifted* from an earlier emphasis on traditional concepts of individual psychology and interpersonal relations to system constructs' (1966, p. vii, my italics). This shift reflects the growing dissatisfaction they felt with the human relations approach after their own studies and after encountering the socio-technical approach in the later material of Trist (1963) and Rice (1963), to whom they refer favourably. Moreover, only an 'open-system' approach can be fully satisfactory for 'closed-system' theory has exhibited a 'failure to develop and understand the processes of *feedback* which are essential to *survival*' (p. 29).

An open-system perspective, they claim, has the advantage of showing the way in which an organisation attains stability by the inputs it receives from the environment of goods and services. An additional input is human motivation without which any social system cannot function. This approach also reveals the functions which the organisation itself performs for other systems. Thus their typology of organisations distinguishes 'productive', 'maintenance', 'adaptive' and 'managerial-political' functions. Finally, they claim that an open system, by drawing attention to the influence of structures on behaviour, permits an integration of the 'macro' concerns of the sociologist with the 'micro' perspective used by psychologists. They go on to outline the characteristics of open systems in a manner which suggests complete acceptance of the organic analogy. 'The following nine characteristics', they suggest, 'seem to define *all open systems* . . . importation of energy . . . the throughput, output, a cycle of events, negative entropy, information input, the steady state and dynamic homeostasis, differentiation . . . and equifinality' (Chapter 2, *passim*).

Katz and Kahn are, however, not unaware of the differences between an organisation and an organism.[11] In particular, unlike biological organisms, organisations have no clear boundaries and are therefore more open; the relationship between their parts may be looser and hence allow a greater variability of behaviour, and finally, social systems are socially contrived and not born. Now it might seem that only two courses of action are possible once a functionalist recognises the vast limitations of the organic analogy; he may, like Merton, concentrate on 'middle-range' theories and only make implicit assumptions about the nature of the social system, or he might forgo functionalism for a less misleading perspective. However, Katz and Kahn find still a third possibility—they argue that, if organisations are unlike biological systems, this need not involve dropping the organic analogy. Instead, we merely take account of the fact that certain ways of meeting system needs are probably more important in organisations than in organisms.[12] Thus, because social systems are not organisms, their 'maintenance' sub-system is particularly important since organisations 'require control mechanisms of various kinds to keep their component parts together and functioning in the required interdependent fashion' (p. 69).

The problem of 'integration' presents a particular difficulty to this form of analysis. If, as they have admitted, organisations are composed of motivated individuals rather than cells, there is less likely to be a mechanical exchange of function between the parts and the variability in behaviour may be greater. Or, to put it in other terms, we cannot exclude the possibility of conflicts of perceived interests in organisations. Their 'solution' to what might appear a dangerous threat to the organic analogy derives from Parsons's notion of the 'central value system'. Roles, they suggest, have a 'normative component'. Thus 'the worker not only plays his part in the interdependent chain of activities but he accepts the norms about doing a satisfactory job' (p. 38). Similarly, organisational members are integrated by their acceptance of the values of the system which, in turn, reflect those of society.

At best this is an approximation of one polar situation; at worst, as a description of all organisations, it involves illegitimate *a priori* assumptions. It is interesting to note that Katz and Kahn take as their example of the acceptance of organisational values the attitudes of members of voluntary rather than economic organisations.[13] They have then conveniently concentrated on precisely that form of organisation where one would least expect conflict of interests and values. But far more damaging to their explanation of integration is their assumption that because there exist 'official' norms about role-playing, the worker necessarily complies with them. The worker's norm about 'satisfactory' work may be very different from that of management. In any event, as Gouldner (1954) has pointed out, we must take compliance with a dominant authority structure as problematical rather than as given.

Katz and Kahn's only other attempt to come to terms with the 'motivated' nature of human behaviour is when they concede that the characteristic of 'dynamic homeostasis' only applies to non-social systems. Again, this might have led them to drop the attempt to predict the course of organisational change by means of the metaphysical 'in-built characteristics' of all systems. Instead, they merely substitute one misleading concept for another. In organisations, apparently, we must talk of the 'system dynamic' which 'moves a given structure toward becoming more like what it basically is' (p. 67). This implies that the System will itself respond to any internal or external threat by attempting to absorb it and to restore itself, as closely as possible, to its previous state. At the same time, the system will attempt to preserve its character through growth and expansion.

Such a position bears an obvious resemblance to Parsons's view that all systems have a tendency to 'boundary maintenance' within a 'moving equilibrium'. If organisations are in equilibrium, moving or not, then the clear implication, as has been noted with Parsons, is that social change occurs because of a new external factor to which adjustment must be made. It is not surprising, therefore, that Katz and Kahn, while acknowledging the possibility that internal forces of change may exist, conclude: 'It is our thesis . . . that these sources of internal *strain* are not the most potent causes of organisational change. The set of conditions which we have called changed inputs from *without* are the *critical* factors in the significant modification of organisations' (p. 448, my italics). The treatment of how pressures for change arise within organisations would require a systematic analysis of the conflicts of interest that may exist and of the balance of power that plays a part in structuring their outcome. The *a priori* reasoning in which Katz and Kahn engage can only suggest that it is this type of analysis which the functionalist theory of organisations precludes.

Katz and Kahn also seek to resolve the first problem of functionalist analysis: the definition of the system and of its boundaries. What the system is, they argue, can be readily established by employing the popular names used to label organisations. Despite the fact that this may be potentially misleading, it has the advantage of conceiving the system in the same way as it is defined by its members and by those who deal with it. This unusual retreat to the actors' perspective indicates how difficult a problem the definition of their system can be for functionalists. On the other hand, they will have no truck with their colleagues who would talk about the goals of the system. They argue that all too often the goal of the system has been determined by examining the goals of its leaders. 'The fallacy here', they write, 'is one of equating the purposes of goals of organisations with the purposes and goals of individual members' (p. 15). Predictably, they conclude from this that instead of attempting to identify the different ends that may be pursued inside organisations and dropping the consensual framework, we should, as far as possible, avoid talking about goals at all.[14]

All that we can legitimately observe, they argue, are the latent functions that organisations perform for their members and for other systems. 'The theoretical concepts that we use', they say, 'should begin with the *input, output* and *functioning* of the organisation as a system and *not* with the rational *purposes* of their leaders. . . . Our theoretical model for the understanding of organisations is that of an energic input–output system in which the energic return from the output reactivates the system' (p. 16, my italics). The further they move from the motivation of the actors, the more nearly they reify their system. The search for objectivity ultimately involves them in subjectivity. The consequences of action are to be considered, but only in terms of the supposed 'needs' of the system; the explanation of causes is to be left to others or, at best, discussed in a circular way so that the 'cause' of any act is that the needs of the system made it necessary. The problem of causation in their work is seen most clearly in their treatment of conflict.

When one examines the entries under 'conflict' in the index of Katz and Kahn's book, one discovers that not only do the references suggest a concern with the consequences of conflict (the total list is 'dysfunctional, functional, hierarchial, objective, resolution of, role, vertical, conflict dynamic') but that there is not one entry relating to its causes.[15] Moreover, conflict is not mentioned in a whole chapter devoted to 'Power and Authority', while these themselves are considered in terms of the contribution they make to the system's needs and, in particular, its need to reduce variability in behaviour.[16] It is not that they altogether ignore conflict. They go so far as to note that: 'Many facts of organisational life can be readily understood if the model of organisations is one which views social patterns . . . as the outcome of a *continuing tug of war*' (p. 108, my italics). They even present Dahrendorf's criticisms about the utopian nature of functionalism. Yet, on the same page, they go on to say that what they find interesting about conflict (*à la* Coser) is the functions it may perform,[17] and the mechanisms which organisations develop to meet it where it might be dysfunctional. A better illustration of the way in which their perspective diverts attention from problems, which even its user considers important, could hardly be found.

A further illustration of the limitations of the Systems approach is provided in their discussion of 'organisational effectiveness'. Katz and Kahn measure such effectiveness solely by reference to the needs of the organisation or of society: for instance, they point out that monopolies may be effective for the former, but not for the latter. Devoting a whole chapter to the concept, they go on to consider 'technical efficiency', which involves the full use of the input of resources into the organisation, and 'political effectiveness', where the organisation attempts to control the nature of its input and the disposal of its output through direct manipulations of its environment. On the other hand, the possibility that we might examine the varying effectiveness of certain organisational structures in attaining the ends of their members is never discussed.

Models are only useful for the illumination they throw on problems at issue. This discussion of the work of Katz and Kahn is, therefore, concluded by considering the applicability of their model to a problem they themselves raise: we shall fight the battle on their own ground. Early in their book, they defend their approach by taking the example of a strike: 'If we want to know more about why a union in a conflict situation voted to strike', they argue, '. . . we would look at such system aspects as the *industrywide conditions*, the utilisation of appropriate *strategies* by management and by the union for handling the causes of their differences, the *power position* of the labour leaders with respect to their followers, and the *power* positions of representatives of management . . .' (p. 11). Their analysis of the elements involved seems to be beyond dispute. What is so difficult to see is how a concern with 'functions' allows one to deal with 'strategies' used by groups with different conceptions of their interests, or how a list of the 'needs' of systems can help one to understand the causes of the distribution of power.

Summary

It will now be useful to summarise some of the points in the preceding discussion.

1. Functional analysis is concerned to explain why the social order persists despite internal and external pressures for change.
2. The nature and consequences of social processes, functionalists would maintain, are often unintended by the human actors. The sociologist must show how apparently isolated and unrelated social phenomena may perform unintended functions for the maintenance of society.
3. A crucial social process is the tendency of social systems to react to forces of change in an adaptive manner. This is called 'homeostasis' or 'dynamic equilibrium'.
4. Functionalists set out to characterise the systemic characteristics of organisations which, in turn, are viewed as sub-systems of more inclusive systems (e.g. the economy, 'society').
   (a) The boundaries of organisations are located by determining to what extent any process is primarily concerned with organisational goal-attainment.
   (b) Organisational needs or functional prerequisites are outlined (e.g. adaptation, integration) and the degree to which any process reflects and/or satisfies these needs is examined.
   (c) Organisations are 'open' systems viewed as receiving resources and reacting to problems coming from other systems.

In critical analysis, both the advantages and the limitations of the structural-functionalist perspective were outlined.

1. Functionalism overcomes a narrow concern with the organisation itself and draws attention to the inter-relation of organisation and environment.

2. Social interaction nearly always has consequences which are hidden from the participants and not intended by them. By focusing on unintended consequences, functionalists have grasped an important aspect of social life.

3. By concentrating on the behaviour of organisations themselves, as influenced by a series of impersonal processes, functionalists run the risk of reifying the systems that they construct. One is not convinced, for instance, that the view that organisations take actions in response to their needs is anything more than a convenient way of explaining history as 'what had to be'. One can always invent needs which made past changes inevitable. By de-emphasising the actors' definitions of the situation and the choices of action that are perceived to be available, functionalists inhibit the predictive power of their approach.

4. Functionalists direct our attention to the consequences rather than to the causes of social phenomena. To ask 'what is the function of these parts' tells one nothing about why the parts are like that in the first place. This is only overcome by teleology (the consequence is the cause) or by postulating certain unacceptable evolutionary assumptions.

Conclusions

Perhaps it is fairest to conclude with the views of a sympathetic critic. Alvin Gouldner writes as a functionalist but, no doubt partly as a result of his brilliantly analysed empirical studies, has some misgivings about the direction in which the model appears to be heading. In the course of a survey of the state of organisation theory, he has distinguished two types of analysis both of which, as Mayntz (1964) has pointed out, are variants of the system model. The 'Rational model' relates to the approach of the classical theory of bureaucracy and need not concern us here. The 'Natural System Model', on the other hand, which asks how organisations 'maintain' themselves or 'survive', is clearly patterned on the functionalists' organic analogy.

The 'Natural System Model', Gouldner (1959) argues, despite the insights it can give us, has severe limitations. By concentrating on unintended consequences, it has minimised the importance of 'rational' behaviour in organisations. Its treatment of the relationships between organisations and their environments has shown a 'lack of systematic concern with the way in which the diverse social identities that people bring to the organisation affect organisational behaviour' (p. 412). It has overstated the necessary level of integration in any system and has not explained differences in the amount of integration which do occur among organisations. Finally, and perhaps most damaging of all, the attempt to define systems in terms of their orientation to goals, either assumes a consensus or 'means no more than that these are the goals of its top administrators, or that they represent its societal function which is another matter altogether'.[18]

A problem in the Sociology of Knowledge now clearly arises: why, despite all its deficiencies, should the functionalist version of a system be one of the most popular ways to understand the nature and structure of organisations? Uncharitably, one could say that functionalism is favoured because it is geared to answer the questions of those in control of systems. Thus, Mayntz (1964) has noted the ways in which the 'Natural System Model' is particularly appropriate to the type of problems that management encounters in the newer, more technologically complex industries. Here the issue has shifted from efficient task fulfilment to the consideration of structures with the necessary flexibility to ensure system 'survival' in the face of rapid change (p. 104). However, by no means all functionalists consult for organisations and, presumably, not all aspire to do so. To explain their choice of approach in these terms imputes an unlikely degree of Machiavellianism. A far more plausible explanation is to be found in the present state of Sociology as a discipline.

Possibly at certain stages in the development of a discipline its scholars become concerned to demonstrate its respectability either because of a need to reassure themselves or to encourage the provision of research funds. In Sociology, this concern has expressed itself in two ways. The first and most obvious outlet was in limited empirical studies which appeared to use the methods as well as the perspectives of the natural sciences. The *importance* of the problem being considered took a very subsidiary place to whether, for instance, it could be quantified.

But claims for the 'scientific' character of Sociology could also be made on the basis of the concepts it used as well as its methods of observation. Therefore, the other direction which this search for respectability took arose in attempts to build up theories with concepts deriving from older disciplines. In particular, it appeared that the terms and point of view of biology could be transported *en bloc* over to the study of social phenomena with a notable gain for 'scientific objectivity'. As Emmet (1958) has noted, 'To consider [social actions] . . . under the aspect of function may claim an advantage of *objectivity* . . . the notion of function thus appeals to the point of view of the external observer. The notion of purpose (i.e. of the ends of the actors), on the other hand, may well be eyed with *suspicion* as imprecise, and indeed subjective' (p. 106, my italics).

Of course, one is not arguing that any discipline can do without agreed concepts. Indeed, nowhere is the difficulty involved in using everyday, commonsense terms more apparent than in the study of society. However, the point is that where these concepts are of doubtful validity, which even Merton feels is true of social 'needs', one of the most central concepts of functional analysis, then the end product is likely to be not 'scientific objectivity' but of value-involvement.

The question remains whether it might not be possible to revise functionalist analysis in order to take account of the sort of criticisms that have been made. Gouldner, for one, believes that this is worth trying: 'More precise formulation', he suggests, 'would require specification of the *ends* of different *people*, or of the typical ends of different parts of strata, within the organisation. Such a specification would indicate that these ends may vary, are not necessarily *identical*, and may, in fact, be contradictory' (1959, p. 420, my italics). While one may agree with all of Gouldner's suggestions, it is difficult, if not impossible, to see how they could be embodied in any theory which could still be called functionalist. Gouldner's attempts to revive such an approach reflects the dominant position it has assumed in Sociology.

REFERENCES

1. The remark is made by Poggi (1965) in a paper which is discussed in Chapter Ten.
2. He has noted that the notion of functional prerequisites or needs 'remains one of the cloudiest and empirically most doubtful concepts in functional theory' (Merton, 1949, p. 52).
3. Another reasoned critique of the assumptions of many functionalists is made by Hempel (1959). He argues that the 'explanations' of functional analysis are teleological rather than causal. Instead of examining the causes which 'bring about' a phenomenon, functionalists explain a situation in terms of ends which determine its nature. This leads Hempel to four criticisms:

    1. Functional analysis can explain the consequences that a phenomenon has for the social system but it cannot explain why the phenomenon in question is as it is. Only hindsight makes it appear that functional alternatives might not equally well have served the same function.

    2. Unless one is prepared to accept that systems necessarily react to potential threats to their existence in an adaptive way, functional analysis is unable to make predictions.

    3. Functionalists are often guilty of using vague, ill-defined terms, e.g. what is meant by 'survival' or 'proper functioning' as applied to social systems.

    4. Many functionalists seem to equate 'function' with 'purpose', but the view that systems have purposes is 'empirically vacuous' (Hempel, p. 300).

    Hempel goes on to argue that functional analysis offers 'a directive for research' (p. 301), rather than a series of *a priori* assumptions. It commands us to look for the self-regulating aspects of social systems and, instead of assuming that self-regulation is a given, to examine the various ways in which parts of the system influence its particular mode of adaptation. Hempel's view of the possibilities and limitations of functional analysis bears a resemblance to Gouldner's (1967) argument (discussed elsewhere) that the parts of a social system may have varying degrees of autonomy and hence system integration is problematic rather than given. Cf. also Scheff's (1967) paper arguing that consensus is not a necessity for social life and that we need studies which focus on the degrees of partiality of consensus in different social settings.

4. His particular contribution in this direction is represented by the 'role-pattern variables' (Parsons, 1951, pp. 58–67).

5. This example has been given in a Parsonian critique of earlier functionalism by Bredemeier (1955).

6. His two 'essential reference points' for a systematic sociological theory are: 'a classification of the functional requirements of a system' and 'the arrangement of these with reference to processes of control in the cybernetic sense' (Parsons, 1965, p. 30).

7. Thus Landsberger (1961) has pointed out Parsons's tendency 'to glide, imperceptibly, from the description of a *possible* model and a definition of its various parts, to statements concerning conditions and relationships necessary and existing *if* a certain system is to be stable and then to assertions about phenomena and their relations as they actually exist' (pp. 225–6).

8. Cf. Gouldner's discussion of the relative autonomy and hence attachment of the participants to any particular social system (Gouldner, 1959 and 1967).

9. 'Total institutions' describe the typical definitions of the situation and pattern of interaction within a certain organisation; by analysing organisations in terms of their function for society, one moves away from the orientations of the actors.

10. He probably has in mind here Gouldner's (1959) Rational Model of organisations; this is discussed later in this chapter.

11. 'Our discussion of the common characteristics of all open systems should not blind us to the differences that do exist between biological and social systems. . . . Otherwise we could know about the political state from the science of cytology' (Katz and Kahn, p. 30).

12. 'Lacking the built-in stabilities of biological systems, social organisations', they suggest, 'resort to a multiplication of mechanisms to maintain themselves . . .' (p. 67)

13. 'For example', they write, 'the political activist may be dedicated to the liberal or conservative values of his party' (p. 38).

14. 'We may want to utilise . . . purposive notions to lead us to sources of data or as subjects of special study, but not as our basic theoretical constructs for understanding organisations' (p. 16).

15. The next entries after 'conflict' are: 'conformity', 'consensus', 'consequences' and 'control' (p. 489).

16. This bears a strong resemblance to Parsons's own concentration on the functions rather than the distribution of power.

17. 'It can lead to heightened morale within a sub-system and . . . to solutions which move more in an integrative than a compromise direction' (p. 108).

18. Gouldner (1959), p. 420. This makes a nice criticism of nearly

all functionalists, for while Parsons and Katz and Kahn attempt
to get round this difficulty, they only find themselves in equally
deep waters by defining organisations in terms of their social
function.

4

Organisational Psychology

THE APPROACHES that will be considered in the next two chapters share a great deal in common. Both approaches have grown out of a similar critique of existing theories of organisations. Each arose at the same time and each traces its intellectual origins back to a common position. If the writers in one group tend to be psychologists and those in the other sociologists or social psychologists, then this has been expressed merely in certain differences of emphasis. In many respects, their points of view are complementary and the perspectives they offer combine the same insights and the same limitations. These two schools may be termed 'Organisational Psychology' and 'Socio-Technical Systems'. The latter we shall deal with in the next chapter.

'Organisational Psychology' can be seen as the 'neo-human relations' school.[1] Its most immediate intellectual ancestor is the Harvard group of Mayo, Roethlisberger and Dickson. It shares with them a reaction to the emphases of 'classical' organisation theory.

Intellectual Origins

1. *Classical theory*. Much of what is understood as classical theory developed from observation of the characteristics of the industrial and political organisations which developed in the later decades of the nineteenth century. Their scale and high level of specialisation provided both administrators and the emerging discipline of sociology with a stimulus which provoked new answers to new problems.

In sociology this period is notable for the study of the central features of organisations and their relationship to society. An example of this is Weber's typology of traditional, charismatic

73

and rational-legal structures. Out of the latter developed a
model of the recurring features of 'bureaucratic' organisations
which can best be expressed in Parsons's later formulation—
in terms of his role-pattern variable dichotomy—of the predominant mode of interaction in industrial societies. Roles
in bureaucratic organisations can thus be seen as achieved,
universalistic, specific, affectively-neutral and collectivity-
oriented.[2] Perhaps unfortunately, in an uncharacteristic
moment of dogmatism, Weber committed himself to a view of
this type of organisation as the 'most efficient'. Written at a
time when, at least if one operates with the popular notion of
'efficiency', this may not have been too far from the truth,
Weber did not foresee the ways in which his 'bureaucracy'
might be inappropriate to the problems of the administrator
faced with a rapidly-changing technology. This line of criticism
has been most developed by the 'socio-technical system'
theorists although at least one organisational psychologist has
spoken of 'the need for . . . flexible structure or autonomy' in
modern organisations, and has criticised bureaucracies for
being too slow to adapt to a changing environment.[3]

Weber's ideal-type has, however, come under most criticism
from psychologists because of its alleged failure to take account
of 'human needs'. These 'needs' are expressed in the informal
patterns of behaviour which were first systematically studied
by the Hawthorne researchers. By appearing to ignore 'informal' organisation, Weber seems, to the psychologists at
least, to have considered only one half of the problem. This is
stated, in its most extreme form, by Bennis (1966), who
attributes to Weber a view of 'organisations as if they existed
without people' (p. 66). Since Weber goes to great lengths to
show the means by which different structures are legitimated
to their members, this criticism is, of course, only valid in a very
limited sense. Weber is uninterested in the personality needs of
individuals but he is very much concerned, as even a cursory
glance at his theoretical and methodological works would reveal, with individuals as social actors.

In any event, the source and presentation of the ideal-type of
bureaucracy were not calculated to cut much ice with those
engaged in managing industry. Yet managers, at the turn of
the century, were not as unreceptive as their predecessors had

been to theories about the efficient running of industrial organisations. A slowly rising class of salaried administrators, without the ascribed characteristics of the former owner-managers, were seeking a new source on which to base their claim to authority and turning to theories which, only a little before, would have been dismissed as unnecessary. The techniques offered by the school of 'Scientific Management' combined, in a most acceptable manner, spurious 'scientific' appeal and practical ideas which seemed in harmony with intuition. These techniques (time and motion studies, economic incentive schemes) stemmed from the assumption that man was an economic creature, limited in his pursuit of gain only by his physiological capacities.

However, the simplistic view of motivation implicit in this approach did not recommend itself to later psychologists. First, they argued, men have other than purely economic motives, or to put it more strongly, 'There are many incentives, of which, under normal conditions, money is the least important.'[4] Secondly, the 'carrot-and-stick' hypothesis about the relationship between behaviour and reward is of doubtful validity. Thirdly, these hypotheses depend very much on a view of the worker as an isolated individual rather than a social being engaged in, and deriving satisfaction from, his interactions with his fellows.

2. *Human relations*. Despite the difficulties inherent in the 'Scientific Management' approach, the original perspective of the Hawthorne team, if they had one, derived from its suggestions about physical working conditions and economic incentives. As might have been expected, since Taylor's schemes had already been tried and found wanting, the Hawthorne workers found little relationship between either of these factors and productivity. Only then did they attempt to develop, *ex post facto*, concepts which might explain the factors affecting worker motivation.

Their arguments centred around a view of Social Man as seeking satisfaction primarily by membership of stable work-groups. The moral for management was also quite clear: rather than operating on 'atomised economic automatons', it should work through the small group by encouraging its members to develop favourable views of their situation and by avoiding creating a sense of frustration or threat. Consequently, various techniques were suggested such as 'expressive' supervision and worker participation, which, it was thought, would promote a climate of good human relations in which workgroups could 'usefully' function.

Certain criticisms of these arguments soon began to be aired. When human relations techniques were tested experimentally, it became clear that they by no means always had the desired effect on productivity and work satisfaction.[5] This led on to the suggestion that factors like communications might not be independent variables but dependent on more basic aspects of organisational structure. Critics also made a great deal of the human relationists' lack of concern with extra-organisational factors. For instance, in his analysis of their research findings, Wilensky has found hardly any evidence about the degree of union militancy, the local labour and produce markets, or the class identifications and mobility aspirations of the persons studied.[6] That this is a real and continuing difficulty is suggested by recent human relations studies which manage almost totally to ignore environmental factors.[7]

Finally, the human relations approach is criticised for a crude management orientation which has led its practitioners to suggest that there is no real conflict of interest between the worker and his employer. This view is represented by a contemporary writer: 'The objectives of employee satisfaction and increased productivity', he suggests, 'are not fundamentally opposed'. He then goes on to note that, unfortunately, 'people are not always anxious to see their objectives in the light of organisational objectives. People have to be influenced'![8]

Much of this critique has been accepted by contemporary organisational psychologists. Many would argue that the managerial stance of human relations has involved an underestimation of the measure of genuine conflict between the satisfaction of individual needs and the satisfaction of the organisation's goal of 'efficiency'. Hence what is good for the individual is by no means always good for the organisation and vice versa. McGregor (1960), for instance, has pointed out that high morale is not always associated with high productivity. This leads on to a criticism of human relations for looking for easy answers in the form of techniques instead of questioning an organisational structure which may be at the root of the problem.

Some psychologists add a new critical perspective deriving from their commitment to the multi-dimensionality of human personality needs. May not Mayo and his colleagues, they ask, have become so obsessed with a Durkheimian emphasis on an individual's need for 'belonging', that they forget other needs which may be equally, or more, important in structuring motivation? In particular, following Maslow (1954), once physiological, safety and social needs have been satisfied, the need to realise one's full potential may become the crucial motivating force.

The Contribution of Post-Hawthorne Social Psychology

We are now in a better position to describe the approaches of organisational psychologists. Since these share a remarkable measure of unity, it will help our exposition if we begin by presenting the major elements of their analysis of organisations before examining the individual contributions of different theorists.

1. Individuals can be seen as having 'personality needs' and/or 'generalised motives'. These needs may be arranged in a hierarchy starting with physiological and safety needs and moving towards the need for 'self-actualisation'.
2. These needs and motives are understood to exert a *direct* influence upon behaviour.
3. Behaviour is thus *explained* when we have shown the need or motive upon which it is based.
4. There is a basic conflict between the needs of individuals and the goals of organisations.[9]
5. This conflict is best resolved not by human relations techniques but by changing the organisational structure.[10]
6. The best form of organisation is one which attempts to optimise individual and organisational need satisfaction by means of the following: the encouragement of the formation of stable workgroups and of worker participation in decision-making; good communications and expressive supervision;

non-bureaucratic structures which function by the setting of objectives rather than through a hierarchy of authority.

Four themes will recur as we consider the exponents of this approach:

1. How do we validate the *existence* of personality needs? Are they 'real' or constructions of the psychologist? How do we establish what they are? Are they universal, or is their expression contingent upon circumstances?
2. To what extent is it legitimate to use needs as *independent* variables? Do they really explain behaviour? Is there a basic contradiction between them and the use of a sociological perspective?
3. Even if needs exist, why do they have to be satisfied inside industrial organisations? Why can they not be met *outside* work?
4. Given the criticisms that they make of it, how different are the organisational psychologists from the human relationists?

While we have stressed the similarities in the approaches of these writers, it will now be valuable to assess their separate contributions. For convenience, these can be considered in terms of Schein's (1965) typology: 'Social Man' who seeks to join groups, 'Self-Actualising Man' who seeks to realise his own potential, and 'Complex Man' who has many motives.

Social Man

Man's primary motivating force can be seen as his 'need' to interact with, and to be accepted by, his fellows. This orientation which is fundamental to the explanations of worker behaviour developed by the Hawthorne researchers, has by no means been discarded by all contemporary psychologists of organisations. In particular, social scientists at Harvard, under the influence of Roethlisberger and Homans, while recognising the existence of other needs, have stressed man's 'social' needs and have concentrated their efforts on the study of the small group.

Homans (1950 and 1954) begins by distinguishing the 'external' from the 'internal' aspects of organisations. The former consists of the technology and the authority and reward structures, the latter is the informal system of group relations. Homans goes on to argue that, since differences of interest are an essential part of any system of authority, the most fundamental source of conflict, or, at least, the source most amenable to change, is to be found within the internal structure.[11] This is because man is basically a social animal: 'The working man comes to the factory a *social* person', he suggests. 'He *needs* and makes an opportunity to become intimate with others. Working men tend to form *cohesive groups* of those doing the same kind of job or working at the same place' (Homans, 1954, p. 56, my italics). The solution to his problem, 'can we make industrial harmony the rule and not the exception?', is thus largely based on giving greater freedom to the workgroup by allowing it to participate in decision-making.

This approach has been taken up by J. A. C. Brown, a British social psychologist influenced by both Mayo and Homans. Brown (1964) rejects models of Economic Man by citing evidence of married women who use the factory primarily as a social centre: 'If one begins with the assumption', he writes, 'that the sole incentive to work is money or fear, then such behaviour is incomprehensible' (p. 188). One must recognise the existence of certain psychological needs at work, among which is the need to be 'treated as human beings'. Such needs can be met by firms conscious of human factors and willing to use sound psychological techniques. For instance, 'the pride and interest shown in the affairs of certain concerns (e.g. the Ford Company, Unilever Limited) by those employed in them, when an adequate information service has publicised the company's achievements, is quite genuine and unaffected' (p. 191). He goes on to acknowledge that 'instrumental' attitudes towards work, which emphasise monetary rather than social rewards, do exist but suggests that these are held either by '. . . socially unattached people who are self-sufficient' or by '. . . others [who] are unattached and *miserable*, the group of neurotic men or women who want to "*belong*" but, for various reasons, fail to do so' (p. 192). He notes further that the former group comprise only a very small proportion of the total working population and that their motivation provides '. . . the least *satisfactory* reason for working' (p. 206, my emphasis).

Apart from the value-judgment implicit in this last statement, one can criticise Brown for failing to consider a third group, namely, instrumentally motivated people who are socially attached but derive their social satisfactions outside the workplace.[12] It is because Brown observes behaviour from inside Mayo's blinkers that he is led to argue that only in work can a new organic solidarity be born. It is hardly surprising, therefore, that he concludes with a note of anxiety about the 'neurotic' unattached: 'That the number of workers in this group is increasing is one of the serious problems of modern industry' (p. 192). That this assertion should be made, despite lack of evidence,[13] is a further illustration of the way in which this theoretical perspective can lead, only too rapidly, from 'ought' to 'is' propositions. Because anomic workers *should* be a problem they *are* one.

Probably the most representative contemporary writer in the Social Man tradition is Abraham Zaleznik from the Harvard Business School. He is clearly influenced by the work of his colleague Roethlisberger. His most developed theoretical work focuses exclusively on the small workgroup. He justifies this by arguing that, 'there are probably few organisational problems in which its structure and dynamics can be safely excluded from consideration . . . the effectiveness of large-scale organisations depends, in large measure, on the development of effective small groups'. This is because it is apparent that man desires, above all, the satisfaction to be gained from close interpersonal relations: 'The *fact* that small groups satisfy important human needs assures their survival as a form of organisation.' Moreover, '. . . the small group is at the center of the influence process. Anyone interested in the formation of attitudes and decisions by the individual needs to understand the effects of group membership.' However, the individual need for group membership by itself '. . . does not assure the development of effective groups and *consequently* effective organisations'. Hence we must take as our primary concern the attempt '. . . to show what forces determine the formation of groups in organisations; how individual and group interact . . . and how problems of group *productivity* and change emerge. . . .' (Zaleznik and Moment, 1964, pp. 3–4).

The criticisms which have already been made of the human

relations school, are, as in the case of Zaleznik, in large measure applicable to the Social Man perspective. Of all the later psychologists they are closest in spirit to the Hawthorne team. They have advanced from them only to the extent that they recognise that other, albeit minor, personality needs exist, and that the pursuit of 'industrial harmony' will require change of organisations in addition to human relations techniques.[14] The other theorists we shall now turn to claim a far greater divergence of perspective from the Hawthorne approach, so it will be interesting to consider whether this claim is justified and to explore the directions in which these writers seem to be moving.

Self-Actualising Man

Some psychologists argue that there are still 'higher' needs than the need for group acceptance. In particular, 'self-actualisation', or the realisation of an individual's own potential, becomes increasingly important as 'lower-level' needs are satisfied. Hence the principal role of management is to harness this need by making work intrinsically more challenging and meaningful.

This theory of motivation derives from the work of A. H. Maslow (1954), who argues that man's 'needs' can be considered in terms of an hierarchy. At the lowest level are *physiological* needs, particularly those of food, water, clothing and shelter: these are paramount in importance until they are satisfied. Next follow *safety* needs from which, according to some commentators, spring such mundane motivations as the desire for economic security. Then come the *social* needs—for belonging and acceptance by one's peers—which the Harvard school have stressed so much. Finally, come the needs for *self-esteem*, *status* and *self-fulfilment* or self-actualisation. Maslow goes on to suggest that only when a lower-level need has been satisfied will a higher need become operative: thus a man without food is unlikely, for instance, to be concerned about status. Hence it is the unsatisfied needs which are important in determining motivation. Quite clearly, Maslow's formulation raises many more questions than it settles. One might ask whether these needs are 'real' or merely a useful model for understanding behaviour in terms of how people would act if they were motivated by them. If it is claimed they are real, how do we validate their existence? If they are simply a model, then may not our explanations in terms of them 'explain' very little and, perhaps, even approach tautologies?[15] Finally, are we to assume that the needs operate in all cultures and situations, or only in some? If the latter is the case, is it legitimate to treat them as independent, explanatory variables? Nevertheless, many psychologists, explicitly or implicitly, make use of Maslow's scheme by stressing the higher-level need of self-actualisation.

As applied to organisations, Maslow's need hierarchy involves a direct criticism of the Economic Man of 'Scientific Management', and also suggests the deficiencies of the human relationists' monocausal view of worker behaviour. It is also clearly relevant to management practice as well as to academic debate. Three American psychologists, Douglas McGregor, Rensis Likert and Chris Argyris, have followed Maslow and sought to bring the insights of psychology to the attention of those engaged in managing organisations.[16] In particular both McGregor and Argyris have contrasted the commonsense assumptions which so often govern managerial behaviour with the more sophisticated view of the social scientist, while Likert has suggested that the latter's knowledge is not purely 'academic' but when put into practice can be shown to be highly effective.

McGregor argues that social scientists are particularly well suited to provide managers with information about the most significant forms of expression of 'human energy' and about the best means to make use of them. This is all the more important, he suggests, since the conventional management view of human nature is many decades out of date. According to this, Man is seen as recalcitrant by nature and resistant to change as such. Management should direct people so that certain of their natural instincts are overcome and appeal to other instincts by means of economic incentives. This 'carrot-and-stick' theory, which bears some resemblances to Taylor's position, McGregor calls 'Theory X' and rejects.

Alternatively, McGregor argues, workers' hostility towards management and its instructions can be viewed not as inherent in their personalities but as a reaction to the lack of satisfaction of their needs inside a given organisational structure. Following Maslow, these needs are arranged in a hierarchy and only those needs that are not satisfied influence motivation and behaviour. Inside organisations, McGregor goes on, the higher-level needs are the typical sources of antagonism. Now, because such needs are generally related to the intrinsic rather than extrinsic rewards of work, they cannot be satisfied directly by management. All that can be done is to provide the conditions which will allow the worker to meet his needs himself. Thus the alternative view, 'Theory Y', follows Drucker in suggesting 'management by objectives' rather than 'management by control'. This is very different from the Scientific Management conception of the worker as a 'glorified machine tool': instead of directing people, management must seek to create opportunities for their self-fulfilment. 'The essential task of management', McGregor therefore concludes, 'is to arrange organisational conditions and methods of operation so that people can achieve their own goals *best* by directing *their own* efforts towards organisational objectives' (1966, p. 15).

In much the same vein as McGregor, Argyris has suggested that there is an incompatibility between any formal structure designed to achieve limited economic goals and the expression of the full potentialities of those who work within it. What is gained by the technical efficiency of, say, a bureaucracy or of a certain technology will be balanced by its human costs. The multiple social and psychological effects of organisational form must therefore be recognised, and a balance struck between the competing requirements of worker satisfaction and efficient production.

While McGregor and Argyris use the insights of psychology in order to suggest the limitations of what management can do in its pursuit of conflicting objectives, Likert (1961) is altogether more confident about the capacity of the new approach. Sophisticated managers who are prepared to take account of the 'major motivational forces' that govern behaviour (presumably the need hierarchy), can assure 'attitudes of identification with the organisation and its objectives and a high sense of involvement in achieving them' (p. 98). Moreover, he suggests that, where this is done, both satisfaction and productivity will increase together: 'Managers with the best records of performance in American business and government', he argues, 'are in the process of pointing the way to an apparently more effective system of management than now exists' (p. 1).

To exhort managers to make decisions that take account of Man's hierarchy of personality needs is one thing; to present specific suggestions about the organisational form which can promote both self-actualisation and economic efficiency is quite another. Yet McGregor and Likert, in particular, seem to have few qualms about bringing their reasoning down to an altogether more practical and prescriptive level. Recipes for happy and efficient organisations are not an altogether new phenomenon and it will be helpful, as their suggestions are discussed, to bear in mind the parallels that may exist with much older approaches.

According to McGregor, men are most able to express their potentialities where they can derive satisfaction from their work and understand its relevance to the tasks of the organisation as a whole. Management, therefore, ought to encourage people to assume responsibility, to participate in decision-making and to join a 'tightly-knit cohesive work group'. Similarly, Likert (1959) argues for the encouragement of workgroup formation, for expressive supervision so that foremen 'treat people as "human beings"' rather than as cogs in a machine', and for workers to be allowed to exert 'at least some influence on the overall objectives and decisions of the organisation as well as to be influenced by them' (p. 205). Implicitly criticising Weber and Taylor, Likert argues that all these are most likely to be effective in non-bureaucratic structure, where 'reliance is not placed solely or fundamentally on the economic motive of buying a man's time and using control and authority as the organising and co-ordinating principle of the organisation' (1961, pp. 98–9). In accordance with his optimistic position, he argues that such a structure would be compatible with both human satisfaction and organisational efficiency. It would maximise the former by allowing for procedures which are 'additive' and 'reinforcing', and would facilitate the adaptation of an organisation to its environment by building into it a mechanism for internal change.

It would be misleading to suggest that the self-actualising approach is no advance at all from the position of Human Relations. For both McGregor and Likert seek to emphasise the importance of the formal structure of an organisation and, in the cause of worker satisfaction, argue for considerably more structural alterations than most human relationists would see fit to consider. They are also both committed to the multi-dimensionality of personality needs, and McGregor, at least, is uncertain that satisfaction and efficiency necessarily amount to the same thing. However, the happy facility with which they suggest techniques for maximising productivity, and their tendency to write off, *a priori*, economic issues as sources of antagonism, bears a clear resemblance to what has gone before. This resemblance is all the more striking since they are writing several years *after* the contribution of certain of their techniques to 'efficiency' and to satisfaction has been severely questioned.[17]

If we follow the assumption of the prevalence of a certain set of personality needs among members of organisations, then the only issue is whether the means by which it is suggested that these 'needs' can be met are in fact either efficient or practical. For instance, it might be argued that worker participation is impractical because, if seriously carried out, it involves an intolerable attack upon what management generally regards as within its prerogative (a view which is often shared, although for quite different reasons, by union officials). Or it might be argued that it is inefficient, because once workers share in management their role-interests change and they are regarded on the shop floor merely as other managers. A different sort of issue, although one that can arise within the same framework, is whether such needs may not be satisfactorily satisfied in the expressive roles played outside work, allowing therefore an instrumental involvement in an organisation to co-exist with work satisfaction.

It is also possible, however, to question directly the assumption upon which the organisational psychologists proceed. The difficulty with assuming certain internal personality needs among the members of an organisation is that there is often very little opportunity to validate their existence. In using a sociological perspective, on the other hand, it would be possible to examine the ends and expectations actually held by certain actors and to attempt to locate these in their social situation both within the organisation, and outside it. Interest then centres upon establishing the range of orientations which people bring to their involvement in organisations and upon the varied relationship of different organisational forms to the actors' chances of attaining their ends and satisfying their expectations. Thus, when techniques for increasing satisfaction and efficiency succeed, this would be explained as a consequence of the congruence of the organisational changes with the role-expectations and historical experiences of those concerned, rather than as a result of the satisfaction of a universal need. When they fail, as they often do, then this would not be because workers have misled themselves or repressed their 'true' needs (an almost Marxist position which, nevertheless, many organis-ational psychologists seem to get themselves into), but because there is no such congruence. The question of needs is then the crux of the difference between the sociological perspective and the self-actualising school of psychology.

This is most clearly revealed in the work of Argyris. Argyris (1964) states a theory of fundamental human needs which can only be met within certain types of structure, although he allows that different cultural environments will affect the way in which these needs are expressed and the means necessary to satisfy them. These needs are very similar to those noted by the other theorists dealt with. They include the need to feel a 'sense of competence', to be 'self-aware', to feel self-esteem and to experience 'confirmation' (i.e. to have one's conception of self validated by others). Unfortunately he does not always appear clear whether these are needs which people *do* have or which they *should* have. He recognises this difficulty but hardly re-solves it: '. . . we acknowledge the existence', he notes, 'of individual differences and the impact of society on the need for psychological success. However . . . we have to begin some-where. We do so by simply asking—what *would* happen if people who aspire for psychological success populated organis-ations . . .' (p. 36, my emphasis). While this is an entirely legitimate question, the level of abstraction towards which Argyris now heads is a direct consequence of the nature of the psychological theory that he uses.

The problems involved in fitting this theory into a sociological perspective become clear when, no doubt answering criticism of an earlier work, Argyris brings 'social class' into his analysis.

At first glance, it might seem that what we know about differential class ideologies and behaviour patterns would conflict with any theory of universal human motives. May not some workers, for instance, actually desire jobs that offer little opportunity for initiative and responsibility?

In response to this argument, Argyris first suggests that workers' needs, even if they are relatively limited in scope, may still not be satisfied, and hence that there remains a psychological problem. This is because management 'will not sanction such working-class behaviour as apathy, "getting by" and "low levels of aspiration" ', although it is not immediately apparent to the reader why this should be so.[18] An alternative argument that Argyris puts forward is that it is possible that the needs of workers are not as different as they seem, that '. . . *"underneath"* the layers of social learning there may be strong but *repressed* needs and capabilities for self-actualisation'. Not surprisingly, he goes on: 'Unfortunately, there are no systematic studies that have focused on this proposition' (pp. 79–80, my italics). It is difficult to know what Argyris means by 'underneath' in this context. As with J. A. C. Brown, it would seem that the desire to assert that psychological problems of this nature actually are a central issue in organisations is closely associated with the feeling that they ought to be. One is left with statements which give the impression that a very unlikely interpretation is being put on the data. One is not convinced, for instance, by a 'hypothesis', which appears to be practically untestable, 'that the lower class worker is still *capable* of aspiring toward psychological success, but he has *suppressed* this desire' (p. 86).

If the claim of organisational psychologists to offer a 'general theory' of organisations, which synthesises the knowledge of the social sciences, must be regarded as premature, a sociological approach can still derive a useful insight from their work. This arises not from their substantive writings and still less in the theory of Maslow upon which these are based, but rather from the important reminder that they indirectly provide of the limitations of positivist sociology. Positivism is often associated with the explanation of human behaviour as a direct reaction to an external stimulus:[19] thus, for instance, a non-social factor such as a certain technical system may be thought to produce, by itself, a given pattern of behaviour. However, as McGregor

(1966) has pointed out: 'human behaviour is seldom a *direct* response to objective reality, but is rather a response to the individual's perception of that reality' (p. 216). This view, which is shared by other psychologists, is important because it emphasises the necessity for explanations of human behaviour to take account of both the 'situation' and of the orientations towards it held by the people concerned: the worker is thus only alienated by a certain technology if he brings to it certain expectations and ends (which are not satisfied).

Argyris quite rightly uses this argument as a basis for a critique of contemporary sociology, much of which has appeared to suggest that a given organisational structure by itself produces a given behavioural response.[20] As he says, one must assume an intermediate variable which mediates between the structure and the human response to it (compare Figure 4.1 with Figure 4.2 below).

Organisational structure → Given behaviour

Figure 4.1

Organisational structure → (?) → Given behaviour

Figure 4.2

For Argyris this variable is provided by the human personality and its needs; hence analysis must take account of both structural and psychological variables. But he never convincingly establishes the case for treating personality characteristics as the intervening variable. The moment we turn to the motivations of different actors as the intervening variable, we are once again brought face to face, notwithstanding Argyris's claim to offer a synthesis of the two approaches, with the different nature of psychological and sociological explanations.

When discussing the 'structural' variables that Argyris mentions, the theorists that we have been discussing do, however, make use of one type of perspective widely used by sociologists. Following the functionalists, they are inclined to view social systems in terms of an organic analogy.[21] Such a position directs our attention to the problem of system stability and to its dependence upon the functions which the parts contribute to the whole. Thus Likert, for instance, chooses to consider 'healthy' organisations and to examine the functions of conflict, while Argyris appears to assume a self-maintaining equilibrium within organisations which can only be disturbed by external forces.[22] While such an approach is not without certain advantages, it has introduced the doubtful notion of system 'needs'. Yet Argyris does acknowledge the danger of reification involved in this concept when he asks: 'Does an organisation *behave*? Can "it" *desire*?'[23] His answer, however, seeks, illegitimately, to move from an assertion of the interrelatedness of phenomena to a suggestion that the outcome of such relationships can itself 'behave'.[24] The coupling in analysis of system and personality 'needs' has thus brought together two vague and rather doubtful concepts. Other psychologists have, however, only criticised the conception of personality needs in the context of establishing a case for viewing organisations as systems.

Complex Man

While being sympathetic to the previous approach, Edgar Schein and Warren Bennis—two social psychologists working at Massachusetts Institute of Technology—have sought to move away from Maslow's need hierarchy. In taking up a far less rigid position, they have argued that motives may vary according to situations. Hence 'Complex Men' may have different motives stemming from their separate experiences and may attach different meanings to the same aspects of 'reality'. As a consequence, managers should avoid being over-committed to certain techniques and 'be prepared to accept a variety of interpersonal relationships, patterns of authority and psychological contracts'.[25]

This view is based on a critique of Argyris and McGregor which has been stated most clearly by Bennis (1966). Argyris argues that individual needs and the demands of the formal organisation are incompatible; however, by means of certain techniques, the gap can be reduced to an *optimal* position where both individual and organisational need-satisfactions are maximised. Bennis suggests that simultaneous optimisation is a 'utopian resolution', and prefers McGregor's 'tragic view' which merely calls for a 'satisfactory solution ... [which] recognises the basic ambivalence and conflicts within the *personality*' (p. 72). However, Bennis is critical of two more basic aspects of the 'self-actualisation' approach: the first arises in its diagnosis of the problem, the second in its suggested cure. First, the objection to the notion of human needs is that it is untestable: 'In order for an abstraction to be meaningful', he suggests, 'there must be empirical and experiential validity for it' (p. 15). Secondly, he questions whether the techniques suggested to meet these needs can achieve what they intend. Can organisations really be redesigned so as to make manual jobs inherently satisfying? Can socially skilled supervisors resolve the basic tension between friendship and authority? Can genuine participation occur if it involves overturning key management decisions?

The most fundamental criticism which both Bennis and Schein make of other organisational psychologists is that they fail to conceptualise organisations as 'systems'. Their cogent criticisms of what remains of human relations leads them, however, directly into the arms of the functionalists. Schein (1965), in asking what are the psychological problems of systems, develops an answer which bears striking resemblances to Parsons's 'AGIL' paradigm (adaptation, goal-attainment, integration, latency).[26] A further parallel is to be found in his view of an organisation existing in an environment to which it is related by the 'processes of import, conversion and export', and consisting of sub-systems which interact with one another and with the wider system (see Figure 4.3 below).

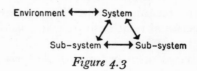

Figure 4.3

'Given a systems concept of organisation', Schein asks, 'how does one assess how well or poorly the system is functioning?' Schein rejects earlier arguments which measure effectiveness in terms of profit, by taking the view that organisations have multiple functions. His own solution derives, once again, from

Parsons: 'Acknowledging that every system has multiple functions and that it exists within an environment which provides unpredictable inputs, a system's effectiveness can be defined as its capacity to *survive, adapt, maintain* itself and *grow* ...' (pp. 95–7, my emphasis). In this argument, he follows very closely Bennis's view of 'organisational health'.

In a chapter entitled 'Towards a Truly Scientific Management: The Concept of Organisational Health', Bennis (1966) criticises Argyris's and McGregor's definitions of efficiency in terms of both high satisfaction on the part of members and effective performance of the organisation in meeting its goals for being essentially static, in that it does not take account of the more or less continuous adaptation to change which occurs in 'healthy' organisations. Instead, he suggests that an organisation should be treated as if it were an organism attempting to meet its needs. Such a view is dynamic because it illuminates the 'processes by which the organisation searches for, adapts to and solves [*sic*] its changing goals ... these dynamic processes of problem-solving . . . provide the critical dimensions of organisational health'.[27]

This Durkheimian conception of disease and health is carried over into Bennis's view of the pathology of conflict, which fails to take into account its social functions as analysed by the more sophisticated functionalist writers.[28] 'Chronic conflicts', he suggests, 'probably dissipate more energy and money than any other single organisational *disease*. Inter-group conflict, with its "win–lose" orientation, its *dysfunctional* loyalty . . . its cognitive distortions of the outsider and its inability to reach what has been called "creative synthesis" effectively disrupts the commitment to truth' (p. 57, my emphasis). Such a facile treatment of the consequences of 'conflict' is only paralleled by Bennis's implicit assumptions about its causes. These become clear when he notes that his 'healthy' organisations, by the 'spirit of inquiry' and 'scientific attitude' which they generate, can resolve inter-group conflict because '. . . rational problem solving is the only means presently known by which organisations may be *rid* of persistent inter-group conflict' (p. 58). To show that he is aware of the difficulties ahead he concedes that, in a full view, '. . . the distribution of power . . . [will] have to be considered.' But apparently it will have to be considered by somebody other than Bennis who devotes no further time to it. Having begun in a tradition which stresses the needs of Man, Bennis has moved over to a primary concern with the needs of the Organisation. To then argue, as he might, that organisational need-satisfaction is not inconsistent with the satisfaction of individual ends is merely, in his own phrase about Argyris's work, to suggest 'a utopian resolution'.

The useful critique which Bennis and Schein make of Self-Actualising Man might have led them to argue that, if the notion of fundamental human needs and motives is of little use, we ought to build up a model which can explain motives and the pursuit of goals in terms of the subjective logic of social situations. Instead, however, they have been attracted by the explanatory power of the organic analogy used by functionalist sociologists. As relatively new adherents to this approach, they have failed to recognise many of its limitations and, as a consequence, have followed a far less sophisticated formulation of it than is currently in use. Unfortunately, as others have noted, such a reaction is not infrequent where converts first come to grips with systems which offer 'total' explanations of reality.[29]

An Evaluation of Organisational Psychology

It was mentioned earlier that the contribution of the organisational psychologists is best assessed by examining their points of departure from other approaches. Human Relations and the Systems perspective are most immediately relevant to the work that has been considered. The arguments that follow take account of the historical link that the psychologists provide between Hawthorne and the Systems frame of reference. We shall consider the similarities between Organisational Psychology and Human Relations; the points of divergence between the two; the move of the psychologists towards systems theory; and the reminder they provide of the limitations of a purely structural sociology.

1. *Similarities with human relations.* The 'Social Man' perspective brings together a group of writers who represent the continuing tradition of the approach to organisations implied by the Hawthorne researchers. They believe that work is the

most important activity to satisfy the social needs of man and to resolve the crises of integration of an anomic society. The possibility of social satisfaction outside work or the emergence of social solidarity other than through economic institutions is not considered.

They focus on the workgroup and de-emphasise the formal structure of the organisation. They suggest techniques for integrating the workgroup into the factory social structure. They are inclined to disregard economic issues or to imply that they are relatively unimportant in motivating men.

2. *Differences from human relations.* A major point of divergence from the Hawthorne perspective is found in the emphasis of certain psychologists on the existence of an ultimate conflict between worker satisfaction and an 'efficient' organisation. Whatever techniques are used, at a certain point it will not be possible to maximise both satisfaction and efficiency: to make workers really happy you may have to give them the day off!

Human motivation is also not quite as simple as the Hawthorne study might imply. Men have a variety of needs arranged in a hierarchy; a higher-level need will operate when a lower-level need has been satisfied.

The emphasis, however, on the multi-dimensionality of needs, and the selection of self-actualisation as the highest-level need of all, is not necessarily convincing. One is not clear whether the notion is intended as an heuristic device or a description of the real world. When Argyris seeks to explain away contrary evidence on the basis of a set of 'repressed' needs, one is given some indication of how cloudy the concept of needs has become. One cannot escape the impression that the humanistic psychologists, like the human relationists, too easily move from 'ought' to 'is', too easily see what they want to see.

3. *Systems.* Many of the writers whose work has been considered in this chapter are critical of the Hawthorne team for an additional reason. In discovering informal organisation, it is argued, they made the mistake of ignoring formal structures. Yet clearly the two aspects of organisation are

inter-related; generally one may not consider the one without the other.

Few would now disagree with such an argument. Yet some psychologists, notably Bennis and Schein, move from a consideration of the inter-relatedness of phenomena to a conceptualisation of organisations as systems. Moreover, we are told that, in many respects, organisations are *natural* systems which are subject to disease and health and which undergo unconscious processes to ensure survival and adaptation. This type of argument is criticised elsewhere in this book and one need only note that this view, in giving power of thought and action to what should be only conceptual categories, is endemically in danger of reifying social constructs.

4. *The limitations of a structural sociology.* To conclude this brief evaluation on a positive note, one owes thanks to the psychologists for re-emphasising the limitations of a purely structural sociology. It is always necessary to clarify the subjective meaning of situations and not to assume that others define the world in the same way as we do. It is not clear, however, that the concept of personality needs provides a universally acceptable means of explaining subjective responses to social objects. The location of actors on a social map is an alternative, and sociologically more satisfactory, basis for explanation.

The Contribution of Victor Vroom

The argument has not suggested that there is no room for psychology in the analysis of organisations: such an assumption would be presumptuous and also fallacious. Rather, the concern has been to criticise certain psychologists. A point of criticism that has not so far been taken up arises in the implicit assumption of certain psychologists that their approach makes it possible to offer a 'general theory' of organisations encompassing all the social sciences: the limitation of such a view is best expressed in their concept of personality needs which has just been discussed. However, there is at least one organisational psychologist to whom there is no need to address these objections.

Victor Vroom (1964) makes abundantly clear, in the preface to his major work, the nature of the perspective he is using: he seeks to explain *individual* behaviour, for 'although research on the behaviour of groups and formal organisations was of interest to me, I doubted that *meaningful generalisations* would emerge which would "cut across" phenomena at different *levels of analysis*' (p. vii, my emphasis). There is no grandiose claim here for a reconciliation of the social sciences. Again, unlike many others, Vroom explicitly states that he is concerned with description and explanation rather than prescription.

Vroom's modest proposition is that 'actions on the part of individuals could, at least in part, be accounted for in terms of their preferences among outcomes and their expectations concerning the consequences of their actions for the attainment of these outcomes' (p. viii). In order to test it, he uses the concepts of 'valency', 'motive' and 'value'. Valence is used, in Lewin's sense, with reference to 'affective orientations towards particular outcomes . . . an outcome is positively valent when the person prefers attaining it to not attaining it. . . .' Motive indicates 'a preference for a class of outcomes', while value refers to the actual as opposed to the anticipated outcome of attaining objects desired. Vroom then goes on to develop hypotheses about the factors affecting occupational choice, job satisfaction and job performance.[30] He illustrates one of these with evidence, albeit largely drawn from human relations sources, that job satisfaction is 'directly related' to the amount of pay received, the amount of consideration that people report they receive from their supervisors, the belief they have in chances of promotion, and their chances of being in a stable workgroup, having a varied task and control over their pace of work.

Vroom is concerned with this analysis because it helps us to understand the patterns of interaction within organisations which people themselves regard as satisfying: 'We must develop', he argues, 'an understanding of the attributes of social interaction which are satisfying and dissatisfying to individuals. The problem which besets the industrial psychologist is to identify the affective consequences of particular forms of social interaction within the work situation' (p. 119). If this is not taken to imply that the valences, motives and values of individuals are universal, this approach is clearly in line with the problem of attachment to organisations—to be considered in Chapter Eight.

The major virtue of Vroom's approach is that he is thoroughly aware of the nature of the perspective he applies and does not seek to pre-empt other sorts of explanation.

Conclusions

Organisational psychology, if its practitioners would only recognise its limitations, provides us with a potentially most fruitful perspective. The analysis of the processes within organisations through which individuals make sense of the social world (e.g. selective perception, psychological 'sets') is something about which sociologists, as Argyris has noted, are most unclear, and is an area in which psychologists clearly have much to contribute.

Throughout this chapter, it has been observed how psychologists, while rejecting the canons of classical organisation theory, have hovered unsatisfactorily between the happy certainties of human relations techniques and the biological simplicities of structural-functionalism. Some are rather more in one camp than the other, others have clearly chosen sides.[31] The same dilemmas arise in theories of organisations as 'socio-technical systems'.

REFERENCES

1. This term is found in Goldthorpe (1966b) who has also distinguished these two schools.
2. Parsons (1951). The application of these variables to organisations has been critically analysed by Banks (1964).
3. Bennis (1966), p. 13. See also Likert (1961), p. 98.
4. Brown (1954), p. 187.
5. This was found particularly to be the case with techniques of supervision, cf. Survey Research Center (1950).
6. As he writes: 'The effect of participation programs might be different with young rural girls on their first jobs in a small pajama factory than on hard-bitten men with long industrial experience and identification with the "working class" and/or a strong union' (Arensberg, 1957, p. 89; cf. also Sheppard, 1954).

7. Cf. Zaleznik *et al.* (1958), who only introduced the social background of their workers as an *ex post facto* variable, and Coch and French (1952), who have only later reluctantly modified their position about the universality of the benefits of participation programmes.

8. W. G. Scott (1962), pp. 48 and 56.

9. Tannenbaum (1966) writes: 'The qualities of personality and motivation that we have discussed are *inconsistent* with the requirements of formal organisation' (p. 32).

10. Tannenbaum goes on to quote a study that he conducted with Seashore: 'Our research was leading us slowly but surely up the organisational hierarchy. It now seemed apparent to us that to get supervisors to behave in optimum ways, one must create conditions in the *organisation* as a whole which make it possible and easy for the supervisor to behave appropriately' (ibid., p. 38).

11. 'When you have put a new group in power,' he writes, '. . . when you have given the working man all the money he can get in your society, you will still find him at his lathe or on the assembly-line. He will still be there' (Homans, 1954, p. 53).

12. Cf. Goldthorpe (1966a) and his explanation of the behaviour and attitudes of Luton car-workers.

13. Blauner (1964) would argue that the latest forms of process technology may in fact limit what he calls 'alienation'.

14. Homans (1954) argues, for instance, that: 'Some characteristics of sheer organisational structure . . . bring it about that persons placed in certain positions . . . feel that their jobs are especially frustrating' (p. 57).

15. For instance, the argument that people *seek* status because they need it; cf. Vroom (1964), pp. 278–9.

16. Cf. McGregor (1966), who argues that the role of management is 'harnessing human energy to organisational requirements' (p. 5); Likert (1961), who points out that his book is 'intended for persons concerned with the problems of organising human resources and activity . . . especially for those who are actively engaged in management and supervision' (p. vii), and Argyris (1964), who takes as his problem 'how organisations might be redesigned to take into account . . . the energies and competencies that human beings have to offer' (p. viii).

17. See, for instance, the University of Michigan, Survey Research Center (1950).

18. Why such behaviour will not be sanctioned or tolerated is not made clear: unkindly we might hypothesise that this will only

occur when managers have been over-exposed to human relations texts telling them about the needs that workers ought to
have. The really interesting question, however, is why managers
develop certain role-expectations of workers and vice versa;
this is taken up as a theoretical issue in Chapters 7 to 9, while
useful empirical studies on this very point have been conducted
by Gouldner (1954 and 1965), Lupton (1963) and Cunnison
(1966).

19. This is one of the meanings of the term discussed by Parsons
(1949).

20. Argyris (1964) gives the example of studies of prisons which
suggest that close control may result in retaliatory action by
the inmates and asks: 'Why should one expect these consequences? There is little question but that they are probably
correct. But such an expectation does not flow from one's
sociologically oriented theory. It requires the addition of a
theory of personality' (p. 286). He seems to make the mistake
here (understandably given the present state of the subject)
that sociology is only able to deal with structural variables.
However, as we seek to show later, the consideration and
explanation of actors' orientations towards situations is central
to sociology.

21. McGregor has argued that an organisation should be viewed
as 'an open, organic, socio-technical system' (1966, p. 238).

22. Likert (1961) argues that 'in every *healthy* organisation there
is . . . an unending process of examining and modifying . . .
organisational objectives' (p. 116, my italics), and Argyris
(1964) concludes that organisations are '. . . so constituted that
[they are] unable to modify [their] internal activities. If changes
were to occur, they would have to be brought into the system
from the environment' (p. 156).

23. Argyris (1964), p. 154.

24. His argument is that '. . . organisations may be said to "do"
something . . . as long as we keep in mind that this phrase
refers to a complicated set of internal processes which exist
simultaneously and therefore defy simple uni-dimensional
description' (ibid., p. 156).

25. Schein (1965), p. 61; he uses the term 'contract' because of his
view that involvement in organisations is based on an exchange
of psychic rewards.

26. The needs of his system are 'recruitment . . . utilising human
resources, integration among the parts of the organisation and
organisational effectiveness—problems of survival, growth and

THE THEORY OF ORGANISATIONS

capacity to adapt to and manage change' (Schein, 1965, pp. 10–15).

27. Ibid., p. 41. It is interesting to compare this view with Burns and Stalker's (1961) 'organic' model of management—see Chapter Four of this volume.

28. For instance Coser (1965).

29. Much the same seems to have happened to some of the disciples of Marx and Freud. For a similar, although not totally uncritical, reaction to the system concept of functionalism see Wiseman (1967).

30. To take one example, he hypothesises that: 'the valence of a job to a person performing it is a monotonically increasing function of the algebraic sum of the products of the valences of all other outcomes and his conceptions of the instrumentality of the job for the attainment of these other outcomes' (ibid., p. 279).

31. For instance, Katz and Kahn (1966), while they write as social psychologists, have so totally assimilated a Parsonian perspective that we have included them in Chapter Three rather than here.

5

Technology and Organisations

Technological Implications

The conceptualisation of organisations as systems has owed a great deal to the way in which technology appears to be intimately related to organisational form and human behaviour. However, by itself, a concern with technology may stop short of the consideration of the characteristic pattern of relationships within organisations as a whole. In other words, it may merely analyse the links between certain forms of technology and various types of worker behaviour and need not be directly concerned with the construction of a theory of organisations. Much American work has been characterised by an interest in these more limited problems and has prepared the way for the development of the concept of a Socio-Technical System.

Human relations' attempts to understand the factors affecting job satisfaction have taken the workgroup as the primary unit of concern. However, as more and more empirical research took place, it became apparent that the nature and role of the workgroup, far from being given because of the needs of Social Man, could vary considerably in different organisational, and especially technological, settings. The nature of the work being done, for instance its pace and degree of cleanliness, could affect the satisfaction of the worker as much as the state of human relations. Indeed, human relations might be dependent on the organisation of work which could shape the possibility of meaningful social relationships within workgroups.[1] The way ahead for those sympathetic to a human relations approach was now clear. Attention could still be directed towards the workgroup, and the assumption of the 'beneficial' effects of strong workgroup ties still be made, but all this would have to take place within a framework which recognised that crude prescriptions about techniques would have to be replaced by a careful analysis of the ways in which behaviour could be shaped by different organisational settings.

W. F. Whyte: *Technological Positivism*

William Foote Whyte (1959) is perhaps the best representative of those on the border line between human relations and 'technological implications'. Drawing on the interactionist critique of human relations, he uses a conceptual scheme deriving from Homans.[2] Organisations are to be analysed in terms of 'interaction', by which he means interpersonal contacts, 'activities', or tasks at work, and 'sentiments', which he defines as 'the way individuals feel about the world around them' (p. 157). These influence each other and are influenced by the 'environment' of the organisation which, following Homans, includes the technology being used (see Figure 5.1 below).

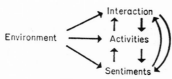

Figure 5.1

Quite clearly, this is an advance on the Hawthorne approach, although Whyte still regards himself as a human relationist: 'If we take seriously the statements presented here regarding the impact of the environment upon the social system', he writes, '. . . then we must recognise that there is no such thing as the good foreman and the good executive' (p. 181). In recognising the importance of the environment, Whyte goes on to use one of its components, technology, as an explanation not only of 'activities', as is obvious, but also of 'interaction' and 'sentiments'. Thus assembly-line technology, the favourite example of this school, itself leads to 'negative sentiments',[3] while the nature of a workgroup is the product of the range of tasks performed and financial rewards of the workers concerned, both of which are themselves largely dependent upon technology. He goes on to use Sayles's concept of 'resonance' to suggest that relative undifferentiation of these factors 'tends to facilitate the formation of a cohesive work-group which acts in a unified fashion in relation to management and the union' (p. 162).

However, it is by no means clear, unless one makes the assumption that all men need and desire to be members of cohesive workgroups, why mere similarities of work and reward should make them form one. The strategies which workgroups adopt seem in no way to be determined by the relative lack of differentiation of their component parts. W. H. Scott *et al.* (1963), for instance, in their study of the Lancashire coalfield found that the behaviour of different groups of workers

Type of → [Universal human needs → Behaviour pre-
Technology   (given)]   dictable from
                                                    knowledge of
                                                    technology

Figure 5.2

Type of → [Definitions of the → Behaviour
Technology   situation and ends of   unpredictable
              the actors (empirically   from knowledge
              open)]   of technology

Figure 5.3

stemmed mainly from their relative position in the balance of power within the organisation and from their status within the community.[4] Whyte thus appears to make the mistake of viewing behaviour and motivations as the *outcome* of technology. This *positivist* explanation of behaviour in terms of a non-social factor is something in which all the members of this school indulge. However, as Argyris has pointed out, this does imply assumptions about an intervening variable on which technology operates and which in turn influences behaviour. On closer inspection this turns out to be the 'needs' of human personalities. It is because these needs are taken as universal, at least within any one society, that members of this school are able to be so confident about the 'effects' of technology.

Whyte's limited view of the components of an organisation's environment directs attention away from the processes through which experiences within the larger society impinge upon the ordering of wants and expectations and upon the meaning which people attach to different aspects of an organisation's structure.[5] If one were to concentrate upon these then the consequences of technology would become problematic (compare Figure 5.2 with Figure 5.3).

L. Sayles: Technology and the Development of Workgroups

An attempt to understand the inter-relatedness of formal and informal structures is also to be found, as in Whyte, in the work of Leonard Sayles. While swift to the defence of human relations ('. . . many researchers who are blanketed-in under the reproachful term "human relations" deal directly and specifically with environmental forces particularly structural forces'), his contribution nevertheless illustrates how slow the adjustment to these factors has been. Even within his own study, he notes: 'Our whole emphasis has shifted from concentrating on the informal group to the relation of workgroup behaviour to the technological and organisational setting' (1958, pp. 168 and 160). But to recognise the role of technology is one thing, to view it as the *determinant* of behaviour, as Sayles seems to do, is clearly another: 'the conclusions of this study', he writes, 'indicate that the technology of the plant . . . *molds* the type of workgroups that evolve . . . the *human* element, so-called, is a resultant of the *technological* decisions and, in part at least, *predictable* from them' (pp. 4–5, my italics).

Four distinct types of workgroup are distinguished by Sayles on the basis of their level of skill and degree of interpersonal interaction (see Figure 5.4). 'Apathetic' workgroups are composed of relatively unskilled men who work individually rather than in groups. They have little sense of group solidarity, low morale and are regarded by management as unsatisfactory employees. Unskilled workers who have a relatively large amount of interaction with one another form 'erratic' workgroups which develop solidarity on occasions but are not usually very shrewd about choosing the right sort of situation in which to express their grievances. They have authoritarian leaders and make unpredictable employees. 'Strategic' workgroups are typical of skilled workers with high interaction at work. They tend to be highly calculating in their strategies and yet are accepted by management. The highest skilled workers of all form 'conservative' workgroups, which maintain a strong sense of group identity even when their members are dispersed and are primarily concerned with the stability of traditional wage differentials.

		Interaction	
		High	*Low*
	Unskilled	Erratic (dockworkers)	Apathetic (labourers)
Skill			
	Skilled	Strategic (skilled steel workers)	Conservative (craftsmen)

Figure 5.4

It is difficult to see how this analysis, based on workers drawn only from 'mass production' industries, can be given any general validity. Even using a technological perspective, it seems likely that the varying proportions of different skills required from industry to industry may affect the nature and aims of work-group behaviour. When we bring in historical and environmental factors, the explanatory power of Sayles's scheme would appear to become rather limited.

Nevertheless, even if Sayles does cling too determinedly to a closed system, his work does represent a further advance by recognising the existence of perceived conflicts of material interest inside enterprises and the use of strategies by the actors. As opposed to the *friendship* and *task* groups analysed by the Hawthorne team, he notes the functioning of *interest* groups arising from the market situations of workers with differing work roles.[6] He goes on to criticise the older view of work-groups as essentially *passive* attempting to maintain group stability merely by reacting to the demands of management as expressed through the formal organisation. Many of his work-groups, on the other hand, acted to *improve* their relative position. 'This is not the traditional concept of the informal group seeking conformity with established norms of conduct,' he notes, 'these are much more free enterprise units interacting in a struggle for maximisation of utility' (p. 158). Workgroups thus play many more functions for their members than merely the satisfaction of their social needs. In a further criticism of Hawthorne, he emphasises that workgroup interaction may not lead to integration and equilibrium but to conflict and instability inside organisations.[7]

Studies of the Assembly-Line

If, however, the relation of workgroup behaviour to technology was to be fully understood, it seemed necessary to study both industrial settings which appeared likely to encourage workgroup formation and those which might prevent it. Assembly-line technology appeared to be the best representative of the latter case and, accordingly, it attracted a series of studies. The work of Walker and Guest (1952 and 1956) established its well-known characteristics: it is repetitious, machine-paced, involves a minimum of skill, the use of predetermined techniques, a minute subdivision of the product and calls for only a limited degree of attention so that the work can be done 'automatically'. Moreover, social interaction between assembly-line workers is limited by the noise, which makes talking difficult, by the need to keep up with the line and to remain in one place to do so, and by the individual nature of each man's work. Workers do not work in groups or teams but each performs an individual task, taking, on the average, one and a quarter minutes per operation. Hence the technology is held to deprive the workers of satisfaction, and this assertion is supported by evidence that men whose jobs approached closest to the ideal-type of assembly-line work had the highest scores on absenteeism and were most likely to give up their jobs.

The instrumental attitude to work which this lack of work-group interaction is held to generate is something, of course, which any manager concerned with good human relations would deplore. Moreover, since it stems from the technology which is basic to the industry, there might appear little to be done. Foremen, for instance, have no room for initiative in attempting to modify the work to meet human needs, for problems of work organisation are decided by experts. Again, since the men work as individuals, there is no workgroup to support supervisory attempts to create favourable definitions of the situation. Hence all the basic conditions for satisfactory human relations might appear to be absent. Nevertheless, Walker and Guest are not without an answer. If there is no workgroup, then the foreman must carry out his functions through individual workers. Indeed, by mediating the anonymity of assembly-line work, by playing an expressive role and by making it clear that they are equally subject to the control of the assembly-line, supervisors can become the focus of the workers' feeling and provide leadership for an otherwise fragmented group.

As Goldthorpe (1966a) has pointed out, the difficulties with Walker and Guest lie not so much in their findings as in the interpretation which they give to them. The most obvious characteristic that this has is an implicit assumption about man's needs at work: the technology is only unsatisfying because these needs are not met by it (see Figure 5.2 above). If, however, these needs are not treated as given but as problematic (see Figure 5.3 above), then explanations may be of a very different nature. What is more, there is some evidence about the nature of the ends operating in this situation. Walker and Guest point out that 90% of their assembly-line workers had previously worked in jobs where the pace of work was not machine-governed, while the previous job of 72% had been non-repetitive. Moreover, a full 15% had come from professional, managerial, clerical or sales jobs, a further 26% from skilled manual work, while 50% were high-school graduates.[8] It is not stretching the evidence too much to suggest that this indicates at least an element of choice in the decision to take up assembly-line work. The reason for this choice is, of course, clear: the large wage-packets which, in good times, car-assembly work can offer. Indeed, as Walker and Guest note, 80% of their workers liked their job for its economic benefits.

What this suggests then, is that explanations of the assembly-line worker's instrumentality in terms of the 'dehumanising' nature of the technology in which he finds himself are, *prima facie*, no more convincing than an explanation in terms of a self-selection of instrumentally motivated individuals into such work. The second explanation is further supported by Goldthorpe's evidence that, while 94% of his sample of Luton car-workers said they got on well with their foreman, 65% of these gave an explanation in terms of their infrequency of contact and only 26% gave reasons which referred to more positive forms of supervisory behaviour. 74% also rated Vauxhall's, where they worked, as better than most employers. Similarly, Walker and Guest's finding of the greater tendency of assembly-line workers to give up their jobs can be reconciled with the self-selection hypothesis. For if, as happens at times of economic slump, the work does not offer opportunities for high rewards through overtime, then it is tempting for the instrumentally-oriented worker to move elsewhere to a more secure job. Equally, if the reasons for the instrumental attitude lose their force, then the worker may move on.

The possibility that Walker and Guest do not consider is that a highly instrumental attitude and a low level of work involvement can co-exist with a high measure of job satisfaction. This is because, as neo-human relationists, they first take as given a set of human needs and then assume that these have to be met at work rather than being satisfied elsewhere. Without the shackles of these assumptions, it is possible to ask, on the other hand, which sort of experiences generate an overwhelmingly instrumental attitude towards work and which do not.[9] Such a question, coupled with an attempt to understand the structuring of group relations inside organisations in terms of the different strategies available to the participants, would enable us to deal far more adequately with the empirical evidence about different behaviour patterns between groups and of varying reactions to the same technology.[10]

Blauner: Technology and Alienation

Following on from the work on assembly-line behaviour, Robert Blauner (1964) has attempted a comprehensive examination of the relative 'alienating' capacities of a wide range of technologies. Accepting that modern technology itself, rather than the social relations of production within a capitalist economy, is the 'cause' of alienation, Blauner hypothesises that some technologies are more alienating than others. To simplify, he argues that work in craft industries is most satisfying, in assembly-line production least satisfying, while process technologies fall somewhere between the two. All this implies a conscious reaction on his part (he approvingly cites Whyte and

Walker and Guest) against the concentration of early human relations studies on interpersonal relations as the crucial variable in work behaviour.

Technology, according to Blauner, is to be seen as the central determinant of behaviour. 'I attempt to show', he notes in his preface, 'that the worker's relation to the *technological* organisation of the work process and in the social organisation of the factory *determines* whether or not he characteristically experiences in that work a sense of control rather than domination . . .' (p. vii, my italics). Since he goes on to argue that the social organisation of the factory is largely a product of the technology (see Figure 5.5 below), it is difficult not to label him as a 'technological determinist'. This view of his work is supported by his later assertion that the technical system structures a worker's sense of powerlessness and self-estrangement, his

Technology $\rightarrow$ Social Organisation $\rightarrow$ Worker's Alienation or Involvement

Figure 5.5

degree of cohesion with his fellows, and the nature of workgroups, if they exist at all. However, he does recognise the difficulties into which his arguments might lead him when he argues that '. . . despite my emphasis on *impersonal* factors, this study does not follow a *totally* deterministic approach . . . the character of the labor force in particular industries and the personalities of individul employees influence their subjective and behavioral responses to objectively alienating conditions' (p. 11, my italics). This could have led him into a consideration of the way in which social factors mediate between the individual and technology, but, in his subsequent chapters, Blauner fails to develop such an analysis. Indeed, all too soon, he apparently forgets his earlier disclaimer: 'His industry', he writes about the worker, 'even affects the kind of social personality he develops, since an *industrial* environment *tends* to breed a distinctive social *type*' (p. 166, my italics).

A further difficulty in Blauner's approach is shown in his conception of an 'objectively alienating condition'. Implicit in this is a moral judgment, drawn in varying measures from

Marx, Fromm and Argyris, about the sort of work which *ought* to be satisfying.[11] This is, of course, rather different from examining the ends and conceptions of job satisfaction which men actually *do* bring to work, and then comparing these with the actual nature of their work. This would not matter if Blauner did not speak about his view of 'alienation' as an 'objective' condition. The problem occurs again in Blauner's later conclusion that '. . . we cannot assume that men are only what they are at present or what they themselves desire to become' (p. 187). Perhaps not, but by not making this assumption we are constructing a moral system rather than explaining action through the accepted methods of observation and analysis.

SOCIO-TECHNICAL SYSTEMS

The somewhat varied group of writers dealt with under the title of 'Technological Implications' share a concern with elaborating the consequences of different types of technology (given certain assumed personality needs of those studied) for job satisfaction and workgroup behaviour. While this illustrates the demands of one structure on another, it is not fully satisfactory from a Systems point of view. This is because such an approach need not ask questions about the nature and causes of system stability and goal-attainment or take account of the resources provided and demands made by the environment in which an organisation is located. The view of organisations as Socio-Technical Systems, on the other hand, stresses the inter-relationships of technology, environment, the sentiments of the participants and organisational form. Since the nature of these relationships will determine the stability and even the survival of any economic organisation, all the variables must be taken into account in empirical analysis and in prescribing change.

Socio-technical system theorists have usually been satisfied that the assumptions of the organisational psychologists, together with certain propositions derived from psycho-analytic theory, provide an appropriate way to deal with the purposes and orientations of the members of organisations (sentiments).

At the same time, they are agreed that the value of much early work was vitiated by a concentration on 'informal' behaviour and its consequent failure to develop a view of an organisation as a system, with inter-related formal and informal structures, which is shaped by and shapes the environment. In the last chapter we saw that two psychologists, Schein (1965) and Bennis (1966), are concerned with the processes whereby the psychological problems of systems can be met and with assessing their relative success in doing so: to meet these problems as Bennis points out, is a 'healthy' response, while not to do so implies a pathological organism. Socio-technicists, as will be seen, are equally committed to this organic view of organisations. Yet there are certain differences between their approach and that of the functionalists.

Structural-Functionalism is a well-developed mode of analysis which has been taken from the realms of sociological Grand Theory and applied to the substantive study of organisations. The Socio-Technical System approach, on the other hand, grew out of observation of behaviour in economic organisations and was only later codified into a set of related propositions. Many of its proponents have been prescriptive in their orientation and much of the work in this tradition has arisen out of attempts to make greater sense of material gathered during consultancy. Finally, socio-technicists have sought to develop an inter-disciplinary perspective, which has drawn on economics, psychology, and even psycho-analysis, rather than to make use of the more strictly sociological frame of reference of the functionalists. It is possible, however, to exaggerate the differences between the two approaches. Both adhere to a Systems position and in so doing manage to ask much the same questions and to derive similar answers.

An organisation may be viewed as a Socio-Technical System in the sense that, while the technology, the formal role-structure and the sentiments of the members are systematically connected, none is of prime importance or necessarily the first target of analysis. All may be seen as inter-related with each other and with the environment in which the organisation is located. Thus the technology, together with the formal structure, is thought to limit the amount of human satisfaction that may be derived from participation and to shape the nature of the output to the outside world. In turn, both are shaped by the demands which the environment makes on the organisation. The problem of this type of analysis then becomes: what kind of formal structure can most effectively relate to one another the varied demands of the environment, of the technology and of the members? Effectiveness is here usually defined as the attainment of the goal or 'primary task' of the organisation.

There is no one most efficient form of organisation; even bureaucracy, the attractions of which were so vigorously presented at the beginning of the century and then equally vehemently denied as knowledge was obtained of the 'vicious circle' (Gouldner, 1954)—an appeal to formal rules can add to instability—and the 'displacement of goals' (Merton, 1949)—a means to a goal may become the goal itself—is, by itself, neither an efficient nor inefficient instrument. It all depends on the nature of the organisational goal and on the demands made by sub-systems (e.g. the members) and by other systems (e.g. the economy) on the organisation. Different organisational forms are, therefore, appropriate to different combinations of demands.

We shall now turn to various discussions of the nature and consequences of the demands made, respectively, by the technology employed, the sentiments of the participants, and the environment.

Joan Woodward: Technology, Decision-Making and Organisational Structure

Joan Woodward's (1958 and 1965) study of industrial firms in SE. Essex suggested to her that production systems could be placed somewhere on a continuum based on degree of technical complexity. At one end would be found the relatively non-complex unit (or small-batch) production; highly complex process production would come at the other end, while mass (or large-batch) production would be located somewhere in the middle. She went on to examine the range of organisational forms that she encountered and found that firms with similar production systems were organised in a similar manner. The levels of authority in management increased with technical complexity, as did the proportion of managers and supervisors to non-supervisory staff. However, there were also certain similarities between firms using unit and process production—the least and the most complex technologies. In the first place, although staff (experts) and line (administrators) were sharply distinguished in mass production firms, there was very little specialisation among the functions of management in the other technical forms. In unit production firms, this was because a smaller number of specialists tended to be employed and line management, therefore, had to be technically competent. On the other hand, the status of expert positions was so high in the process production enterprises that it was often impossible to distinguish between the specialist's role of advice-giving and the administrator's role of decision-taking. Moreover, in such organisations, even those most directly concerned with administration require a level of technical expertise in order to grasp the complexities of the production process.

A second similarity between the extremes of technical complexity was that the organisations concerned tended to have relatively non-bureaucratic structures as opposed to the more rigid bureaucratic form often found in mass production. This arose, Woodward suggests, because the 'central problem' of unit and process technologies (respectively, product development and marketing) involves the need to innovate; and decisions made through a formal hierarchy might be slow and unoriginal. On the other hand, in mass production the central problem is the efficient administration of production and bureaucracy is clearly appropriate.

The number and nature of policy decisions arising in each technical system also have an influence on the organisational form that is most efficient. In unit production, while a relatively large number of decisions needs to be taken, these tend to have only short-term consequences which commit the firm for the period during which an article is produced. It is most appropriate, therefore, to have decisions made on the spot by those with the most competence for the problem at issue, instead of having to work up through a bureaucratic hierarchy. In mass production, fewer decisions are taken but these tend to commit the firm further into the future (for instance, compare the limited consequences of a decision made by an haute couture dressmaker with the long-term consequences of a motor firm deciding to produce a new car). However, Woodward argues, these decisions often affect only one function of management (e.g. production, sales or research) and can be taken by the senior executive responsible for that function through the normal bureaucratic channels. In process technologies, however, while the fewest policy decisions of all are made, these tend to commit the firm furthest into the future and cannot be taken by one individual. Instead, they require the pooling of all the expert knowledge on the topic at hand—irrespective of the formal position of the expert in an authority hierarchy. In this situation the limitations of bureaucracy are further revealed as decision-making becomes far less dependent on 'hunches'; it is therefore difficult to establish a separate administrative function for the non-expert.

E. Trist: Technology and the Needs of Workgroups

Woodward's work points out the limitations of the view that there are principles of management valid for all situations by showing the different demands that technical systems made on organisations. An organisational form may be right for the technology and economic tasks of the enterprise, yet fail to satisfy other important demands. This was the conclusion of a study of the process of mechanisation in the coalmines of NW. Durham conducted by Eric Trist and others (1963). Their research convinced the writers of the intimate relationship between the technical, economic and social aspects of organisations. The traditional technology of the mines ('single-place working'), where small teams of men worked their own part of the coal-seam, had facilitated the formation of multi-skilled, self-selected, largely autonomous workgroups. This allowed a great deal of independence within the workgroup and generated a relatively high level of job satisfaction. Since the workgroups did not compete with one another, their relations were normally harmonious.

This technology was, however, being replaced by mechanical coal-cutting and specialisation of workers by shift: one shift cut the coal with a mechanical coal-cutter, the next loaded the coal on to a conveyor, and the third shift propped up the roof and moved the conveyor and the cutter for the next shift. This 'conventional longwall method' was technically efficient but had dysfunctional social consequences. It broke up the self-selected workgroup and destroyed some of the loyalties and cohesion necessary in dangerous work, especially since the members of each shift were not always able to get along with each other. Moreover, the specialisation by shift necessitated greater co-ordination from the surface to ensure that each shift completed its part of the cycle. Supervision became closer and the men reacted strongly against having to forgo still more of the inde-pendence which they had traditionally enjoyed. The end pro-duct of the change was technical and economic inefficiency and social disturbance.

However, a different form of work organisation, Trist argues, could maximise the benefits of technical advance and minimise the dangers of unrest and conflict. According to the 'composite longwall method', the three-shift cycle remains but there is no sharp division of tasks between shifts; miners are allowed to make use of their multiple skills. At the same time, supervision is lessened and the workgroup retains its autonomy by being given the responsibility for the deployment of men to each shift. Thus it permitted, Trist would suggest, an optimum relationship between the often opposed claims of technical, economic and social systems.

Woodward and Trist deal with the demands which tech-nology and the social ties of the participants make upon organi-sations. Other socio-technical theorists have concentrated on the ways in which the characteristics of an organisation's en-vironment (especially those associated with the nature of the market in which it operates) shape what would be the most appropriate organisational structure. This problem has been taken up notably by Burns and Stalker (1961) and by Emery and Trist (1965).[12]

Environment and Organisational Structure

In the course of a study of twenty British firms, Burns and Stalker became convinced that management systems could use-fully be seen in two ideal-typical forms. The Mechanistic Model approaches Weber's bureaucratic type and is charac-terised by a clear hierarchy of offices involving strict specialisation, vertical communication, and the implicit assumption that 'somebody at the top' is responsible for making sure that everybody's specialism is relevant to organisational goals. The Organic Model, on the other hand, has no clearly defined hierarchy and involves a continual re-definition of roles and hence a lack of formal job titles. Functions are co-ordinated by frequent meetings between managers, and communications are lateral and regarded as providing information and advice rather than instructions. There is no longer an omniscient person at the top to whom consideration of action in terms of organisational objectives can safely be left. Instead, individuals are expected to perform their tasks in the light of their knowledge of the overall aims of the enterprise.

Burns and Stalker now go on to note that *neither* Model is necessarily efficient or inefficient; it all depends on the nature of the environment in which the firm is located. The Mechanistic type is most appropriate for enterprises operating under relatively stable market conditions and using an unchanging technology. In these situations, the routinisation of behaviour which it generates is functional for the unchanging tasks which must be dealt with. An Organic structure, on the other hand, mobilises expert knowledge without too much regard for the formal place of the expert in the hierarchy. By not freezing at a certain point of time the amount of authority given to different tasks, it is appropriate to an unstable situation in which the organisation is continually experiencing relatively unpredictable new tasks and problems.

The Open System perspective, which Burns and Stalker's study implies, seeks to take account of the full range of inputs into an organisation. In the same manner (but influenced by the general system theory of von Bertalanffy, 1967, and his use of concepts drawn from the natural sciences), Emery and Trist (1965) advocate an Open Systems Model and consider various types of environment, each of which makes different demands on organisational structure.

In a 'placid, randomised' environment, there is no causal connection between the unchanging and separate parts, and relatively small, undifferentiated organisations can flourish. In a 'placid, clustered' environment, organisations must develop a measure of specialisation and adopt strategies, as distinct from tactics, in order to meet a setting where aspects of their environment are causally related. In a 'disturbed-reactive' environment there are organisations pursuing similar goals and each one must decide between competition, co-optation and co-operation with the others. Finally, in 'turbulent fields', where the environment itself is changing in addition to the changes deriving from the interaction of organisations, organisations must adopt non-bureaucratic structures and attempt to develop a consensus of values about their forms of relationship. Such a consensus provides an 'organisational matrix'.

Underlying what Emery and Trist are doing, and perhaps confused by the terms that they bring in from the physical sciences, is an assumption that the situations which organisations were originally designed to meet may no longer exist. As technical and economic change accelerates, an attempt must be made to make the unpredictable predictable, or at least to create structures which will be prepared to deal with rapidly changing conditions. This point of view has its parallel in the work of Bennis, and in the studies of Burns and Stalker and of Woodward. It is interesting to note that the 'open-system' concept, when based on an organic analogy and concerned with the way in which environments serve to meet the 'needs' of organisations (which in turn perform 'functions' for other systems) becomes indistinguishable from structural-functional analysis. This is particularly clear in the emphasis of Emery and Trist on an evolutionary process of differentiation in social systems which bears striking resemblances to the views of Parsons.

Miller and Rice: Task Systems and Sentient Systems

Rice (1963) has also been explicitly concerned with the analysis of organisations as Open Systems which 'can only exist by the exchange of materials with their environment' (p. 184). However, unlike the other writers so far discussed, he considers together the impact of the various components of the system on each other and provides a means of assessing the relative success of an enterprise in adapting to the demands made upon it. An organisation is successful to the extent that it manages to attain its 'primary task'. This concept is central to the development of Rice's approach but is not developed until a later volume.

Miller and Rice (1967) define primary task as 'the task it [the organisation] must perform if it is to survive' (p. 25). If this seems somewhat tautological, they add that it is a descriptive rather than normative category and hence is not to be identified with the commonsense view within the society about what the primary task of an organisation should be. A better way of establishing the nature of the primary task is to examine the statements which the leaders of an enterprise make about the goals of their organisation. However, these views can be 'wrong', 'if through inadequate appraisal of internal resources and external forces, the leaders of an enterprise define the primary task in an *inappropriate* way' (p. 27, my italics). If this is so, then the very survival of the organisation may be jeopardised. Thus one is only left with inferring the primary task from observation of the behaviour within the organisation and of the criteria by which it is judged by those taking part. This allows us to argue that 'This enterprise is behaving as if its primary task were . . .', or that 'This part of the enterprise is behaving as if the primary task of the whole were . . .' (p. 28).

The means by which organisations attain their primary task are embodied in the formal structure, or what Miller and Rice call the Task System. This is distinguished from the informal structure, or Sentient System, which directly commands the loyalty of the members. Sentient Systems derive from the personality needs which motivate the human participants. Following the Hawthorne approach, individuals are assumed to need to belong to small face-to-face groups at work: in return for the security provided, loyalty must be shown towards group norms. Hence, in a view not unreminiscent of a much older analysis, it follows that, unlike task systems, sentient systems are non-rational: 'At the level of task performance', they suggest, 'members take part as rational, mature human beings; at the level of assumptions they make about each and the group, they go into collusion with each other to support or to hinder what they have met to do' (p. 18).

The concept of a socio-technical system is arrived at by suggesting that the task system operates directly upon the sentient system. Thus Miller and Rice write: '. . . the nature of the task and of the activities involved in its performance can provide the individual with *overt* satisfactions . . . or . . . deprivations . . . it can also provide satisfaction and deprivation by reciprocation with the *inner* world of *unconscious drives* and needs for defence against *anxiety*' (p. 31, my italics). So the personality needs of the workforce provide a limiting factor on the type of organisation used to achieve the primary task; that is why we must talk about socio-technical systems. The goal of analysis must, therefore, be that set down by Trist in his development of '. . . solutions that [take account of] . . . the technical requirements of the task and the human needs of those performing it. The assumption was made that the "right" organisation would satisfy the *task* and *social* needs' (pp. xi–xii).

Thus an organisation needs a structure to 'ensure the commitment of its members to enterprise objects and . . . to regulate relations between task and sentient systems' (p. xiii), so that, as far as possible, human needs and the task system coincide. Three situations are possible: the tasks performed may preclude a coincidence with the sentient system, as in the case where people have commitments to task systems outside the organisation (for instance 'cosmopolitan' professionals); a 'natural coincidence' may occur, as in the case of a family business where task and sentient groups coincide; or there may be a 'contrived coincidence' such as Trist claims is provided by the composite longwall method of mining. Such a contrived coincidence will need to ensure that the method of work allows 'internally led, quasi-autonomous, primary work groups' (p. 255) to survive and flourish.

An Evaluation of Socio-Technical Systems

This brief treatment of the literature has had to impose a false measure of unity on a range of different positions. As with Structural-Functionalism, therefore, it is difficult to evaluate an approach which has no clear orthodoxy. Nevertheless, the socio-technical theorists do share certain views in common, not least because of their situation on the eastern side of the Atlantic and their commitment to abstracted empiricism in preference to grand theory.

The advantages of the approach, while they are by no means insubstantial, can be speedily dealt with. They can be seen most clearly by a comparison with the perspectives that historically preceded it. Unlike them, it has taken account of the inter-relatedness of formal and informal, and of organisational and extra-organisational. Unlike them, it does not imply that there is one most efficient form of organisation which is appropriate for all situations. Finally, unlike them it has been able to offer fairly convincing explanations of the differences between organisations which comparative studies have revealed.

The limitations of the Socio-Technical System approach arise, firstly, in the orientation which it suggests towards what are taken to be the problems of systems. Thus, like Structural-Functionalism, its usefulness depends on how far one is prepared to concede that social institutions are similar to biological organisms and that their functioning is best understood in terms of a series of adaptations to an often hostile environment.

The connection of their System with organic analogy is found most clearly in the work of Rice: 'This book', he states in a recent work, 'seeks to establish a series of concepts and a theory of organisation that treats enterprises . . . as living organisms' (1963, p. 179). The organism has demands made upon it by other systems and reacts by seeking to stabilise itself. The concept of 'primary task' provides a referent by which to judge the health or disease of the organism: where the primary task is secured, the System has made a healthy response to the demands which it experiences; where it is failing in performing adequately (in terms of the primary task), the System must be restructured so as to bring the parts into a better balance.[13]

The deficiencies of the organic analogy as applied to social life have been discussed elsewhere, and it is only necessary to raise the more obvious questions. Does patterned social interaction depend upon a primary task? Is social action best understood as a response to demands perceived by the observer but not necessarily by the participants? Is it useful to conceive of social forms in terms of health and pathology?

Of more practical importance than these issues, is the problem of whether the Systems perspective can deal adequately with 'why' questions concerning the origins and causes of social phenomena. While, if you accept its assumptions, it can explain rather neatly the manner in which social systems adapt to one another and, thereby, maintain social order (both 'how' questions), it has considerably more difficulty in explaining *why* systems have their present characteristics and why they react in different ways, and to a varied extent, to external and internal threats to their stability. Although it can, for instance, suggest the means by which an organisation can be more successful or adaptive, it provides very little in the way of an explanation of the causes of this initial non-adaptiveness. Thus Parsons's view that organisations become inefficient when too much attention is paid to integration and 'latency' rather than to adaptation and goal-attainment is more a definition of in-efficiency than an explanation of its causes. Without reference to human motivation it is arguable that one cannot explain why social life has the characteristics that it does.

This is tacitly recognised by many System theorists. Burns and Stalker (1961), for example, while they begin by stressing the objective demands of the environment, ultimately resort to the definitions of the situation which are held by the participants in order to explain why organisations respond in different ways to the same market conditions. Thus, the political and status commitments of the actors influence the way they interpret the situation, while the response to a given rate of technical or market change is shaped by the orientations of top manage-ment—or what Burns and Stalker call, 'their capacity to lead'.[14] This is because each organisational form is not only 'objectively' better for a certain set of economic conditions but is also assessed from the point of view of the ends of the mem-bers.[15] The action which they take will be governed by their definition of the situation rather than that of the observer.

If the objections to a Systems perspective are put on one side, serious limitations to the work carried out in the tradition of Socio-Technical Systems remain. These arise from a failure to distinguish 'is' and 'ought' propositions; from a commitment to a primarily prescriptive frame of reference; from an insufficient attention to the different types of attachment to economic organisations; and from a consideration of environment in almost exclusively economic terms. Each of these four criticisms are briefly discussed below.

1. *Is or ought:* It is one thing to say that technology, market pressures, and the needs of the participants ought to be important in organisations, it is quite another thing to maintain that these factors actually do determine organisational form. A limitation of socio-technical analysis is that one is never quite sure whether it is being argued that such factors are the causes of an organisational structure or merely variables that require attention in any attempt to change the organisation. While each of these factors is supposed to be given equal weight in analysis, it becomes apparent on reading the literature that an implicit distinction is made between what may be called 'operational' variables which shape an organisation *if left to itself*, and 'evaluative' variables which are used to judge the efficiency of an existing structure. Technology and the pressures of the market, it seems, determine organisational form (e.g. Woodward, Trist *et al.*). But since this may mean that insufficient attention is paid to the personality needs of the participants (Miller and Rice, Trist), or to the rate of environmental change (Burns and Stalker, Emery and Trist), a certain amount of planned organisational change is necessary.

Distinctions between 'is' and 'ought' propositions are clearly essential if one is to come to grips fully with the nature of what is being studied or to predict how it is likely to change. Yet, as with Parsons, one is never quite sure whether what is being attempted is a description of how organisations actually work or an abstract discussion of the conditions necessary for their stable functioning. The notion of a Socio-Technical System thus requires a more conscious distinction between those factors which determine organisational form and those which can be used to judge its efficiency.

2. *Prescription.* Part of the confusion over 'is' and 'ought' no doubt arises out of the dual role of many socio-technicists as academic analysts and as consultants to business organisations. Consultancy, despite the solution it provides to the problem of access, by its nature involves a prior orientation to the question of how an efficient organisation can be constructed. While this

clearly does not imply that the consultant cannot pay attention to the highest standards of rigorousness in the collection of his data, it does mean that he is likely to be immediately concerned with social rather than sociological problems, and that theories and empirical material which do not have a direct bearing on the task at hand may not be taken up. This impression is supported by the tendency of their works to refer almost entirely to other socio-technical writers, to the exclusion of much that one might have thought was common ground in the literature.[16]

Consultancy necessarily implies a commitment (if only temporarily) to the problems of those who are paying one's salary, the concerns of other members of the organisation being important only in so far as they affect the task at hand. This is not meant to suggest that consultants deviate in any way from the highest ethical standards; indeed many of them are quite aware of the limitations of their position and admit to it freely.[17] It reminds one, however, as R. K. Brown (1967) has pointed out, that observation depends upon the spectacles being used and that the difficulties of an organisation may well be a polite name for the difficulties of those in positions of authority.

Two further consequences of the consultancy posture should be noted. First, it is no coincidence that the theory that has been developed is specifically applicable to economic organisations, since it is in these that most consulting has occurred. Certainly it would be rather difficult to incorporate the emphasis on technology into an approach to all organisations. Secondly, a commitment to problem-solving as a first priority is usually associated with an attempt to mobilise all perspectives that might be useful. Socio-technical theorists thus tend to make use of a wide range of disciplines.

Opinions vary as to the fruitfulness of an inter-disciplinary approach. What is gained by the collapse of artificial boundaries is balanced and sometimes outweighed by the failure to make use of the full insights of any of the constituent disciplines: a good partial approach is to be preferred to any number of hastily constructed general theories. Nevertheless, even as a general theory, one is struck by the absence of a sociological perspective or of due attention to the sociological literature in the work of some socio-technical theorists. Instead, their primary orientation often seems to be towards psycho-analysis in the understanding of motivation, and economics and some-times biology in the study of organisation-environment relations.

3. *Attachments.* The weakest part of the Socio-Technical System approach is the regular failure of its proponents to discuss adequately the sources of the orientations of members of organisations. Sentient Systems are supposed to derive from what is often a hotch-potch collection of human needs which group together in equal measure the Social Man of classical Human Relations, the theory of Self-Actualisation of the Organisational Psychologists and Melanie Klein's psycho-analytic Object-Relations theory. Instead of examining the different types of involvement in organisations, they argue that men are (or should be) morally attached to their work and that organisational form is only satisfactory (from the point of view of efficiency as much as of the men themselves) when it pro-vides for such an attachment. Trist (1963), for instance, sug-gests that, by showing how large autonomous workgroups can function effectively in a modern technology, his study has a general relevance for industry. Yet this is to assume that the type of attachment to work of a Durham miner is repeated among other workers and that all would be satisfied in the same work-setting. In a similar way, with similar objections, Wood-ward (1958) argues that assembly-line production has a poorer record of industrial relations because, as a mass production industry, it limits the amount of job satisfaction and frustrates the workers' desire to belong to stable workgroups.

4. *Environment.* Adequate analysis of the orientations of mem-bers of organisations would require attention to the specific ways of perceiving situations which they bring from their extra-organisational experiences. However, the socio-technicists have generally considered the environment in purely economic terms as a series of market demands upon organisational structures. While sufficient for some purposes, this gives no means of ex-plaining the different reaction of those in authority to the same objective set of demands or of predicting the pattern of social interaction that will develop.

These four limitations are not inherent in Socio-Technical

System analysis. If attention is paid to them, then there is no reason why an adequate analytic theory, as opposed to a series of prescriptions, could not be constructed. Such a theory, it seems likely, will be much more intimately related to Structural-Functionalism with which it will share the same conceptual apparatus.

REFERENCES

1. Lupton (1963) describes a garment workshop where the technical system prevented workgroup formation. For a critical analysis of the view that there is a mechanistic relationship between technology and behaviour see Reeves (1967).

2. For the interactionist critique see Mouzelis (1967), pp. 105–7.

3. 'Most human beings', he writes, 'seem to find the assembly-line environment an exceedingly severe one. . . . This leads to negative sentiments towards the job, and this, in turn, seems to affect worker sentiments towards higher management and the company in general' (Whyte, 1959, p. 160).

4. This affected their morale which, in turn, influenced whether they expressed their grievances in organised conflict, i.e. as a group, or in unorganised conflict, i.e. as individuals.

5. Following Homans, the environment consists of the technology and the authority and reward structures.

6. The bargaining position of each group is particularly important, as affected by its opportunities for promotion, degrees of indispensability in the technical system, and the ability of management to measure its output precisely.

7. 'On the basis of this study', he suggests, 'we might expect that certain combinations of pressure groups actually involve the organisation in increasing instability—a trend towards disequilibrium' (Sayles, 1958, p. 158).

8. It seems reasonable to assume that this figure of 50% is considerably higher than the national average among semi-skilled workers in the United States in the early 1950s when this study was carried out.

9. Goldthorpe suggests that mobility experiences, age and family ties may be of importance in structuring the subjective meaning of work. In this connection, it is interesting to note the relatively low average age (27) of the car-workers which Walker and Guest studied.

10. For instance, it might help to explain why there is more manifest conflict in some car-factories than in others, or why some

assembly-line workers are less strike-prone than workers engaged in more 'satisfying' work.

11. 'Along with Marx, Erich Fromm and Chris Argyris', he writes, 'I assume that work which permits autonomy, responsibility, social connection and self-actualisation furthers the dignity of the human individual . . .' (Blauner, 1964, footnote, p. 15).

12. These studies were briefly discussed in Chapter One.

13. The difficulty in this, as R. K. Brown has noted, is that, 'though a biological system has an obvious "primary task" in relation to its environment, the same is not true of a social system' (Brown, 1967, p. 45).

14. They explain that 'to lead' is 'to interpret the requirements of the external situation and to prescribe the extent of the personal commitments of individuals to the purposes and activities of the working organisation' (Burns and Stalker, 1961, p. 96).

15. 'As soon as the span of considerations we bring into play widens beyond that of organisational analysis, it is clear that "dysfunctional" types of management system are developed . . . [and] are seen to be entirely effective in appropriate parts of the social organisation in which they serve rationally as means to specific ends' (Burns and Stalker, 1961, preface). I am grateful to Prof. Burns for drawing my attention to this statement.

16. There is, for instance, no mention of Dalton, Crozier, Gouldner or Selznick in the text or in the bibliography of Miller and Rice (1967).

17. 'The elaboration of theories about organisations and the collection of data to support [sic] hypotheses', Rice notes about their work, 'have usually had the severely practical objective of attempting to clarify the difficulties that my clients and I were meeting' (1963, p. 4).

6

The Action Frame of Reference

THE DISCUSSION of the System perspective in Chapter Two
referred to an Action approach and gave certain indications
of its nature. For instance, while behaviour may be viewed as a
reflection of the organisational structure and its problems, it
was argued that it is equally as valid to suggest that an organisation itself is the outcome of the interaction of motivated
people attempting to resolve their own problems. Further, it
was noted that the environment in which an organisation is
located might usefully be regarded as a source of meanings
through which members defined their actions and made sense
of the actions of others. In this chapter, it will be necessary to
pull the threads together and to present a coherent exposition
of what has been called 'the action frame of reference'.[1]

Many writers have made use of an Action approach and the
works that are discussed here include Weber (1947), Schutz
(1964), Berger (1966), Berger and Luckmann (1966), Berger
and Pullberg (1966), Rose (1962), Goffman (1959), Cicourel
(1964), and Cohen (1968). Instead of providing a summary,
at this point, of these various views, I shall try to present an
ideal-typical action theory. This will fail to do justice to the
separate arguments of each author, but it will have the advantage of presenting clearly the essential features of the perspective.

Seven propositions are presented below and the rest of the
chapter will be devoted to a discussion of them.

1. The social sciences and the natural sciences deal with entirely different orders of subject-matter. While the canons
   of rigour and scepticism apply to both, one should not expect
   their perspective to be the same.
2. Sociology is concerned with understanding action rather

than with observing behaviour. Action arises out of meanings which define social reality.

3. Meanings are given to men by their society. Shared orientations become institutionalised and are experienced by later generations as social facts.

4. While society defines man, man in turn defines society. Particular constellations of meaning are only sustained by continual reaffirmation in everyday actions.

5. Through their interaction men also modify, change and transform social meanings.

6. It follows that explanations of human actions must take account of the meanings which those concerned assign to their acts; the manner in which the everyday world is socially constructed yet perceived as real and routine becomes a crucial concern of sociological analysis.

7. Positivistic explanations, which assert that action is determined by external and constraining social or non-social forces, are inadmissible.

1. *The distinction between the social and natural sciences.* The view that the natural sciences provide the most appropriate model for the study of social life has a long and distinguished history in sociology. It suffers, however, from the fatal defect that it fails to take into account whether social and natural phenomena are the same in kind. The behaviour of matter may be regarded as a necessary reaction to a stimulus. Matter itself does not understand its own behaviour. It is literally meaningless until the scientist imposes his frame of reference upon it. There is no possibility of apprehending its subjective intentions and the logic of its behaviour may be understood solely by observation of the behaviour itself. The action of men, on the other hand, is meaningful to them. While the observer perceives water boiling when it has reached a certain temperature, men themselves define their situation and act in certain ways in order to attain certain ends. In doing so, they construct a social world. Social life, therefore, has an internal logic which must be understood by the sociologist; the natural scientist imposes an external logic on his data. As Weber (1964) and Schutz (1964) have observed, this situation is both a source of problems *and* a distinct help to the social scientist.

If social action derives from the meanings which those concerned attribute to their social world, the observer is limited by his inability to experience the experience of another. Schutz points out that the scientist's individual biography and view of society may make him perceive what is going on in a way which distorts its meanings to those involved.[2] His best defence is to develop a 'scientific' frame of reference, for the distinction between the natural and social sciences does not affect the common rules of procedure which they share (rigour, scepticism, and so on). But this is very little use if the observer fails to come to grips with the problem of the subjective meanings that the actors themselves attach to their acts. Fortunately, the social scientist has one distinct advantage. He is not limited merely to the observation of uniformities of behaviour: 'In the case of social collectivities', Weber suggests, 'we can accomplish something which is never attainable in the natural sciences, namely the subjective understanding of the action of the component individuals' (1964, p. 103).

The generalisations which the social sciences develop are also fundamentally different from the laws of the natural sciences. The former are based on the probability that actors will act in terms of certain typical motives or intentions, the latter on the necessary reaction of matter to a stimulus (providing other stimuli are controlled for). Both the data and the form of explanation of the two types of science are thus fundamentally different: they share only a commitment to a systematic and rigorous analysis of their material.[3]

2a. *Action not behaviour.* According to one view, observable patterns of behaviour provide the social scientist with his most reliable source of data. While what goes on in the minds of people is difficult to assess, their behaviour is concrete, quantifiable and easily susceptible to scientific analysis. Such a position has been taken by behaviourists generally, and is also favoured by those who take the Interactionist view of organisations which, while taking account of attitudes, concentrate mainly on interpersonal contacts ('interaction') and work tasks ('activities').[4]

However, the mere observation of behaviour has its own set of difficulties. In order to make sense of an act, the observer must place it within a category which he can comprehend. He might distinguish, for instance, between an act associated with work and, say, an act of friendship. At the same time, however, the act will have a certain meaning to the person who carries it out and to the people at whom it is directed. What the observer takes to be merely the repetition of the same physical action may imply totally different meanings to those concerned according to the way in which they define each situation. By concentrating on the behaviour itself, it is possible to miss totally its significance to the people involved and, therefore, to be unable to predict with any accuracy the way in which those at whom it is directed will react to it. This difficulty has made itself felt most strongly among anthropologists who have to come to terms with a culture very different from their own, in which the subjective significance of actions is difficult to grasp. Even in his own society, however, the observer is still frequently an untutored outsider unable, without further knowledge of the commonsense assumptions being used, to comprehend the implications of the behaviour he is observing.

As has already been suggested, problems of this nature are specific to the social sciences. Matter, on the other hand, does not act, it 'behaves'. Moreover, the logic of its behaviour may be understood through an observation of the behaviour itself. The action of men, however, stems from a network of meanings which they themselves construct and of which they are conscious.[5] Weber put the relationship between social science and action clearly when he argued that sociology is concerned with: 'The interpretation of action in terms of its subjective meaning' (1964, p. 94), where action is 'all human behaviour when and insofar as the acting individual attaches a subjective meaning to it' (p. 88).

2b. *Action arises from meanings.* Behaviourists argue that behaviour can be broadly explained as a response to a stimulus whose objective characteristics are perceived by the scientist. The reaction of subjects to this stimulus (e.g. 'expressive' supervision) may thus be observed and laws formulated which relate the observed response to the stimulus (e.g. expressive supervision tends to be associated with a high level of morale among those who are exposed to it).

This fails to take account, however, of the 'internal' logic of the situation. People assign meanings to situations and to the actions of others and react in terms of the interpretation suggested by these meanings.[6] Thus they may respond differently to the same objectively-defined stimulus: the same supervisory behaviour may be interpreted as a friendly act by one group of workers (who, because they also desire supervision of this nature, react in a favourable way), or as an illegitimate attempt to win their sympathy in order to accomplish objectives opposed to their own. The same individual even may, at different times or in different situations, assign varying meanings to what appears to an observer to be the same act.

Action occurs, therefore, not as a response to an observable stimulus but as a product of what Parsons (1951) has called a 'system of expectations' arising out of the actor's past experiences and defining his perception of the probable reaction of others to his act. At the level of cognition,[7] the actor defines his situation in this way and becomes aware of alternative courses of possible action. Since action is goal-oriented, that is concerned with the attainment of certain subjectively-perceived ends, the actor chooses, from among the means of which he is aware, the action that seems most likely to produce what he would regard as a satisfactory outcome. At this analytical level, to use Parsons's term, he is concerned with 'evaluation'. Any instance of action (a unit act) thus stems from the ends that the actor is concerned to attain, his definition of the situation, including the range of alternative actions that he perceives to be available to him, and his choice of a means which is likely to be effective, bearing in mind the likely reaction of others to his act.

3. *Meanings as social facts*. Since action stems from meanings, it is legitimate to pose the question—'from where do these meanings arise?' One valid answer would be that meanings are given to men by their society and the past societies that preceded it. Such a reply would draw heavily on the perspective of Emile Durkheim, who argued that men are constrained by social facts which determine their actions and consciousness. The suicide rate, to take Durkheim's favourite example, is separate from the intentions of individual men. It is a social fact which

stems from the organisation of society and is thus both external and constraining to individual actors.

If we follow Durkheim, it seems clear enough that meanings reside in social institutions. Society is composed of an inter-related series of institutional orders each of which is composed of a hierarchy of status positions to which are attached rights and obligations. This hierarchy usually persists even though the occupants of offices change. Meanings are, therefore, associated with an institution itself, both in terms of the general areas within which its members are supposed to act (e.g. the economy, the law) and of the specialised expectations attached to each office. Individuals are thus located on a particular social map. They live in a particular society and play roles in some at least of its component institutional orders. By partici-pating in society they are given expectations about the appro-priate acts of themselves and of others when in various status positions. They are able to apprehend the meanings associated with the actions of other people and to form a view of self based on the responses of others.

The question that now arises is why people should meet the expectations of others; one comprehensive answer to this has been offered by Parsons. According to Parsons (1951), society motivates its members, while respecting their personalities and biological needs; by this means it is able to prevent too much deviance from expected ways of behaving. People *learn* the expectations contained in different social roles through the process of socialisation. They *conform* to them because these expectations become part of their definitions of themselves (or are 'internalised', as Parsons put it) and because they want to retain the good opinion of those around them. Conformity thus expresses a set of shared values which is central to the existence of any society. While Parsons acknowledges that people can engage in interaction for their own private purposes, he holds that, unless one is prepared to be led 'straight to the Hobbesian thesis [of a war of all against all]', common values must pre-dominate if the system is to survive.[8] Action thus necessarily derived not only from shared expectations or norms, but also from shared values. 'Considering that we are talking about the conditions of relatively stable interaction in social systems', he writes, 'it follows from this that the value-standards which define institutionalised role-expectations assume to a greater or less degree a *moral* significance' (Parsons, 1951, p. 41, my italics).

The meaning of the social world is given to us by the past history and present structure of our society. Social reality is 'pre-defined' in the very language in which we are socialised. Language provides us with categories which define as well as distinguish our experiences. Language allows us to define the typical features of the social world and the typical acts of typical actors—it gives us a set of what Schutz (1964) calls 'typifications'. Typifications deal with symbols, highly abstracted from everyday experience (e.g. art, religion, science); with categories of people and the implied pattern of behaviour in which each may legitimately indulge (e.g. policeman, friend, neighbour); and with particular people with whom one has had the opportunity to interact face-to-face (e.g. a helpful policeman, a reliable friend, an unpleasant neighbour). These typifications may be viewed as composing a set of concentric circles of knowledge which vary in diameter according to our degree of familiarity with the person or object involved. Typifications provide the individual with a frame of reference which he can use to shape his own actions and to make sense of the acts of others.

4. *Meanings are socially sustained.* It is true that society constrains us; it is also true that society provides us with the belief that, rather than bowing to constraints, we are acting in a manner which expresses 'what commonsense suggests'. Even in our routine compliance with role-expectations, we believe we are acting 'naturally' in the only way which it is possible to act. Society, as Berger (1966) has pictured it, is both a prison and a puppet-theatre, in which we are manipulated while maintaining that we are doing 'what any reasonable man would expect'.

In viewing society as a social fact, sociologists reflect the commonsense view of members. Man experiences the social world as an external and unquestioned reality. People have always acted in a certain way, they will go on acting in that way because it is 'natural' that they should do so, and an individual's wants and intentions are as nothing before 'what has to be'. Society is perceived to be something out there and we believe we have no choice but to meet its requirements. The social world is a taken-for-granted world governed by what we understand as 'the laws of nature'. 'We experience the objects of our experience', Laing puts it, 'as *there* in the outside world. The source of our experience seems to be outside ourselves' (1967, p. 33).

We can best apprehend the limitations of the commonsense view of the nature of society by asking how it is that members come to perceive the social world as an external, routine, non-problematic facticity.

To answer this question we need to take account of two phenomena: men 'know' the social world through a shared stock of knowledge and the 'correctness' of this knowledge is continually made apparent in the actions of other men. The social stock of knowledge is a series of assumptions about appropriate behaviour in different contexts. I know how I ought to behave as a teacher and I know how my students ought to behave towards me. I know what purposes may underlie their actions and I know how my purposes may appear to them. Moreover, my view is usually confirmed by the everyday actions of others which appear to stem from the same set of assumptions. I do not doubt that I am a teacher and that this man is a student because he continues to act as I imagine a student should and, by responding to my actions in the way that I expect, he confirms my impression of myself. As such reciprocal typifications develop out of interaction, expectations become institutionalised and social roles are objectified or made part of the 'natural order of things'. In this way, it becomes thought necessary, proper and natural that the roles of student and teacher should be defined in a particular manner; it is no longer noticed when subsequent generations of actors continue to meet these assumptions—after all, what other way could they behave?

This glimpse at an aspect of the everyday world, while it stresses the routine nature of interaction, paradoxically makes social order seem more problematic. To be believable, the reality of the world-taken-for-granted must be continually re-affirmed in the actions of men. Meanings are not only given, they are socially sustained. 'The realisation of the drama', as Berger and Luckmann point out, 'depends upon the reiterated performance of its prescribed roles by living actors. The actors embody the roles and actualise the drama by presenting it on the given stage. Neither drama nor institution exist empirically apart from this recurrent realisation' (1966, p. 75).

Social order depends upon the co-operative acts of men in sustaining a particular version of the truth. In conversation, for instance, we find it convenient to accept the prevailing definition of reality within a group and not to question the major aspects of the views of self which are being presented. When actors act in unexpected ways, however, or when, as Goffman (1959) shows, events occur which cast doubt upon an agreed definition of a situation, that part of the social order is, for the time being, no more.[9] The fact that the stock of knowledge upon which action is based tends to change rather slowly reflects the vested interest that we all have in avoiding anomie by maintaining a system of meanings which daily confirms the non-problematic nature of our definitions of ourselves.

Man makes the social world. The existence of society depends upon it being continuously confirmed in the actions of its members. Social structure, therefore, 'has no reality except a human one. It is not characterisable as being a thing able to stand on its own ... [and] exists only insofar and as long as human beings realise it as part of their world' (Berger and Pullberg, 1966, p. 63). We reify society if we regard it as having an existence which is separate from and above the actions of men: social roles and institutions exist only as an expression of the meanings which men attach to their world—they have no 'ontological status', as Berger and Pullberg put it (p. 67).

The phenomenological position adopted by Berger, Luckmann and Pullberg has clear parallels with the view of social relationships presented by the Symbolic Interactionists. If, as Rose (1962) notes, Man lives in a 'symbolic environment' and acts in terms of the social meanings that he ascribes to the world around him, then roles are merely 'clusters of related meanings' perceived to be appropriate to certain social settings (Rose, p. 10); structure, once more, refers only to meanings, in this case the meanings that define the social setting itself and the appropriate relationships between the role-players that are expected to be part of it. Both roles and structure merely provide a framework for action; they do not determine it. Both 'are the product of the activity of acting units and not of "forces" which leave such acting units out of account' (Blumer, 1962, p. 189). Industrialisation, to take one example, does not determine the family form. This will, as Blumer points out, depend on the interpretations which the actors concerned place on the industrialisation process.

If society is socially constructed, then the logic behind some sociological investigations becomes highly questionable. For to relate one structural variable to another, for instance organisational form and economic environment, may fail to take account of the orientations of the people involved and the meanings which they attach to 'efficiency', 'the economy', and so on. It is out of factors like these that action is generated: to pay insufficient attention to them can involve the sociologist in an empty determinism in which things happen and processes occur apparently without the direct intervention of human purposes. Indeed, what has already been said should indicate a need to extend what have been regarded as the canons of satisfactory explanation of social phenomena; a need, as Berger and Luckmann argue, for 'more than the casual obeisance that might be paid to the "human factor" behind the uncovered structural data'. Instead, we must be concerned with a 'systematic accounting of the dialectical relation between the structural realities and the human enterprise of constructing reality—in history' (1966, p. 170).

5. *Meanings are socially changed.* If the reality of the social world is socially sustained, then it follows that reality is also socially changed—by the interaction of men. Indeed, the only alternative to explaining social change by an historical examination of past interaction is to assume an evolutionary scheme through which the needs of social systems are 'necessarily' met.

The most obvious instance of changed meanings resulting from interaction is when disruptive events occur which bring into question a certain aspect of reality. Goffman gives the example of an inquisitive guest who wanders into a room where he is not expected and discovers pulp magazines which he reveals to the others present, much to the consternation of his host who had successfully defined himself as a great intellectual. The implication that roles are not just given but socially sustained and changed casts some doubt on Parsons's emphasis on the socialisation-internalisation process as a non-problematic source of social order. Roles are normally only defined to a limited extent, and there are varying motives which underlie compliance to role-expectations.

Our behaviour is not completely determined by role-expectations. Even when we accept the conventions associated with social roles as constraining, there remains, as Dahrendorf (1968) has pointed out, an element of choice in role-playing. Role demands may refer to role behaviour or role attributes (dress, manner, and so on). Since the latter are usually defined in a far more imprecise manner than the former, the actor's individual biography becomes important in shaping his particular pattern of behaviour. Role demands are also usually defined by exclusions rather than prescriptions and this permits the 'arts of impresssion-management' to be used by an individual as he presents an image of himself to others (Goffman, 1959). The components of a role in fact include varying levels of perceived compulsion, each of which is supported by different kinds of sanction and reward. It is necessary to distinguish, therefore, between the actor's perception of 'must', 'should' and 'can' expectations (Dahrendorf). Failing to meet a 'must' expectation usually involves breaking the law; social exclusion usually results from breaking a 'should' expectation; one merely loses popularity by failing to comply with a 'can' expectation. This allows an element of choice in role-playing and implies the possibility of change through interaction. Dahrendorf does not directly dispute, however, Parsons's assumption that men are socialised into a common value-universe. Only when we question the notion that learning a norm necessarily implies a valued attachment to it, can we fully explain social change. This argument is taken up in an important paper by Dennis Wrong.

Wrong (1967) points out that Parsons and others may have exaggerated the extent to which conformity derives from the shared values which men learn. Even if social norms are internalised, one ought not necessarily to expect them to be expressed in behaviour. Men can act in a certain way and feel guilty about offending their conscience only retrospectively. At the same time, there may be internal conflicts in the values that men learn in society. While men may generally seek approval, they may also be more concerned with the approval of certain types of men than of others and be prepared to offend the latter in the hope of satisfying the former. In doing so they continually re-define social reality as experienced by themselves and others. Parsons may, therefore, be criticised for having adopted an 'over-socialised conception of man' which overlooks the fact that role-expectations are not just given by society but arise from and depend upon on-going human interaction. Social order is, therefore, problematic. A more complete analysis would need to take account of the range of motives underlying conformity to the expectations of others, and to pay attention to the possible role of coercion in *imposing* a normative definition of the situation on others.

Weber had already noted, many years previously, that in social relationships the parties may (and to some extent always do) attach different meanings to their interaction. It is certainly true that interaction may involve shared values (Weber gives the example of a father–child relationship), but very frequently the meanings involved may not be shared and the relationship will then be, as he puts it, 'asymmetrical'.[10] What is to the shop steward, for instance, a means of 'delivering the goods' to the workers he represents, may be regarded by the manager as a necessary relationship in order to settle disputes with the minimum interruption to production. The shop steward and the manager come together not because they have the same values (indeed, each may hope one day to overturn the authority of the other) but because, for a while at least, their differing ends may be served by the same means.

Social relationships, then, need only involve the ability of the actors to predict the likely actions of others by means of the common stock of knowledge which they share. At the same time, there always exist what Schutz calls 'finite provinces of meaning', sets of orientations which govern the nature of the involvement in any particular social relationship and derive from the various experiences of different actors (their 'individual biographies', to use Schutz's term). Moreover, if conformity to the expectations of other partners in this relationship is not generated by shared values, then analysis of its origins may reveal that it derives from the attempts of certain actors to attain their own personal ends and is merely tolerated by others. To take an extreme example, the relationship between the slave and master in a plantation society, while occurring on the basis of common expectations of the likely behaviour of the other, may originate in the ability of the master to impose his definition of the situation upon the slave. It need not, therefore, involve shared values, while the degree of attachment to it (and hence the measure of commitment to its continuation) may vary considerably between the participants. It becomes necessary to examine, in a similar manner, the processes through which any body of knowledge comes to be socially established as reality (i.e. institutionalised) and to take account, as Berger and Luckmann (1966) put it, of the fact that: 'He who has the bigger stick has the better chance of imposing his definitions' (p. 101).[11]

The existence of different definitions of situations indicates the advantages of an action perspective and reveals certain limitations of analysis from the point of view of the system. As Berger (1966) has noted, in an extremely useful little introduction to Sociology, the System approach tends to be concerned with analysis from the viewpoint of the authorities and is primarily concerned with the problems involved in the management of social systems. However, what is a problem to one actor is often a more or less efficient means to an end from the point of view of another.[12] A situation may, therefore, be usefully examined from the vantage points of 'competing systems of interpretation', and this will provide important clues as to how it arose, why it continues in its present form, and what circumstances may make it change.

It is important to recognise that the social order is threatened not only by particular circumstances, such as revolutionary change, culture contact or marginal groups (Berger and Pullberg), but by its very nature. '*All* social reality is precarious', as Berger and Luckmann put it, '*All* societies are constructions in the face of chaos' (1966, p. 96). While people take everyday life as non-problematic, as reality, they continually step into situations that create problems which have not yet become routinised. Our normal reaction is to seek to integrate the problematic sector of reality into what is already unproblematic: we look around for an already learned definition of the situation to apply to the 'new' reality. However, this is not always possible: 'certain problems "transcend" the boundaries of everyday life and point to an altogether different reality' (ibid., p. 24).

6. *Explanations in terms of meanings.* The form of explanation which the foregoing analysis suggests is concerned with 'verstehen', that is, it begins with 'the observation and theoretical interpretation of the subjective "states of mind" of actors'.[13] This may take the form of 'the actually intended meaning for concrete individual action ... [or] the average of, or an approximation to, the actually intended meaning' (Weber, 1964, p. 96). More usually, however, explanations are in terms of ideal-typical actors whom we take to be pursuing certain ends by choosing appropriate means on the basis of a subjective definition of the situation. 'It is not even necessary', Schutz argues, 'to reduce human acts to a more or less well known individual actor. To understand them it is sufficient to find typical motives of typical actors which explain the act as a typical one arising out of a typical situation' (1964, Vol. II, p. 13). He goes on to suggest how the acts of priests, soldiers, and so on, may be explained in this way.

Ideal-typical explanations, according to Weber, must be adequate on the level of meaning and also causally adequate. They must make use of what is known about the actor's definition of the situation and his ends. They must show that the action to be explained is in practice related to these meanings: that is, where the act is present, so must be the meaning. Ideal-typical explanations usually involve the assumption of rational action or the continuous weighing by the actors of means, ends, and the secondary consequences of their actions (Weber calls this type of action 'zweckrational'). It then becomes possible to examine the non-rational elements in actual behaviour—the extent to which those concerned diverge in practice from such a weighing process. As Schutz notes, it is easiest to come to grips with the subjective meanings of actors where their behaviour is most rational and, therefore, most standardised and anonymous.

Action explanations make a great deal of what Schutz calls 'in order to' motives. An action is explained when the meaning which the typical actor attributes to it has been demonstrated. At the same time, action is motivated on the basis of the actor's background and environment: this is its 'because' motive. I act in a certain way, therefore, not only in order to attain certain desired ends but also because I see myself as the sort of person who engages in acts of this nature. However, it is illegitimate to say that my action is *caused* by certain characteristics of mine which only the observer perceives. 'One reifies action', as Berger and Pullberg put it, 'by claiming that it is performed *because* . . . the actor is an X-type person' (1966, p. 66). This is to detach an act from its performer, who is viewed merely as a collection of roles. In the same way, 'roles are reified by detaching them from human intentionality and expressivity, and transforming them into an inevitable destiny for their bearers' (ibid., p. 67).

7. *The rejection of positivism.* In equating the methods of studying social and natural reality, positivism may take any one of three approaches. It may try to explain human behaviour in terms of universal psychological forces (e.g. aggression), non-social factors (climate or technology), or reified social constructs (social facts). Since most contemporary sociologists reject the first two, the discussion here will be concerned with the third.

Berger (1966) has accused much Sociology of viewing society as a 'prison' or as a 'puppet-theatre'. According to the former position, society is external to men and constrains them through the operation of impersonal social facts; according to the latter, society enters into the minds of men through the process of socialisation which gives them their social roles and determines how they will in future respond. 'That this sort of intellectual edifice is inviting to many orderly minds', he remarks, 'is demonstrated by the appeal that positivism in all its forms has had since its inception' (p. 190). None the less, there is an alternative view. Society may be seen as populated by living actors and its institutions regarded as dramatic conventions depending on the co-operation of the actors in maintaining a definition of the situation. As he puts it, the way in which this position 'opens up a passage out of the rigid determinism into which sociological thought originally led us' (p. 160), is best illustrated by the methodology of Max Weber.

Weber stands firmly against the reification of concepts by the observer. The State, for instance, does not itself act; it is merely a representation of certain meanings held by actors and is reducible to those meanings.[14] When these meanings change, the State changes: 'for sociological purposes there is no such thing as a collective personality which "acts". When reference is made in a sociological context to a "state" . . . a "corporation" [or] a "family" . . . what is meant is . . . *only* a certain kind of development of actual or possible social actions of individual persons' (Weber, 1964, p. 102). Such sets of meanings constrain only in the sense that they are objectified by actors who orient their actions to them: 'The social relationship thus *consists* entirely and exclusively in the existence of a *probability* that there will be, in some meaningfully understandable sense, a course of social action' (ibid., p. 118, his italics). He goes on: 'It is vital to be continually clear about this in order to avoid the reification of these concepts' (ibid.).

In attributing a causative role to the constructs of the observer (system needs, system dynamics) and losing sight of the meanings which actors attach to their actions, many contemporary sociologists have cheated themselves of a rich source of data. Parsons, in his introduction to Weber's most substantial work, accuses him of failing to use the insights of a functionalist system perspective; but it is clear that Weber very sharply saw the difficulties involved in explanations in terms of the nature of the whole and, in particular, its need for survival.[15]

The Action Frame of Reference and the Systems Approach

The Systems approach tends to regard behaviour as a reflection of the characteristics of a social system containing a series of impersonal processes which are external to actors and constrain them. In emphasising that action derives from the meanings that men attach to their own and each other's acts, the Action frame of reference argues that man is constrained by the way in which he socially constructs his reality. On the one hand, it seems, Society makes man, on the other, Man makes society. It is hardly surprising, therefore, that each approach should appear to stress, as was noted in Chapter Two, merely one side or another of the same coin. When the relative merits of the two approaches are discussed, it is usually suggested that they are complementary to each other. This appears to be the argument in a recent work by Percy Cohen (1968).

Cohen distinguishes a 'holistic' from an 'atomistic' approach: the former seeks to explain the action of parts of a system in terms of the nature of the whole, while the latter views the system as an *outcome* of the action of the parts. The tension between the two is provided by the fact that knowledge of the social system does not tell one everything about the action of its parts, just as information about its human parts does not in itself provide a complete description of the nature of the system. Cohen argues that this is because the members of society have biological and other characteristics which are separate from the nature of the whole system. Secondly, individuals have choice over which aspect of the whole to respond to, especially where it makes demands which are mutually inconsistent (Cohen, 1968, p. 14).[16] Thus both approaches have difficulty in explaining facts which the other is able to take for granted: the Action approach tends to assume an existing system in which action occurs but cannot successfully explain the nature of this system, while the Systems approach is unable to explain satisfactorily why particular actors act as they do.

The way in which each approach is affected by these sort of limitations has been taken up in a paper by Helmut Wagner (1964). Wagner distinguishes two sorts of atomistic model: 'Reductionist' theories explain the behaviour of the parts in terms of their individual biological or psychological make-up and, because they apply the same general laws to the parts and the whole, have no difficulty in also explaining the characteristics of society. Social action theories, on the other hand, are concerned with explanations in terms of interpersonal human action and are, therefore, best fitted to explain 'micro' problems involving particular patterns of action. When they seek to comprehend 'macro' processes, action theorists at once come up against 'the apparent machine-like character of large social systems which seem to follow their own mechanical laws'. It is almost impossible, in this situation, 'to submit adequate interpretations of large-scale societal structures and processes, without resorting to non-voluntaristic (i.e. positivist) explanations' (Wagner, 1964, p. 583). Attempts to do so, from an action position, inevitably raise the problem of what he calls 'a displacement of scope'.

As Touraine puts it, however, the view that: 'The action approach says little about the characteristics of the social system' (1964, p. 7, my transl.) and, therefore, 'does not attempt to substitute for an analysis of social systems but to complement it' (ibid., p. 11), is severely challenged by several of the writers who have been discussed in this chapter. The work of Berger, Luckmann and Pullberg, for instance, supports the argument that, by its examination of the sense in which society *does* make man, the Action approach can offer a means of explanation of the nature of social systems and need not depend on Systems analysis for, as it were, the other half of the picture. 'The paradox', as Berger and Luckmann note, is 'that man is capable of producing a world that he then experiences as something other than a human product' (1966, p. 57).

The possibility that Action and Systems explanations offer conflicting rather than complementary frames of reference is strengthened by the view that they are concerned with different types of problem. Cohen argues that holism and atomism are alternative means of coming to grips with the same basic issue: the problem of social order. However, as Dawe (1969) suggests, contemporary Sociology is also concerned with a second problem—'the exertion of human control over hitherto-inviolable institutions' (Dawe, 1969, p. 116). This latter issue was a major concern, as he points out, of the Enlightenment and it underlies Berger and Pullberg's discussion of 'objectivation' and reification.[17] A commitment to the insights of phenomenology may in practice prove difficult to reconcile with an acceptance of the positivist position. Even if both approaches are ultimately concerned with social order, their views of its nature and consequences are very different.

The debate about the complementarity or opposition of the two approaches is, however, marginal to the main purpose of the present work: the illustration that the action frame of reference can be a useful source of propositions in organisational analysis. Chapter Seven will take up the arguments presented here with special reference to organisations.

REFERENCES

1. This is the term used by Parsons (1949 and 1951). His work will be discussed in this chapter although, as it will become apparent, he is not in sympathy with the view of action theory taken by most of the writers discussed here. For a further examination of his work, with special reference to organisations, see Chapter Three.

2. The problems to which this gives rise have been vividly expressed by Laing: 'If, however, experience is evidence, how can one ever study the experience *of the other*? For the experience of the other is not evident to me, as it is not and never can be an experience of mine. . . . Since your and their experience is invisible to me as mine is to you and them, I seek to make evident to the others, through their experience of my behaviour, what I infer of your experience, through my experience of your behaviour. This is the crux of social phenomenology' (1967, pp. 16–17).

3. Laing has also pointed out the error of attempting to follow blindly the approach of the natural sciences in the study of the social world: 'The error fundamentally', he suggests, 'is the failure to realise that there is an ontological discontinuity between human beings and it-beings. . . . Persons are distinguished from things in that persons experience the world, whereas things behave in the world' (1967, p. 53).

4. Cf. Whyte (1959), discussed in Chapter Five.

5. Schutz (1964) notes that: 'The distinguishing characteristic of action is precisely that it is determined by a project which precedes it in time. Action then is behaviour in accordance with a plan of projected behaviour: and the project is neither more nor less than the action itself conceived and decided upon in the future perfect sense' (Vol. II, p. 11).

6. Rose (1962) points out that: 'All social objects of study . . . are "interpreted" by the individual and have social meaning. That is, they are never seen as physical "stimuli" but as "definitions of the situation" ' (p. x). Similarly, Cicourel (1964) argues that 'the actor's awareness and experience of an object are determined not only by the physical object as it is . . . given, but also by the imputations he assigns to it' (p. 220).

7. This discussion is not concerned with 'cathection'—or reaction in terms of innate personality drives—which Parsons takes as another level of human response.

8. Parsons acknowledges that an actor's sentiments may not be

involved in his action: 'But, in a general sense in social situations, the circumstances of socialisation preclude that this should be the predominant situation in permanent social systems which involve the major motivational interests of the participant actors' (1951, p. 40).

9. Goffman considers the definition of the situation which the actors project in face-to-face interaction. He goes on: 'we can assume that events may occur within the interaction which contradict, discredit, or otherwise throw doubt upon this projection. When these disruptive events occur, the interaction itself may come to a confused and embarrassed halt. Some of the assumptions upon which the responses of the participants had been predicated become untenable, and the participants find themselves lodged in an interaction for which the situation has been wrongly defined and is now *no longer defined*' (Goffman, 1959, p. 12, my italics).

10. 'The subjective meaning', he notes, 'need not necessarily be the same for all the parties who are mutually oriented in a given social relationship . . . "Friendship", "love", "loyalty", "fidelity to contracts", "patriotism", on one side, may well be faced with an entirely different attitude on the other. In such cases the parties associate different meanings with their actions and the social relationship is in so far objectively "asymmetrical" from the points of view of the two parties. . . . A social relationship in which the attitudes are completely and fully corresponding is in reality a limiting case' (Weber, 1964, p. 119). The appeal of the 'non-routine', in the form of a charismatic leader, was also a central concern of Weber's sociology—see later.

11. What the 'stick' actually consists of will vary according to the meanings attached to various sanctions by the actors' stock of knowledge. Excommunication, for instance, is at certain times a far more significant threat than more material 'sticks'.

12. 'Organisations', as Touraine puts it, 'can be thought of as social systems, but also as means limiting or providing the opportunity for the actor to attain his ends' (1964, p. 7, my transl.).

13. Parsons, introduction to Weber (1964), p. 87, footnote 2.

14. Compare this to the view of organisations as concrete things which Haworth (1959) follows—Haworth's view is presented in Chapter One.

15. Weber notes that sociologists have used an organic analogy in discussing society and goes on: 'this functional frame of reference is convenient for purposes of practical illustration and for provisional orientation . . . at the same time, if its cognitive value

is overestimated and its concepts illegitimately "reified", it can be *highly dangerous*' (1964, p. 103, my emphasis). Similarly, Berger and Luckmann term functionalism 'a theoretical legerdemain' and suggest that: 'A purely structural sociology is endemically in danger of reifying social phenomena' (1966, p. 170).

16. The same point is made by Rose (1962), who argues that actors possess choice especially where a culture is internally inconsistent. Of course, if reality is socially constructed, then the maintenance of any definition of a situation is the outcome of choice by the actors—however much they may experience the situation as constraining.

17. While the problem of order 'gave rise to a social system approach', Dawe remarks, '. . . the problem of control gave rise to a social action approach, with its emphasis on the actor's definition of and attempts to control his situation, and upon a distinctively "social science" view of the nature of social enquiry' (1969, pp. 116–17).

7

Action Analysis of Organisations

ORGANISATIONS WERE defined in Chapter One as social institutions with certain special characteristics: they are consciously created at an ascertainable point in time; their founders have given them goals which are usually important chiefly as legitimating symbols; the relationship between their members and the source of legitimate authority is relatively clearly defined, although frequently the subject of discussion and planned change. The Action approach, the main elements of which were outlined in a necessarily abstract form in the previous chapter, does not, in itself, provide a theory of organisations. It is instead best understood as a method of analysing social relations within organisations.[1] Three problems—the explanation of the origin of organisations, the nature of behaviour within them, and organisational change—provide a convenient means of discussing the main features of this method.

The Origin of Organisations

Any explanation of the origins of organisations must clearly take into account the nature of the society in which they arise; it is an indication of the tendency to view organisations as relatively *closed* systems that so little attention has been paid to this problem. Nevertheless, from the Systems point of view it has been argued, in general terms, that organisations (as sub-systems of society) arise as part of an evolutionary process of internal differentiation of system parts. In order to explain the number and nature of organisations that are created at any time, it is necessary, therefore, to consider the stage of development of a society and the kind of environmental conditions to which it must adapt.[2] An explanation in terms of the Action

147

approach, on the other hand, would begin from the fact that organisations are created by a specific person or group. It therefore becomes necessary to ask: who are these people and what is the nature of the ends and definitions of the situation which cause them to form an organisation with a particular goal? How does the pattern of expectations and type of legitimate authority within the organisation relate to the stock of knowledge characteristic of the society and to the finite provinces of meaning of its founders? A. L. Stinchcombe has paid systematic attention to the relationship between organisations and society and, in so doing, has suggested ways in which these questions may be answered.

Stinchcombe (1965) is concerned with why a far greater number of organisations tend to be created in post-industrial societies. In such societies, where the population is highly urbanised, literate, and used to the processes of a money economy, the potential founders of organisations are more likely to have the necessary financial and intellectual resources and to be aware that they and their group can gain by organising. At the same time, the replacement of traditional with rational-legal types of legitimate authority means that the actors are likely to be aware of more alternative courses of action, to perceive that they are less likely to be defeated by vested interests, and to make use of a calculable system of laws and taxation in predicting the chances of success of a new organisation.

Once created, Stinchcombe points out, organisations reflect the prevailing meaning-structures of their time in their internal pattern of social relations. Thus organisations originating within a bureaucratised society will tend to be created with a bureaucratic structure—even when, one might add, they are designed to overturn the political system of that society (e.g. radical political parties, trade unions). This is because the founders of organisations, whatever their aims, will usually take their ideas about efficient organisation from the stock of knowledge characteristic of their society at that time. While the original pattern of social relations tends not to be altered very rapidly (people often find it convenient to continue to pay lip-service to a set of symbols that would be difficult to alter formally), the actual nature of interaction can change very considerably over the years as the expectations of certain actors are not met and as new personnel enter the organisation. These changes may subsequently impinge on the prevailing meanings and pattern of interaction within the outside society. Stinchcombe argues, for instance, that the extent to which superiors in organisations are dependent on the consent of inferiors will influence the nature of class relations in a society. The importance of this is that it suggests a two-way relationship between organisational and societal structures.

Action in Organisations

Many empirical studies have been concerned with linking observable aspects of organisational structure (e.g. technology, nature of authority, promotion opportunities) to the behaviour of those concerned (cf. especially Blauner, 1964; Sayles, 1958; Turner and Lawrence, 1965; and Walker and Guest, 1952). Each aspect is associated with the nature and level of rewards offered, for instance opportunity for better-paid work or contact with fellow workers and supervisors. The presence or absence of these will, it is held, *determine* the response of members of the organisation. It soon became apparent, however, that knowledge of these objective characteristics of an organisation was an inadequate predictor of behaviour (cf. Goldthorpe, 1966; Turner *et al.*, 1967; and Cunnison, 1966).

An alternative approach, favoured particularly by psychologists, developed out of the work of Morse (1953). She suggested that satisfaction is determined not by the rewards alone but by the extent to which they diverge from what is desired. Expectations thus become of prime importance: where they are very high, one would generally expect satisfaction to be lower than when not very much is expected. Much of the work in this tradition has, however, not sought to relate these expectations to the other orientations of the same people or to examine the extent to which they consider them legitimate. In short, it has failed to take account of the *meaning* attached to the expectation.

This argument has been taken up by Karpik (1968), who has concentrated on what he calls 'social' expectations. These have a variety of subjective meanings depending on their social context, and the impact of experience upon satisfaction is, therefore, very varied. He illustrates his point with a study of several hundred French workers which shows that expectations have different consequences among town and country workers. In the town, high expectation of work signifies a desire for a more interesting and better-qualified job and tends to be associated with low satisfaction. In the country, high expectation implies high satisfaction. This is because in the country a high level of expectation usually means that the worker has accepted an industrial frame of reference as opposed to the prevailing rural values; he finds work satisfying because it offers him a symbolic participation in modern society.

If the social meaning of an expectation cannot be understood, as Karpik puts it, 'independently of the individual's orientations, his social position and the situation within which he acts' (1968, p. 350), it follows that analysis in terms of the actors' expectations, while an advance on positivist assumptions, is still insufficient. It is here that the action frame of reference is so useful. For the action of members of an organisation can be explained when their definition of the situation and ends have been understood. The first task of organisational analysis is, then, to distinguish the orientations (finite provinces of meaning) of different members (ideal-typical actors). But why should these orientations differ and what are the consequences of these differences?

Orientations differ, firstly, because actors bring different ends and expectations to their membership of an organisation. These derive from their various historical experiences (e.g. unemployment, rural background, experience of a paternalistic management) and from the multiple statuses which they hold at the time (e.g. husband, member or official of voluntary association, member of ethnic or religious minority). These variations arise, secondly, from the different experiences of actors within the organisation which encourage or discourage certain ends and expectations and generate others. Chinoy (1955), for instance, has noted a 'chronology of aspirations' held by car-workers: an active concern for self-advancement is held largely by the young, while in a short time the majority of the workers develop goals unrelated to advancement (a 'reasonable' standard of living, a steady, relatively pleasant job).

The consequence of these different orientations is that the nature of involvement in the organisation varies considerably among the members and has an impact on the way in which they respond to the behaviour of others, whether equals, subordinates or superiors. It is important, therefore, to distinguish the type of involvement, which can range from moral to alienative (Etzioni, 1961), and the ways in which it expresses itself, as for instance in clique membership (Dalton, 1959).

The nature of involvement is likely to be affected by whether authority is maintained by consensus or superior power. Thus the relationship between the junior hospital doctor and the consultant, just as much as that between the prison warder and the inmate or the worker and the manager, need not

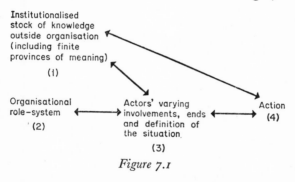

Figure 7.1

derive equally from the ends which each is trying to attain. This is not meant to suggest, of course, that all such relationships are based on an element of coercion or that, where coercion is used, it necessarily derives from the superior alone. Warders are dependent on the co-operation of prisoners and, as Eisenstadt (1965) has demonstrated, bureaucrats rely on an acceptance of the legitimacy of their position by even the poorest and most illiterate client. All parties must, therefore, use strategies (Crozier, 1964) to preserve and enlarge their area of discretion. As illustrated in Figure 7.1, the pattern of interaction and related meanings (2) that is then built up (the role-system of the organisation) reflects the consequences of the behaviour of the various actors (4) as well as the stock of knowledge that they bring in from outside (1). Workers expect supervisors to behave in an indulgent, bureaucratic or authoritarian way, not only because their life in the wider society has led them to this expectation but also because what they have expected has or has not been confirmed in their actual experiences of supervisory behaviour in the particular organisation. As a consequence, they may or may not attempt to alter the prevailing system of expectations.

The organisational role-system thus denotes the system of institutionalised expectations about the likely action of others without which social life cannot proceed. It expresses the rules of the game which all groups tend to accept for the time being, either because they feel they can do nothing to alter them or, more importantly, because of the rewards which stable group relations offer to all those concerned. Organisations are not, therefore, as Crozier (1964) and Burns (1961 and 1966) have pointed out, merely systems of power. But it is also true that the *values* of actors (3) are involved to a greater or lesser extent in any particular role-system. They may, therefore, be more or less continuously involved in seeking to maintain or to alter the rules of the game.

Organisational Change

Organisational change may be understood as a change in either the rules of the game (2) or in the attachment of actors to them (3). Both are related: if attachment weakens sufficiently the rules change. According to the model that has been presented, the sources of change may be located externally in the environment and internally—that is, as arising out of the interaction of the actors.

A great deal of organisational analysis has tended to concentrate on the external sources of change—Katz and Kahn (1966) even argue that such factors are always the most crucial.[3] This is hardly surprising if one remembers that organisations are often assumed to have an inherent strain towards internal equilibrium which is only halted by disturbances generated from outside. An organisation is seen as seeking to adapt, and the frequency and nature of its change is to be explained as the outcome of an impersonal process through which it attempts to satisfy its needs in the face of an often recalcitrant environment.

Now clearly one would not seek to deny that the society in which an organisation is located plays a crucial part in change; indeed, the approach that has been suggested would emphasise the dependence of explanations of organisational behaviour upon analysis of the nature of the particular society. Nevertheless, it is necessary to point out that the relationship between organisational structure and a changing environment will not be mechanical but will be governed by the definitions of the situation used by the participants. For instance, whether a technical innovation is incorporated into an organisation will be determined not by an impersonal process whereby the organisation 'itself' acts to maximise efficiency but by the relevant structure of social relations and orientations. The physical character of the environment, only sets limits—a highly specialised, technically complex organisation could hardly arise in a small, undifferentiated and economically backward society—but within these limits the environment may be interpreted in widely different ways, and the reaction of members of different organisations is likely to vary. If, then, attention is to be paid, as it ought, to the place of the environment in organisational change, it would seem to be most useful to concentrate on the impact of the stock of knowledge in the outside world. Where this changes as, for instance, when new orientations are brought into an organisation this is likely to affect not only the attachment of the actors, but ultimately, perhaps, the rules of the game.

The great merit of the Action approach, however, as Cohen (1968) has noted, is that it is able to explain how change arises out of the interaction of the actors. For the action that occurs confirms certain expectations of the actors and refutes others. It also involves the attainment of certain ends, while suggesting to the actors that other ends are unattainable. They eventually reorientate their actions in the light of a new definition of the situation (3), while their interaction has some sort of effect on the stock of knowledge in the organisation (2). All this does not imply that what the actors subjectively want to happen as a result of their acts will necessarily occur: it is important, in other words, to take account of both the intended and unintended consequences of action. Some at least of the consequences of action are always subjectively unpredictable because of the participants' partial knowledge of the intentions of other actors and of the resources at their command—although the extent to which an actor may be able to predict accurately the consequences of his own and of others' behaviour is, as Crozier (1964) has remarked, a very useful resource.

It is now possible to suggest the path along which an Action analysis of organisations might proceed. It should look at six inter-related areas in the following sequence:

1. The nature of the role-system and pattern of interaction that has been built up in the organisation, in particular the way in which it has historically developed and the extent to which it represents the shared values of all or some or none of the actors.

2. The nature of involvement of ideal-typical actors (e.g. moral, alienative, instrumental) and the characteristic hierarchy of ends which they pursue (work satisfaction, material rewards, security). The way in which these derive from their biographies outside the organisations (job history, family commitments, social background) and from their experience of the organisation itself.

3. The actors' present definitions of their situation within the organisation and their expectations of the likely behaviour of others with particular reference to the strategic resources they perceive to be at their own disposal and at the disposal of others (degree of coercive power or moral authority; belief in individual opportunity).

4. The typical actions of different actors and the meaning which they attach to their action.

5. The nature and source of the intended and unintended consequences of action, with special reference to its effects on the involvement of the various actors and on the institutionalisation of expectations in the role-system within which they interact.

6. Changes in the involvement and ends of the actors and in the role-system, and their source both in the outcome of the interaction of the actors and in the changing stock of knowledge outside the organisation (e.g. political or legal changes; the varied experiences and expectations of different generations).

The character of this approach, in particular the way in which it is proposed to analyse both the sources of action and its often complex consequences, can best be understood when it is applied in practice to the study of a particular organisation. Using Gouldner's *Wildcat Strike* as a base on which the Action method can be presented, his description of a pattern of events and the theoretical apparatus he uses to understand them will be compared to the method of treatment suggested earlier in this chapter.

'Wildcat Strike' and a Social Action Perspective

In *Wildcat Strike*, Gouldner implicitly foreshadows his later explicit rejection of explanations of change in terms of a Natural System reacting to meet its needs when faced with threats to its survival.[4] In posing the apparently obvious question of 'What is going on here?', he rejects prescription in favour of an analysis which describes and seeks to explain the actors' changing interpretations of the situation. By presenting a picture of social relationships within the organisation which, in some respects at least, will have been unpalatable to all those concerned, he emphasises that competent sociological analysis is most easily conducted without any commitment to the ends of one group—especially where these are viewed as the problems of the organisation—or to the observer's, as opposed to the actors', notions of 'goodness', 'badness', or 'efficiency'.

1. *The pattern of events.* 'Wildcat Strike' is a study of a gypsum mine drawing its personnel from a small rural community where social status was as dependent upon length of residence as upon occupational position. Workers and managers were frequently neighbours or friends outside the workplace and the distinction between expectations appropriate to contractual relations at work and those relevant to primary group interaction was very unclear. There arose in this situation what Gouldner calls an 'Indulgency Pattern', whereby management did not seek to supervise workers closely and allowed them a great deal of discretion in the job they performed, their pace of work and use of company materials and tools for private

purposes. The system appeared to suit all concerned, for while the workers found their expectations satisfied, management had little unrest to deal with: it was able to recruit personnel at relatively low rates of pay, and maintain friendly relations with them outside the mine.

This relatively stable situation was disturbed when, as part of an expressed desire by the head office of the company for greater efficiency, the deceased factory manager was replaced by an outsider who introduced new machinery and a far more 'strict' administration of the mine. Faced with the break-up of the Indulgency Pattern and the possible threat of redundancy, the workers grew dissatisfied with the return for their involvement in the organisation. The fact that their grievances were expressed in demands for considerably increased wages rather than in pressure for the restoration of the old social pattern might appear to be somewhat surprising. But, as Gouldner shows, the continued existence of the Indulgency Pattern had always been recognised by both sides as a non-negotiable issue, since even workers saw it to be of doubtful legitimacy and dependent on informal expectations which could not be revealed in public bargaining. Wages, on the other hand, involved no problems of this nature, since the demand for a wage increase did not threaten managerial prerogatives, could be readily understood by people outside the mine and would provide some recompense for the loss of less tangible rewards.

The wages issue was eventually settled, but the mine and the factory which processed the gypsum on the surface were now tense with minor crises. The wildcat strike, which occurred less than two years later, Gouldner explains as the outcome of grievances arising from the original attack on the indulgency pattern. A third factory manager, even more efficiency-minded than his predecessor, had been introduced and had made 'strategic replacements' among middle and lower management in the belief that new men were needed to work the new system. Not only because of the demands made on them by the manager, but also because they were unable to get on close terms with the remaining members of the organisation, the 'successors' were forced to give orders in a manner which called for deference and to emphasise their formal claims to authority. At the same time, the changed technology created further instability when management's experiments with different speeds of work threatened workers' expectations about 'reasonable' levels of production and involved far closer supervision than in the past. Suspicious of the new management and feeling that the best way to deny the legitimacy of its claim to authority was to refuse to co-operate, workers rid themselves of any residual loyalty to the company and did as little work as possible. In return, management regarded the workers' grievances as non-legitimate, while their resistance was strengthened by the view that the cost of giving in to them would not be calculable.

A classic 'vicious circle' then ensued: for not only was each group resisting the other's demands, but the forms of reaction available to them only confirmed suspicions on both sides. Management, unable to use the informal methods of its predecessors, was forced to attempt to resolve the situation by the use of still closer supervision and of the formal channels of authority. In reply, workers resisted still more, and management reacted by once more tightening the screws. Three months after a second succession of manager, the workers walked out and, because the union official structure was unwilling to support them, a wildcat strike began. The conflict was resolved by an agreement which involved the still further bureaucratisation of the factory with clearly defined functions being attached to each position and formal rules being applied to all interaction. Thus impersonal attitudes were reinforced and both sides in time gave up the assumptions which had supported the indulgency pattern. Social relationships were now defined by the participants on a new basis.

2. *Gouldner's theory of group tensions.* The appeal of the agreement, Gouldner suggests, lay in the segregation which it brought about between supervisors and workers who did not share complementary expectations about each other's role. The stable expectations about rights and obligations within a bureaucratised structure provided a solution to a situation where the traditional role-relationships, assumptions and practices, had broken down. If what happened at the gypsum mine can best be understood by examining the expectations of the parties about each other, then, Gouldner argues, why not repeat this method in the study of other organisations? The

'theory of group tensions' which he then goes on to outline is more of a guide to important factors than a general theory of organisations and Gouldner himself acknowledges his 'pragmatic' rather than 'axiomatic' approach to theory. Three major elements may be distinguished:

(*a*) *Roles*. The role-expectations of the participants can first be established by observing the complaints that they make about each other. To complain is to imply that what one regards as a reasonable expectation of the role-obligations of another has not been fulfilled. Thus, as Gouldner shows, when workers complained about a production engineer who had sworn at a shop steward, they were not worried by the swearing itself, which went on all the time in the factory, but by the ability of superiors in the new regime to go against their expectations of leniency and avoidance of the use of authority for its own sake. At the same time, groups assign varying degrees of legitimacy to their expectations; and, as we have seen in the case of the indulgency pattern, in order to predict how they will behave when these are violated it is necessary to distinguish what a group would *like* to happen from what it feels it has a right to *expect* to happen.

(*b*) *Group tensions*. Given two role-players, Ego and Alter, Gouldner argues, tension will arise to the extent that there is a discrepancy in their role-expectations, because, for instance, they are mutually incompatible, vaguely defined, or have recently changed without both parties being consulted or informed.

(*c*) *Social conditions*. Since Gouldner is seeking to explain the social roots of conflict, he is primarily interested in group tensions as the product of certain forms of social situation, rather than of the personality characteristics of group members. Among the conditions which maximise conflict are large power differentials between the actors, so that Ego is able to satisfy his expectations despite the resistance of Alter, or where those past experiences of Ego in which his expectations of the behaviour of Alter were not satisfied govern his present perceptions.

Despite the links that he sees between his work and that of Parsons, Merton and Selznick, it should be immediately apparent that there is no contradiction between Gouldner's 'theory' and the action frame of reference: to examine the definitions of the situation held by the participants, and to explain what happens in organisations as the outcome of their motivated behaviour and of the choices that they make in the light of these definitions is what the action approach is all about. Despite his occasional genuflections towards the Natural System model, I would argue that this is what Gouldner actually does.[5]

3. *A social action interpretation.* Given Gouldner's competent handling of his data within a set of assumptions that are not very different to those used here, there might appear to be little point in further analysis of his material. But by illustrating the way in which the action perspective can be used to handle the evidence about one particular situation, it will be possible to establish its capacity to make systematic sense of organisational behaviour. The history of the gypsum mine during this period can be understood in four stages: stability, instability, attempts to restore stability, and the new stability. Each period will be examined by means of the method of analysis that has been suggested.

(a) *Stability.* The period before the managerial succession was characterised by the shared orientations of the actors towards the role-system of the organisation and the expectations of head office. While certain generalised expectations of the appropriate role-relations of managers and workers (an idealised contract relationship) were part of the stock of knowledge of American society and were incorporated into the expectations of head office, the particular expectations evolved in the local community had favoured the development of a relatively deviant role-system. This Indulgency Pattern satisfied the workers and allowed managers to fulfil their role-commitments in the community. The actions of each group were oriented to maintain this pattern, although each side had some doubts about the legitimacy which it might be accorded outside the community. However, the head office grew dissatisfied with the economic return of the mine and pressed far more strongly than in the past for its own conceptions of 'efficiency' to structure management–worker relations. Thus, in the long run, the unintended consequence of the behaviour of the actors at the mine, given their ultimate dependence (for resources) on the head office, was to create a situation of great instability. This is illustrated in Figure 7.2 below.

Role-system	Characterised by consensus—has arisen out of shared values. Workers' diffuse expectations of management. }Indulgency Managers' specific expectations {pattern of workers.
Involvements	Workers' and managers' involvements largely *moral.*
Definition of present situation	Favourable. Moral persuasion as the major strategy—although some use of bargaining power (e.g. promotion rules).
Actions	Embodied acceptance of role-system.
Consequences	*Intended:* groups obtained desired rewards. *Unintended:* stability of role-system only in short run; intervention by head office.
Sources of change	Head office's lack of support for values upon which system based—always possibility of outside succession to mine manager's job.

Figure 7.2: The Indulgency Pattern—Stability

(*b*) *Instability.* With the more clearly defined role-expectations of head office and a new manager drawn from outside the community, the organisation took on an entirely new appearance. Despite the unchanged orientations of the existing managers and men, the 'successor', mobilising his authority and making use of an accepted managerial prerogative, introduced a new technology and bureaucratised the relations between managers and men. While the new role-system satisfied the ends of the successor and his 'strategic replacements' in middle and lower management, it offended the values of many workers and their existing supervisors. The involvement in the organisation of both these latter groups moved from almost moral to alienative and, after a trivial incident which seemed to them to symbolise the changed order (an engineer brought in to the organisation to solve some difficulties which had arisen over the new machinery swore at a shop steward), they walked off the job. The strike that developed was a wildcat because the official union hierarchy was not in a position to understand the way in which the situation had developed and the president of the local branch, who was aiming at a job in management, failed to give it his support. The intended consequence of their action was that the new manager was brought face to face with their viewpoint; the unintended consequence was that the instability created by their resistance to his role-expectations was instrumental in leading to a tightening of the very system to which they were opposed (see Figure 7.3 below).

Role system	Conflict of expectations and values: management expected 'contract' relationship, workers expected continuation of Indulgency Pattern.
Involvements	Workers *alienatively* involved in organisation. Managers instrumentally involved.
Definition of present situation	Situation regarded as intolerable by all parties; both prepared to use coercive measures against the other.
Actions	Wildcat strike.
Consequences	*Intended:* expression of grievances. *Unintended:* vicious circle, further bureaucratisation.
Sources of change	Perceived unsatisfactory situation.

Figure 7.3: The Wildcat Strike—Instability

(c) *Attempts to restore stability.* The unexpected outcome of the strike was an agreement which further bureaucratised the organisation. The reason for this is to be found in the working through of Gouldner's 'vicious circle'.

Immediately before and during the wildcat strike, the incompatibility of the role-expectations of the actors meant that the role-system was highly unstable. In such a situation, each side was unable to predict with any certainty how the other was likely to act or the probable reaction of the other to its own actions. This instability was disliked by all actors whatever their other orientations. The form of stability which they would have preferred, however, varied. 'Traditionalist' workers wanted a return to the practices associated with the Indulgency Pattern; the new managers and the union officials wanted a structure which would allow them to re-assert their authority; while other workers were prepared to accept a more contract-like relationship between managers and men providing they were recompensed with higher material rewards.

The solution, in the form of an agreement which involved the bureaucratisation of the organisation, can best be understood by beginning from the ends of the factory manager and his definition of the situation that faced him. To restore the Indulgency Pattern, while it would have won him the support of many workers, would have meant a loss of face hardly conducive to the establishment of his authority, and would also have gone against pressing instructions from head office. Moreover, such action was precluded, as Gouldner points out, by the manager's lack of knowledge, as an outsider, of the assumptions and cues upon which the old role-system was based. Bureaucratisation, on the other hand, would provide a formal prop to his authority, it would impose an impersonal system on actors with very strained personal relations, and, because of the stability it offered and the higher wages that went with it, might both attract new workers and be accepted by the less traditionally-oriented members of the existing labour force. The intended consequence of the agreement was to create a new stability; the unintended consequences can best be understood by taking account of the dysfunctions of bureaucracy from the point of view of management.

(d) *The new stability.* The bureaucratic form of organisation that developed attracted to it 'contractually-oriented' workers who were instrumentally involved in the organisation. Thus there was now a congruence between the expectations and orientations of all those concerned and the role-system in which they interacted. However, Gouldner suggests that sources of instability remained. In the first place there was no longer an informal system of relationships between managers and men which could be mobilised to support managerial action. Upward communications now became, therefore, at the best problematical. Moreover, given an instrumental involvement on the part of the workers, conflicts over material rewards could recur—especially at times of economic depression—and would not be resolved by managerial 'indulgency'. Gouldner thus leaves the gypsum mine not in a happy state of internal equilibrium but in a situation where the contradictions arising in the different ends of the actors have only temporarily been resolved (see Figure 7.4 below).

Role system	Characterised by shared expectations. Contract-type role-system prevailed.
Involvements	All sides instrumentally involved.
Definition of present situation	Favourable—while instrumental rewards obtained. But prepared to use coercive tactics if the situation demanded it.
Actions	Workers' acts embodied their acceptance of managerial authority.
Consequences	*Intended:* all groups obtained desired rewards. *Unintended:* new sources of instability (according to variations in economic rewards).
Sources of change	No longer an informal system of relationships; situation could change rapidly from within especially where changes occurred in relative bargaining power of each side.

Figure 7.4: Bureaucracy—The New Stability

The Contribution of a Social Action Perspective

Renate Mayntz (1964) has suggested that the study of organisations is likely to develop in two rather different directions. 'Prescriptive theory', inter-disciplinary and primarily concerned with the problem of efficiency, will continue to have the largest proportion of research time. A more distinctly sociological approach will, however, assert itself in the direction of issues of some theoretical significance. In particular, unlike a great deal of earlier work, it will seek to take systematic account of extra-organisational factors, on the assumption that supposedly 'organisational' processes can only be understood in their wider social context. While Mayntz does not herself develop an Action perspective, her preferences fit well into the approach that has been offered in this study.

In order to make clear the contribution that the Action frame of reference can make to the study of organisations, it will be useful to make a simple distinction. By being equally relevant to an analysis of the orientations of the actors as well as the role-system that emerges from their interaction, it suggests problems of both 'macro' and 'micro' proportions. At the micro level, it is particularly well fitted to explain the orientations and behaviour of members of occupational groups (e.g. miners, nurses, clerks), or of more narrowly defined role-players in particular organisations (e.g. a 'successor'). Instead of explaining action away, say as a mechanistic reaction to their place in the organisation or as a mere reflection of the nature of class relations, it can show how it derives from the definitions of the situation and the ends of the actors as shaped by their prior expectations (associated with their extra-organisational statuses) and their historical experiences of past interaction. Thus by beginning from, and attempting to make sense of, the definitions of the situation held by the actors, the Action perspective provides a means of understanding the range of reactions to apparently 'identical' social situations within one or more organisations. In a wider sense, it contributes to an understanding of the relationship between work and non-work and, thereby, since occupational position is normally taken as a crucial predictor of behaviour, to a fuller picture of the nature and consequences of social stratification.

To say that explanations in terms of action are also concerned with tracing out the macro issue of the relationship between the various actors in an organisation hardly establishes the originality of the perspective. Functionalism, for instance, can rightly claim to have taken the problem of how the parts fit together as its central interest. However, it is possible to view this relationship either as the outcome of the system itself adjusting in order to meet its needs *or* as the generally unintended consequence of motivated social action. In terms of the Action approach, there is no reason to suppose that assumed system needs of adaptation or survival will govern the reactions of members of organisations to the actions of others or to the changing characteristics of the environment. While different individuals and groups may equally pursue 'efficiency' or 'adaptation', the sort of organisational structure that would provide them with this may be very different because of their other ends. What actually occurs in such a situation will, therefore, be the outcome of the relative capacity of different actors to impose their definition of the situation upon others, rather than of a mechanistic relationship between an organisation's needs and the problems with which the system is faced.

It is possible, then, to move from an examination of the micro problem of the action of particular actors to the macro problem of the system of expectations that is established as they pursue their ends in the context of the meanings and symbolic resources which they and other actors import from the wider social structure. In particular, instead of assuming as Parsons appears to do, that a particular pattern of interaction between the actors generally implies shared values, one can go on to establish the extent and nature of the consensus, if any, between them.[6] For while interaction presumes certain shared expectations between the parties, these may be maintained for a wide variety of reasons. This is sometimes missed because a lack of consensus does not necessarily imply overt conflict: people may fulfil the expectations of others in varying ways and for different purposes, which is why we distinguish between *norms* and *values*. Knowledge of the attachment of different actors to the rules which they follow can be of crucial importance in any attempt to predict the degree of stability of an existing pattern of interaction.

To be concerned with stability is also to be concerned with explanations of change. The chief merit of the Action approach is that, while it takes account of the influence of external factors, it can explain how changes arise from the interaction of the actors. For every action has consequences, intended and unintended, for the way in which actors define the situation and perceive others, and hence for their subsequent behaviour. Moreover, the reaction of participants to perceived threats need not be adaptive in terms of organisational 'needs'—as Gouldner's analysis of the 'vicious circle' clearly shows.

Many of these processes have already been examined within one organisation (the gypsum mine); the rest of this chapter will consider the questions that the Action approach raises about the micro problem of organisational roles and the macro issues involved in the comparative study of organisations.

Organisational Roles

The normal method of explaining the attitudes and behaviour of members of an organisation has relied heavily on the objective facts of their situation within the organisation. Thus, to take an important example, certain types of technology have been linked with the alienation of the worker (Blauner, 1964).[7] This approach rests, however, upon certain rarely explicit psychological assumptions: it is only reasonable, for instance, to expect that technical systems will have certain effects upon all workers if one assumes some given universal personality needs in regard to the nature of work. The weakness of this assumption is revealed by the frequent failures of researchers to explain behaviour satisfactorily by the use of this (or any other) organisational variable (cf. Zaleznik *et al.*, 1958, and Turner and Lawrence, 1965). Members of an organisation are found to respond differently to what appears *to the researcher* to be the same stimulus. Only at this point, *ex post facto*, are extra-organisational factors introduced; a particular type of response is now, for instance, shown to relate to a certain class or religious background.

The common failure of organisation research to begin with the construction of hypotheses relating both to factors within organisations and outside them is happily not replicated in other areas of Sociology. Thus, when examining family behaviour, few researchers would seek explanations in terms of purely familial roles, but would introduce at an early stage in the analysis the social context in which the observed interaction occurs—including, for instance, the occupations of the parents and the community setting. This is clearly important if one is to take account of the meanings that the actors themselves attach to the roles that they play.

Thus, in the study of organisational behaviour, both sets of factors, the internal *and* the external, need to be given their due attention before we can understand the sense that the actors make of their situation. This is not, it ought to be stressed, to suggest anything very original: Goldthorpe (1966) for car-workers, Cunnison (1966) for workers in a garment factory, Scott *et al.* (1963) and Gouldner (1954 and 1965) for miners and Hopper (1965) for supervisors, have all recognised the necessity for such analysis. It is still important, however, to emphasise that what has sometimes been characterised as an interesting but primarily anthropological approach is not merely one of many perspectives but, we would argue, the only one that can give substance to the present rather arid explanations of organisational behaviour. This argument will be illustrated by looking at one case in a little more detail.

The clerk, or routine white-collar worker, provides an interesting example of the limitations of analysis purely in terms of the work situation, that is by means of organisational (and structural) variables. Superficially, the clerk seems to share the same occupational life-chances as the manual worker, yet the behaviour and attitudes of many clerks have always been more similar to those of management. One way of looking at this is to explain it away as 'false consciousness', an incorrect reflection of the true position. The other method has been to treat it as neither right nor wrong but as a fact that must be explained. Thus the work situation of the clerk and certain elements of his market situation have been re-analysed and differentiated from that of the manual worker (Lockwood, 1958). A study that the present writer recently conducted sought, following in the line of this tradition, to examine the objective sources of clerical behaviour (Silverman, 1968b). It was also intended to identify, by this means, different groups of clerks and to consider the factors preventing or encouraging a common identification among them.

It is a depressing commentary on much organisational analysis that it is often satisfied to take certain readily estab-lishable behaviour patterns at their face value and does not try to seek out the varying motives which underlie them. In the case of clerks, this has been reflected in the distinctions drawn between union and non-union members as if they necessarily represented different social types.[8] Since it seems that the fact of union membership is likely to be less important than the reason for joining (at least when anything more than the grossest generalisations are intended), this writer's study attempted to establish the orientations of clerks in a far more direct manner by the use of questionnaire items designed to tap their economic worldview and status consciousness. These 'ideological' elements appeared to divide clerks among themselves to some extent, but also to separate them as a whole from manual workers.

The hypotheses which were eventually developed attempted to relate market and work situation to ideology. It was expected that contact at work with manual workers would be associated with relatively high status awareness; lack of contact with relatively low status awareness. This hypothesis arose from a pilot study which had suggested that clerks in contact with manual workers were more likely to be status conscious. They would more probably use manual workers as their comparative reference group and compare themselves unfavourably in economic terms with such workers. At the same time, they would experience attempts to deny white-collar status in their contacts with manual workers.

According to the second hypothesis, prospects of upward mobility would incline the clerk to identify with management, while the lack of such an opportunity would prevent such an identification and foster a 'collectivist' rather than an 'individualist' ideology. Four organisations were chosen to approximate to each of the four cells formed by the possible combinations of the positive and negative values of the two independent variables (see Figure 7.5 below).

Opportunities for contact with manual workers

		Yes (1)	No (2)
		Identify with management	
		Individualist ideology	
	'Good'	More status concerns	Less status concerns
Prospects of upward mobility			
		More status concerns	Less status concerns
	'Bad'	Don't identify with management	
		Collectivist ideology	
		(3)	(4)

Figure 7.5: Hypotheses about Clerical Ideologies

While initial analysis of the data suggests that both hypotheses will not be refuted, it seems probable that the questionnaire was too limited in scope to provide satisfactory explanations of the range of responses to these variables. In particular, it would be useful to have additional information about the orientations which the clerks concerned brought to their organisation. Such material would go a long way towards explaining the meaning attached to, say, promotion opportunities and hence the response to their availability. Certain clerks, for instance, may not particularly want promotion and may have self-selected themselves for an organisation which was better able to provide other types of reward. In such a case, there is no reason to suggest that a 'bad' market situation will be associated with a lack of pro-management sentiments. This seems particularly important since the influx of individuals with working-class backgrounds into office jobs means that attitudinal differences among clerks may relate as much to their different social background as to their current experiences.

Further research on the clerks must, therefore, focus not only on the organisations for which they work, but on the social assumptions that they bring to their work roles. As mentioned earlier, there are hopeful signs in the study of other occupational groups that attention is being paid to the nature and the sources of the meanings which the actors attach to their work roles.

A Theory of Organisations

A theory is a statement in general terms about the likely relationship between two or more phenomena. It suggests hypotheses that it is possible to test and, where necessary, refute. A theory of organisations would explain why organisations are as they are and examine the factors that make them change. It would set out to offer an explanation on both organisational structure and dynamics. In the same way as there is not, in this sense, *a* theory of society, so there is not, of course, *a* theory of organisations. Indeed, it is at least arguable that such a theory is further off in this area of the social sciences than in others, although the reasons advanced to explain this situation would vary considerably from writer to writer. Nevertheless, if there is not *a* theory, then there are many *theories* of organisations which deal differently with the macro issues involved in comparative study.

Most attempts to construct such theories have tended to take both the definition of organisation to be used and the theoretical perspective as non-problematic. Representative students of organisations, such as Etzioni and Blau and Scott have argued, respectively, that sociologists should treat organisations 'as having common *problems*' and that the study of the latter is 'less complicated' than that of other aspects of society because, implicitly, they are more easily viewed as 'closed' systems.[9] The nature of the link between such statements and certain well-defined theoretical positions was discussed in Chapter Two; all that need be noted here is the association of a great deal of organisation theory with a particular form of sociological analysis (i.e. system theory). If one rejects the viewpoint of the latter, then it is tempting to dismiss the theory of organisations as inseparably tied to one rather limited model of society.[10]

In support of this conclusion, it has been further suggested that the differences between organisations are often more interesting than their similarities. This point has been taken up by Mayntz (1964). 'There will always', she notes, 'remain questions to be asked about prisons, armies, labour, unions, etc., which are not generalisable and hence not the proper subject of a general organisation theory' (p. 111).

Yet, to take these arguments in reverse order, the attempt to examine together (say) armies and prisons reflects a worthy preference, whose usefulness Mayntz would not really deny, for the adoption of a comparative perspective. Thus, while their role-structures and degree of self-selection of their members may differ, there may be certain similarities in their predominant forms of interaction as suggested in Etzioni's 'coercive-alienative' category (1961a), and Goffman's (1968) view of a 'total institution'. It is not necessary, however, to argue that the organisations themselves have 'problems' or, indeed, that these are similar. Thus, because a common attempt to construct a theory of organisations has been in terms of their assumed goals and/or problems, this provides no reason not to develop an alternative view while retaining the same aim.

There is no necessary link between such a theory and a reified conception of an organisation.

The Comparative Study of Organisations

As was implied by the previous discussion, the development of a theory of organisations can only proceed by the use of a comparative perspective. Burns (1967) has suggested that comparative studies are principally concerned with answering the question 'what is it?' by seeking to identify the major features of organisations and to account for individual differences. It is, of course, unlikely that all observers will agree about the importance that ought to be attached to any feature of an organisation. This is to be expected where different orders of questions, deriving from varying approaches, are being asked. One approach, for instance, sees the effectiveness with which organisations adapt to the demands of their environment as the crucial problem, and different organisations may be identified as 'high' or 'low' effective systems (cf. Lawrence and Lorsch, 1967); certain other approaches seek to compare organisations on a very different basis.

It is thus impossible to separate comparative study from the observer's preference, implicit or explicit, for a particular typology of organisations. As was suggested in Chapter One, certain typologies concentrate on the relationship of the organisation as a whole to its environment, while others are concerned with a certain aspect of the internal relationships of organisational parts. More importantly, typologies (and hence comparative study) may be directed at the problems of organisations as systems or at an analysis of the motivated action of actors and the pattern of interaction that develops between them without any reference to system needs. In pursuing the last of these, the Action frame of reference suggests questions about the characteristic sets of meanings that arise in different organisations. More specifically, the comparative study of organisations, according to this perspective, is concerned with the following issues:

1. The nature of the predominant meaning-structure and associated role-system in different organisations and the

extent to which it relies on varying degrees of coercion or consent.

2. The characteristic pattern of involvement of the actors; differing attachment to rules and definitions of their situation.

3. The typical strategies used by different actors to attain their ends.

4. The relative ability of different actors to impose their definition of the situation upon others. The nature and sources of the symbolic 'sticks' (resources) available to the actors; their relative effectiveness.

5. The origin and pattern of change of meaning-structures (institutionalisation and de-institutionalisation of meanings) in different organisations.

Comparative study of organisations is essential for coming to grips with issues of this nature especially where it is not confined to one society or one period of history. As Burns has pointed out, both historical (diachronic) and cross-cultural (synchronic) studies are invaluable if significant generalisations about interaction within organisations are to be made. This is why the material presented in, say, Bendix's (1956) book on managerial ideologies or Crozier's (1964) study of the French bureaucratic system is so helpful: for both help us to understand the wide range of meanings which people have used to make sense of their actions in different societies and at different times.

The study of non-Western organisations is particularly useful for throwing into relief many features of Western European and North American organisations which are often part of the taken-for-granted world of the observer as well as that of the participant. While there is some comparative material on organisations in non-industrial societies (e.g. Udy, 1959), there is also available a great deal of work on non-Western industrial societies. The case of Japan is particularly interesting in this respect and a debate continues about whether her industrial organisations are characterised by sets of meanings deriving from kinship relations and even feudal loyalties (Abegglen, 1958), or whether the paternalism of the Japanese factory is a fairly recent development and simply a strategy used by management to ward off Government interference and to attract a stable labour force (Taira, 1964).

Concluding Remarks

The Action approach offers a method for the analysis of organisations and suggests certain questions which this method can be used to answer. In this chapter, the nature of these questions was considered in relationship to the problems of the origin of organisations and organisational behaviour and change. The chapter was concluded with a discussion of the contribution of the Action perspective to the micro issue of the orientations and behaviour of particular actors and to the macro issue of the pattern of interaction that arises between them. The existing literature on organisations reflects some interest in these questions and the next two chapters will consider the manner in which substantive studies have gone about posing and answering them.

REFERENCES

1. Cohen (1968) has stressed the status of the Action approach as a method but not a theory.
2. The evolutionary assumptions behind this reasoning have been stated by Talcott Parsons in his 'Evolutionary Universals in Society', *Amer. Sociol. R*, 29, June 1964, pp. 339-57.
3. They recognise that internal forces of change may exist but conclude: 'It is our thesis . . . that these sources of internal strain are not the most potent causes of organisational change. The set of conditions which we have called changed inputs from without are the critical factors in the significant modification of organisation' (Katz and Kahn, 1966, p. 448)
4. Gouldner (1959 and 1967).
5. The bureaucratisation of the mine could, for instance, be explained in terms of the System adapting to new demands in order to satisfy its needs. Yet Gouldner explicitly rejects this mechanistic model: 'In fine', he argues, 'the participants did not respond simply to the needs of the "organisation as a *whole*", but to those threats which impinged upon their *status* privileges, and in those ways which safeguarded these privileges' (Gouldner, 1965, p. 123). Again, although he goes on to talk about 'organisational defences', he soon makes it clear that he is

referring to the actions of motivated actors and not to the behaviour of a reified System.

6. This follows the distinction that Lockwood (1964) makes between 'system integration' and 'social integration'.

7. It is only fair to point out that another important tradition has focused on the subjective experience of work situations; cf. Hughes (1958), discussed in the next chapter.

8. Prandy (1965) has treated membership of a union by a technical or scientific worker as an indicator of a 'class ideology', while Sykes (1965) believes that it demonstrates anti-management sentiment. Both appear to pay little attention to the meaning which those concerned attach to their membership.

9. Etzioni (1961a) argues that 'while there are many significant differences between a church . . . a factory and a trade union, sociologists have found it helpful to treat all these organisations as having common *problems*' (p. 132). Blau and Scott (1963) consider it possible to explain reactions to supervisory behaviour in terms of purely organisational factors (p. 14, *passim*).

10. This is what I argued in an earlier publication (Silverman, 1968a). The reasons why I have changed my position are outlined in the text below.

8

Attachments and Strategies

ALTHOUGH THERE is no distinct Action tradition in the study of organisations, the literature provides many examples of the use of aspects of the approach. An examination of the material already available provides the best means of considering the work that remains to be done.

In order to handle the mass of available data, it is necessary to specify quite clearly the questions that are being asked of the literature. Three central areas have been selected: the types of attachment to the role-system of an organisation; the nature and source of the strategies that are used in the pursuit of given ends; and the pattern of interaction that emerges from the recurrent behaviour of the actors. The material that is relevant to each of these areas will be considered in this and the following chapter. It should be noted, however, that each problem is only analytically distinct and the assignment of certain work to one area rather than another has been somewhat arbitrary; it does not imply that the authors concerned have limited themselves to the topic under discussion.

The Types of Attachment

To join an organisation is to become involved in an organisational role(s) containing certain generalised expectations about your behaviour and, perhaps, your characteristics as a person. When a member joins voluntarily (e.g. employee, member of a voluntary association or volunteer recruit to the armed forces), it is assumed that he will meet at least some of these expectations of his own volition, for he would not have joined had he found them distasteful and he can usually leave if he dislikes them in practice. Where membership of an organisation is involuntary (e.g. some mental patients, convicted prisoners or conscripted soldiers), then the authorities may have to intimidate the new member and even to threaten his conception of self in order to produce tolerable (i.e. rule-meeting) behaviour (cf. Goffman, 1968).

In *both* situations, however, the attachment of the member to the dominant system of expectations may be less than complete, and his compliance with the demands of authority may be carried out for different purposes and with varying degrees of enthusiasm. As Goffman (1959) has shown, actors may identify with their role and regard it as a sincere expression of their view of themselves, or, at the other extreme, may create a gulf between their performance and their true self-conceptions (role-distance). The source of these differential attachments is to be found in the social expectations and ends that actors bring to their involvement[1] and the manner in which their experience of the organisation validates (or denies) these expectations or generates new ones.

Many studies of organisations have tended to assume, however, that the character of the attachment of members is determined either by the nature of the organisation or the psychological propensities which they bring to it.[2] This is particularly apparent in early theories of behaviour in economic organisations which, as Bendix (1956) has pointed out, both reflected and created managerial ideologies about the essential characteristics of work. According to Taylor (1913), for instance, Man is an economic animal who responds directly to financial incentives within the limits of his physiological capacity and the technical and work organisation which is provided for him. Again, economic theories of the firm, by assuming that the participants share in the goal of an organisation because they accept a contract relationship, have reached the same conclusion by a slightly different path. Reacting against this sort of perspective, Roethlisberger and Dickson (1939), as a result of their researches at the Hawthorne plant of Western Electric, emphasised the unconscious and non-rational elements in behaviour in a manner that was clearly influenced by the work of Freud and Pareto. The importance of economic motives was minimised and the small workgroup with its autonomous norms was discovered. Man's primary desire was now to be seen in his 'groupishness' and, far from reacting directly to the incentives and controls of management, the worker would respond most to the social pressures of his peer group.

Both the Scientific Management of Taylor and the Human Relations of Roethlisberger and Dickson share the view that Man's attachment to economic organisations is non-problematic. If Taylor stresses economic motives, then the Hawthorne researchers point out Man's social needs and the members of their school emphasise that: 'There are many incentives, of which, under normal conditions, money is the least important' (Brown, 1964, p. 187). Instead, however, of assuming the universality of one type of orientation or another, it seems more useful to examine the range of ways in which people are attached to organisations. Differential attachments stem from factors both internal and external to the organisation. As March and Simon (1958) have noted, these include the nature of the recruitment, background and interaction of certain members of the organisation, the extent to which they compete for scarce resources and see the possibility that their interests will be furthered by the attainment of the organisational goals. This 'subjective operationality' of the formal goals of an organisation is an important source of different types of attachment. For, while certain members completely identify with such goals (e.g. members of a radical political movement or religious sect, some 'converted' inmates at mental hospitals), others have to be offered various inducements, which are unrelated to the attainment of these goals, in order to make them want to participate (e.g. most members of economic organisations).

The varying attachments or types of involvement which are generated by these and other factors have been documented by Etzioni (1961) in a study which was discussed in an earlier chapter. Involvement of what Etzioni calls 'lower-level participants' may be calculative (implying a commitment of low intensity), moral, or alienative (a negative commitment of high intensity). Each type of involvement reflects a form of compliance with a particular variety of power and there is a strain towards congruent power/involvement types, e.g. coercive power/alienative involvement, remunerative power/calculative involvement. While this is a useful typology, it is limited, as has already been noted, by a Systems perspective which allows Etzioni to suggest that the strain towards congruence exists because congruent types are more effective, but which provides him with no means of explaining how organisations become incongruent in the first place. Again, different participants may bring varying orientations to the organisation and, as a consequence, perceive the authorities to be using different forms of power. In this case, a congruence between involvement and organisational form (as observed by an outsider) need not develop and different members of the organisation may maintain different attachments to it.

This would suggest that even where power is apparently of a remunerative type (e.g. an economic organisation), lower-level participants need not be instrumentally involved. This, of course, was the argument of the Human Relations school. It does not follow, however, that because a model of Economic Man is unrealistic, all or even most men either have or, as human relationists would argue, are *capable* of having, a moral attachment to an economic organisation. Nevertheless, it is necessary to explain how organisations such as Gouldner's gypsum mine are able to attain a high measure of involvement by their workers even when they offer relatively low material rewards.

In an attempt to find an answer to this problem, Ingham (1967) has noted that low rewards and smallness of scale are frequently associated with a low degree of bureaucratisation. This, in turn, tends to be related to greater possibilities of job rotation and the encouragement of more diffuse skills, more informal interaction, more 'personalised' authority relationships and, as a consequence, less dependence of promotion opportunities upon universalistic criteria. Ingham does not argue, however, that situations of this nature are necessary for the satisfaction of the social needs which, according to the human relationists, are the major motivating force of men at work. Instead, he suggests that the appeal of an organisation of this nature will depend upon the varying orientations of different actors. The orientations of workers towards their job take three ideal-typical forms: '*instrumental*', where material rewards are the sole basis for involvement in work; '*instrumental-expressive-negative*', where, in addition, the worker seeks to exercise control over his work situation and to organise in order to challenge managerial prerogatives; and '*instrumental-expressive-positive*', where work is expected to be satisfying and to offer opportunities for close contacts with people in positions of authority. These orientations may be termed, respectively, 'Economic Man', 'Marxian Man' and 'Hawthorne Man'. Only in the final case will the worker be attached to a low-reward, non-bureaucratised organisation. This is illustrated in Figure 8.1 below:

	Organisational Form	
	Bureaucratised High Remuneration	Non-Bureaucratised Low Remuneration
Orientations of the Worker		
'Economic Man'	+	−
'Hawthorne Man'	−	+
'Marxian Man'	±	−

Figure 8.1: Orientations of the Worker, Organisational Form and Attachment of the Worker to the Organisation

Two important points need to be made about Ingham's typology. First, the orientations that he distinguishes do not represent personality types but depict the various meanings that work is given in different communities, and at different stages of the life-cycle of a worker. Secondly, a congruence between worker-expectations and organisational form is not thought to be 'necessary' and, indeed, in the case of Marxian Man is unlikely to occur at all. To the extent that there is a strain towards congruence, this stems not from the needs of the system but from a self-selection of differently-motivated workers into the types of organisation they perceive as likely to be satisfying. Explanations of the involvement of members of organisations must, therefore, pay attention to the ends that they pursue and the manner in which they define different situations.

In much the same way as Ingham's arguments take us out-side the work situation, so Goldthorpe's (1966) analysis of the attachment of car assembly-line workers to their employing organisation stresses the importance of understanding how they define their situation in the wider society. In explaining the instrumental orientation which they have towards their work, Goldthorpe rejects as positivist the view that this can be seen as a mere function of the technology with which they are involved (cf. Walker and Guest, 1952; Blauner, 1964). Instead, one ought to begin with the factors which influence the ordering of wants and expectations relative to work. The meaning that people attach to their job may thus arise in the non-work roles that they play. If one's primary orientation is the desire for material rewards, it is possible. to be only instrumentally engaged in work and yet to be highly satisfied and favourable to the employer, as long as the rewards are maintained.

Goldthorpe's arguments fit very neatly with Dubin's (1958) earlier study of industrial workers' worlds which pointed out that almost three-quarters of them do not see work as a central life interest. If, as Dubin suggests, nine out of ten such workers prefer primary interactions elsewhere than on the job, then studies of involvement must pay a great deal of attention to non-work factors. Particularly important, in this respect, may be the influence of the worker's image of his society. This has been the concern, among others, of Bott (1964), Lockwood (1966), Popitz (1957) and Hopper (1965).

Bott distinguishes between two views of society which are embodied in 'Power' and 'Prestige' Models. According to the Power Model, society is composed of two conflicting groups with opposed interests and with very little mobility between them. This being so an oppressed group must organise in order to maximise its bargaining potential and any gains that its members make must be generally collective gains—gains by individuals being the result of luck or 'influence' rather than ability. According to the Prestige Model, society is best represented as a ladder. There is very little difference between adjacent rungs which are separated by minute increases (or decreases) in status, and the ladder may be climbed by individuals with ability who are prepared to make the effort. To take collective action would, however, be to admit an individual's limitations and, therefore, to accept a loss in status.

Neither of Bott's models is, of course, a true or false picture of any society. The point is that each will be meaningful to different types of actors who use them to make sense of the social world in which they live. Bott argues that the dichotomous view of society embodied in the Power Model will typically be used by manual workers. In this, she is supported by Popitz (1957), who suggests that industrial workers as a whole distinguish between those who are at the bottom of society (us) and those at the top (them). However, Popitz suggests, there are internal variations within this worldview. Thus society may be seen as an Ordered System which necessarily is evolving towards (or has achieved) social harmony; as an Insurmountable Dichotomy which no action on the part of the group at the bottom can affect and, finally, as a Class System which may be overturned by collective effort.

Popitz goes on to argue that there are two sub-variants of each of these ideologies. The ordered system may be seen as Static (Type 1), that is already harmonic and requiring each man to keep to his station in life, or Progressive (Type 2), that is moving in the favour of the workingman because of the efforts of his trade unions. Society as an insurmountable dichotomy may be a Collective Fate (Type 3) which is not questioned, or may be the perception of certain clear-sighted individuals who none the less respond to their situation with feelings of Individual Resignation (Type 4). Finally, the class system may be seen as susceptible to Democratic Action (Type 5) or only to Revolution (Type 6).[3]

Unlike both Popitz and Bott, Lockwood (1966) suggests that a dichotomous or what he calls a 'proletarian' worldview is by no means typical of all manual workers. It tends to arise in isolated working-class communities whose members are engaged in large-scale enterprises which offer them little contact with management. In predominantly middle-class or rural communities, on the other hand, a 'deferential' ideology which stresses an hierarchical view of society may emerge. Despite their differences, however, both worldviews are traditional in the sense that they develop usually among workers engaged in declining industries and living in relatively isolated communities. A 'privatised' worldview, which is associated with a pecuniary model of society, differs from both these in that those who adhere to it tend not to be conscious of the claims of group membership and separate people by the amount of money they earn rather than by their position in the class or status structure of society. Both their place of residence (very often a new housing estate) and their frequent experience of geographical mobility are related to their instrumental attitude to work and little desire to participate in workgroups.

These different images of society are clearly important in structuring the attachment of people to organisations, for they influence the meanings which men put on their own actions and the actions of others. One illustration of the relationship between worldview and organisational behaviour is to be found in an exploratory paper by Hopper (1965) on the response of workers to different supervisory styles.

Hopper points out that we should expect no direct relationship between our observation of the behaviour of the supervisor and the response of the worker. The orientations which both bring to the organisation, and hence the way in which they define their situation, are the crucial factors in any explanation of their behaviour. In particular, Hopper suggests, the worker's satisfaction with the authority system of the organisation as a whole and with his own position in it will shape his response to the actions of superiors. The 'traditionalist' worker is satisfied with the nature of the hierarchy and his place in it, the 'ritualist' is happy with his own position but not the system. The middle-class 'individualist', on the other hand, supports the system but wants to change his position in it, and the 'instrumentalist' is satisfied with neither. Hopper then goes on to argue that the individualist and the ritualist, unlike the traditionalist and the instrumentally-involved worker, will both reject close supervision—the individualist because he defines himself as a potentially high-status member of the organisation, the ritualist because he is committed to his present role and feels that he needs no encouragement to carry it out.

The insights that may be generated by taking full account of the images of society held by members of organisations applies equally well to higher-level as to lower-level participants. In this respect it is possible to draw not only on Bendix (1956) and his analysis of managerial ideologies but on the growing literature on the varying commitments of professionals to their employing organisations. Thus typologies of involvement in a profession have been developed to measure the degree of commitment of an individual professional to his colleague group or his employing organisation. For instance, there is the cosmopolitan/local distinction used by Merton (1957) and Gouldner (1957) and the public/private/instrumental trichotomy used by Box and Cotgrove (1966). The professional's orientations have been related to the nature of his socialisation by the professional association as well as to the character of the organisation in which he works.

This is not to say that the attachment of people to an organisation is given for all time by the initial orientations which they bring from their experience of the social world. The involvement of the actors is also clearly influenced by their experience of the organisation itself, in particular the way in which it may invalidate prior expectations and generate new ones. Thus Dalton (1959) has shown how cliques develop in management not only because of the varying orientations which people bring to their employment but also because of the differing positions which they occupy in the social structure of the organisation. On the one hand, differences in age, ability and expectations cause people to view their work in a different light and to vary in the extent to which they identify with the existing role-system. On the other hand, the division of labour, with the consequent isolation of personnel into departments, creates different conceptions of interest, with members of each department attempting to magnify the importance of their tasks and to minimise those of others. This is emphasised, as Burns and Stalker (1961) have also shown, when changes in technology or markets, with the consequent introduction of new methods or personnel, make the organisation either more or less satisfactory from the points of view of its members.

Change by itself does not, therefore, provoke an unfavourable reaction: as Scott et al. (1956) have argued, resistance to change is not inherent in Man; what is important is the meaning which different groups attach to this change. Touraine (1965) has suggested that past experiences of change tend to solidify an ideological position towards future changes: the 'Pessimistic' position is opposed to change because it is feared that it will destroy existing occupational values (e.g. craftsmen); the 'Utilitarian' attitude judges change according to its perceived immediate economic consequences, while the

'Collective Bargaining' attitude looks for benefits in economic *and* other respects; finally, the 'Voluntaristic' position recognises the potentialities of change for the interests of workers and actively seeks to encourage it.

Attachments to an organisation thus reflect the meanings which those concerned bring in from the wider society *and* the finite provinces of meaning specific to the organisation. Together these generate different types of involvement which may change during a member's stay. When Goffman (1968) refers to 'the moral career of a mental patient', he is thus describing a process which, while more obvious in total institutions, is true to some extent in all organisations.

The Sociology of Work: The Chicago School

One of the objections to action analysis is that, by playing down the importance of organisational determinants of work orientations (e.g. technology, incentive systems), it appears to imply that *only* factors external to the organisation (e.g. community type, types of experience of social mobility) are important. The approach used by the Cambridge group, which grew out of the studies of the Luton motor workers, seems to be susceptible to this line of attack. A quick reading of their analysis of the Luton material (Goldthorpe, 1966a; Goldthorpe, 1966) could easily lead to the conclusion that the action frame of reference is correctly, and perhaps completely, characterised by an assumption that external factors alone shape orientations to work.*

It is fairer to say, however, that the Cambridge group are only seeking to criticise the conventional wisdom which appears to deny the significance of broader social conditions (external factors), that they do not mean to replace one simplistic assumption with another, and that they recognise the role of the work experience itself (i.e. internal factors) in relation to the worker's orientations and actions. One important objection to this type of analysis, nevertheless, remains. By arguing that work orientations are determined by a combination of internal and external factors, one may miss the way in which people's view of themselves and of their situation is the

* Geoffrey Ingham made this suggestion in a seminar paper.

outcome of an on-going process, i.e. never fully determined by one or another set of structural constraints but always in the act of 'becoming', as successive experiences shape and re-shape a subjective definition of self and of society.

This perspective on men in organisations is most fully developed in the work of the Chicago School of Everett Hughes and Howard S. Becker. Through their own studies of many occupations and professional groups, based largely on the techniques of participant-observation, these writers have encouraged successive generations of graduate students to come to a closer understanding of what it feels like to be involved in a particular kind of role, whether dance-hall musician, medical student or, as in the work of Goffman, mental patient. Their sociology of work has stressed the concept of 'career', the typical series of opportunities and dangers, rewards and disappointments, that confront the new entrant into an occupation. It has further sought to emphasise the subjective experience of various kinds of career-passage, for instance the nature and extent of particular types of commitment to an occupation and/or to an organisation and the characteristic forms of occupational cultures. But always in their works one is encouraged to view subjective experience *in process.**

The work of the Chicago School, unhappily, has not had very much influence on British social scientists. It may prove useful, therefore, to give an example of the material that is currently being produced from within this tradition. Fred Davis (1968) has studied the process whereby student nurses come to exchange their lay view of the profession for that of practising professionals—he calls this a process of 'doctrinal conversion'. His emphasis throughout is on subjective experience of professional socialisation, i.e. 'the feeling states, inner turning points and experiential markings which, from the perspective of the subject, impart a characteristic tone-meaning and quality to his status passage' (p. 237). On this basis, six analytically distinct stages in the process of doctrinal conversion are established. The newly-recruited student nurse is characterised by 'initial innocence'—she views the profession

* The on-going process whereby successive experiences alter one's view of a situation is best expressed in Becker's classic study, *On Becoming a Marijuana User* (*Amer. J. Sociol.*, Vol. 59, 1963, pp. 235–42).

in lay terms, as being generally concerned to 'do good'. She is soon likely to recognise that nursing school is not quite what she expected and to articulate and label what it is that troubles her—'labelled recognition of incongruity'. From perceiving a clash over legitimate role-expectations, she moves on by attempting to guess, by observation or by inference, the role-model expressed in the actions and words of teaching staff—Davis calls this, using an American term, 'psyching out'. Once she has learnt the role-model, she tries to act it out while retaining her distance from it—'role-simulation'. The student nurse's doubts about the inauthenticity of her performance become less, however, as her behaviour evokes favourable responses from those around her. 'Internalisation' of the profession's norms is still only 'provisional' at this stage, as some doubts linger on. 'Stable internalisation' has occurred when the nurse fully identifies with professional rhetoric and with the sincerity of her own performance. She can now look back on her 'immature' impressions of the profession, as reinterpreted from her present standpoint.*

The Strategies of the Actors

The attachment or involvement of an actor indicates the nature of his perception and acceptance of the predominant set of social expectations within an organisation. When this subjective definition of the situation is expressed in action, one may speak of tactics and strategy. An actor may be said to use a strategy when he *regularly* acts in accordance with one established view of what is likely to produce a response from other actors which is favourable to several of his valued ends; a tactic refers to a particular course of action which may be pursued in only one situation and is designed to attain a single limited end.

This does not imply that actors are wholly rational in the sense of continuously weighing the relative effectiveness of

---

* A study of the professional socialisation of teachers, which, together with other members of the Department of Sociology, I am at the moment conducting at Goldsmiths' College, is making use of Davis's model of 'doctrinal conversion'—although it seems clear that the socialisation of teachers and nurses differs in important aspects.

different means and the attainability of various ends. Tactics and strategies which are once perceived to be successful may continue to be used even when they no longer deliver the goods or are even harmful to the desired ends of action. Such ritualistic behaviour is not uncommon in social life. Even when men do pay attention to alternative courses of action they are never fully rational. Their rationality is bounded, as Simon (1959) has noted, by their incomplete knowledge of the resources and dispositions of other actors and by a tendency in many cultures to settle for an alternative that is good enough but not necessarily best (i.e. in Simon's terms, Man satisfices not maximises). They are further limited by a series of assumptions—the world taken-for-granted—which they do not frequently question.

From the point of view of the actor, his action is always a response to the acts or expected acts of others; in turn, for other actors, this action defines the situation to which they must respond. It will prove useful, however, to distinguish strategies which are primarily *defensive* in nature since they are used to resist perceived threats to an existing situation, from those which are *aggressive* in the sense that they involve the initiation of certain courses of action which are designed to change the situation including the relative position of certain actors.

Selznick's (1949) study of the Tennessee Valley Authority provides an important example of the use of a particular kind of defensive strategy by top administrators.[4] Although the TVA, as an experiment in grass-roots administration, was formally committed to take account of local opinion, it had not arisen out of the action or stated purposes of local residents many of whom were unfavourable to change. As a consequence the administrators of the TVA frequently had to engage in what Selznick calls 'self-defensive behaviour', the most important aspect of which was co-optation: the attempt to avert external threats by absorbing the threatening elements into the leadership of the organisation. Formal co-optation occurs when participation is publicly offered to representatives of the general public as a response to widely-voiced questioning of the legitimacy of particular actions or as a means of resolving certain practical and administrative problems. On the other hand, when specific individuals or groups exert a great deal of private pressure which may threaten the position and programme of top administrators, they are often informally co-opted by secretly being offered certain rewards as a means of gaining their future support. As an example of informal co-optation Selznick discusses how the tacit support of local community leaders for an electric power programme was bought by giving them unofficial control of fertiliser policy. This type of co-optation, for obvious reasons, is much more likely to result in an actual sharing of power.

While Selznick's administrators attempted to defend themselves against the unfavourable responses of members of the community to change, the managers that Burns and Stalker (1961) studied were themselves concerned to resist changes which had originated outside the organisation. When laboratory teams were established in several electronics firms at the behest of a government agency, the response of management was often to isolate the newcomers both administratively and geographically from the existing structure.

Existing top management did not really understand the technical nature of the development programme and felt their authority threatened as a result of the influx of the new research teams which they had not even been able to select for themselves. In a bid to maintain their traditional prerogatives they arranged for communications difficulties and limited possible interaction between staff and line.

Burns and Stalker go on to argue that these sorts of defensive strategies are used when existing political and status structures are threatened by change. The political structure is based on the degree of control each actor may exercise over the organisation's resources, the direction of the activities of others, and over patronage (e.g. promotion and other rewards). Closely linked to it is the status structure which is based on the concerns of the actors about the rank they occupy and the prestige attached to their functions. The rewards that people desire, whether power or prestige, derive both from the orientations that they bring to their involvement in the organisation and from the nature of the hierarchy itself, which locates them in different perceived positions and provides them with resources of varying effectiveness. In order to defend these rewards, they make use of the resources available to them and, as Burns and

Stalker show, the possession of relatively rare information is an important strategic counter.

While it might appear that those in positions of authority have more resources to play with, lower-level participants in organisations (e.g. workers, rank-and-file members of voluntary organisations, inmates of institutions), while they lack formal authority, often come to exercise considerable power and influence. Mechanic (1962) has argued that the source of this lies in their frequent access to information, and so to control (over people and resources) which is supposed to be totally in the hands of superiors. Long-serving subordinates accumulate information which superiors passing through an organisation cannot generally possess. Weber (1964) has demonstrated, for instance, how this operates in the relationship between senior civil servants and their political chief, and Gouldner (1954) has shown the inadequate knowledge of a successor to top management about the workings of social relationships in the firm as compared to that possessed by formal subordinates. There are many other examples of this in studies of prison inmates, hospital attendants and non-commissioned officers in the armed forces.

It is impossible for those at the top of the hierarchy, as Galbraith has pointed out, to have full information or to be able to make all (including even the most routine) decisions. They must, therefore, delegate responsibility and, in so doing, relinquish some of their power. Even when they themselves make rules they know, or soon find out, that no rule can cover every possible situation. Thus lower-level participants are able to make strategic use of their ability to interpret and apply rules even though they have not made them. Finally, those in positions of authority are dependent to some extent on the consent and co-operation of people below.[5] As Eisenstadt (1965) has shown in a study of the Israeli reaction to new immigrants, the bureaucrat cannot carry out his task without a measure of co-operation from the citizen. Where the latter is uninformed, the bureaucrat must step outside his formal role in order to encourage compliance with the proper rules of procedure.

The classic case of the use of a defensive strategy by lower-level participants is the restriction of production by industrial workers first discussed by Roethlisberger and Dickson (1939) in their study of the Hawthorne plant. They argued that such behaviour was an outcome of deep yet unreasoned distrust of the intentions of management. The introduction of incentive schemes is perceived by workers as a skilfully planned attack by management upon the security of their workgroup. This view of the motivations of superiors is a myth which is necessary, as Sorel has argued in a different context, to maintain group solidarity. The actions which it occasions thus have psychological functions for the individual and the group, for by restricting production the worker announces his independence from management and his loyalty to the group. An informal code emphasising group solidarity thus develops and sanctions are employed against potential deviants; they are effective because people desire primary group membership much more than immediate economic rewards. Economic explanations of their actions, whether offered by an observer or by the men themselves, are, therefore, inadequate because the fears of the workers about the jobs at Hawthorne were not justified by their experiences or by management's policy. Such explanations must be seen as rationalisations (Pareto would call them 'derivations') by the workers of underlying sentiments (Pareto's 'residues') which are not readily expressed.

The critique of the Hawthorne view of restriction of production raised two types of problem. On the one hand, a re-analysis of the studies themselves by Landsberger (1958) and Carey (1967) has cast a great deal of doubt on whether the data allowed Roethlisberger and Dickson to draw such conclusions (particularly as the men studied were laid off at the end of the experiment), and on the methods by which the data itself was gathered. On the other hand, later material on the behaviour of workgroups suggested that restriction of production ought only to be regarded as non-rational if one assumes that maximisation of their immediate income is the sole aim of all workers. In fact such action may be usefully regarded as a defensive strategy which increases job security, prevents competitive conflicts between workers and, by increasing the unpredictability of their actions to management, enlarges workers' control over their environment. The economic aspects of this argument are supported by Roy (1954) and by Lupton (1963), who, by

analysing the earnings of a 'jobspoiler' and of a group con-
former, demonstrated that the establishment of a norm for
output had an important impact on family budgeting by
increasing the stability of earnings. Lupton, moreover, suggests
that the term 'restriction of production' is itself misleading
since it depends on normative definitions of a fair day's work
which are only objective in the sense that they may be shared
by the participants.

Defensive strategies used by lower-level participants have
also been noted in a study by Blau (1955) of an employment
agency. In the particular case on which Blau concentrates,
management had created a measure of employees' performance
by collating statistical records on the number of clients which
each operative had placed in jobs. The tactic employed by the
participants was initially to maximise their number of job
placements irrespective of the interests of their clients. They
placed applicants in positions which they knew would be
unsatisfactory and went so far as to steal the folders of cases
from off the desks of their colleagues and to threaten (illegally)
their clients with termination of unemployment benefits in
order to improve their own performance. In the long run,
however, this gave way to a collective strategy according to
which the operatives arranged among themselves to give the
impression to those in authority that there was little difference
in their relative effectiveness. Thus co-operation replaced
competition.

It would be misleading to suggest, however, that defensive
strategies are used only for limited ends such as job security,
status or power. Organisations provide an environment not
only for competition over scarce resources but for the generation of images of the self. The set of expectations which are
predominant in an organisation define the basic features of the
character of different actors as well as prescribing their proper
activities: they involve, that is, 'a discipline of being—an
obligation to be of a given character and to dwell in a given
world' (Goffman, 1968, p. 171). Where these expectations are
unacceptable to an individual, his defensive strategy becomes a
protection of his view of himself. Such threats to the self are,
of course, far more common and more dangerous in total
institutions, where the members are unable physically to step

outside the constraints which they experience into a different and more favourable social world.

The most widely used means of adaptation to such a situation is summed up in the concept of 'role-distance': the person continues to meet the formal expectations to which he is subject although he is perhaps conscious of playing a part based on assumptions which he does not accept. This is what Goffman calls his 'primary adjustment'. However, by playing the game in this manner, the member avoids the danger of continual punishments and this opens up the possibility of a secondary adjustment defined as: 'any habitual arrangement by which a member of an organisation employs unauthorised means, or obtains unauthorised ends ... [and thus] stands apart from the role and the self that were taken for granted for him by the institution' (ibid., p. 172). Thus the member learns to make-do and to work the system in his favour, sometimes enjoying so much the act of manipulation that he 'colonises' the institution because he has developed a more satisfactory self-image within it than he has experienced outside. Make-do's thus become important not only for the immediate instrumental benefits which they bring (e.g. better conditions or food) but for their role in the defence of the self.[6]

The discussion so far has centred on defensive strategies which are used as protection against perceived threats to desired rewards. It is interesting that the literature seems to concentrate so much on purely defensive strategies. This may reflect the strategic value to be gained by a group defining its actions (however aggressive in intent) to others as 'what they have been forced to do', because of the 'untimely acts' of certain third parties. This is, no doubt, particularly important in cultures where traditional types of legitimation are significant. Aggressive strategies—concerned with the initiation of certain courses of action designed to change the position of the actor—can be distinguished from these only by the different intentions of the actor associated with each type of strategy. This is important because the same tactic, for instance the withholding of information from others, can have entirely different strategic purposes. It may be intended to resist change or to initiate change, to allow the actor to fit within an existing structure or to overturn the system itself. By paying attention to the 'in-order-to' motives of the participants, it becomes possible to predict the likely response of others: the use, for example, of the doctrine of the Official Secret as a defensive strategy at time of war may be regarded as entirely legitimate behaviour, while its use as part of an aggressive strategy might be strongly resisted by others. In turn, knowledge of the intentions of the actor helps in understanding the manner in which he will perceive the reactions of others to his tactics and whether he will feel obliged to continue his strategy.

Dalton's (1959) study of clique development within management is an interesting example of both defensive and aggressive strategies pursued by relatively stable groups. Dalton distinguishes cliques by whether they include managers of the same rank (horizontal) or of different ranks (vertical). Among vertical cliques are the 'Symbiotic', in which a top manager gives his patronage to a junior in return for information about possible rumblings of discontent among the lower ranks of management, and 'Parasitic', where an individual in a senior position feels constrained to offer support because of family or friendship links with a subordinate. This is parasitic because the nature of the relationship will eventually be discovered and the senior partner's career will be damaged.[7]

Horizontal cliques may be defensive or aggressive in nature. Defensive horizontal cliques develop in response to crises which are experienced as threatening by certain managers of the same rank but in different departments—a good example would be the response of Burns and Stalker's (1961) management to technical innovation. Aggressive horizontal cliques are concerned with a cross-departmental drive to effect rather than to resist change, while 'Random' cliques draw their membership from managers who are not in any of the more functional cliques. The latter are relatively weak, because their members learn few secrets, and are often based expressly on friendship.

The work of Goffman and Dalton illustrates how a 'bounded' rationality governs the actions of members of an organisation. That is, given their definition of the situation, their action may be understood as involving the selection of means in the pursuit of ends. The importance of this approach lies in the limitations it reveals in the view, by no means confined to the early human relationists, that the formal organisation is the embodiment of an external rational purpose, while the action of the participants (especially those in the lower reaches of the organisation) is conditioned by what the Hawthorne researchers termed 'the logic of sentiment'. According to this type of argument 'informal' behaviour is the outcome of the expressive needs of individuals which come into conflict with the impersonality of the formal structure.

What such a view fails to take into account is that the 'formal' system itself is the outcome of past interactions among the actors and of their relative ability to get others to accept (or to have imposed upon them) one particular definition of the situation. There is thus not one rationality (residing in the work organisation or the official goals of the system), but a *multitude* of rationalities each of which generates the 'in-order-to' motives of the participants and allows them to make their own sense of the actions and intentions of others.

Concluding Remarks

This chapter has moved from the types of attachment to the role-system of an organisation held by the participants to the nature of the strategies (both defensive and aggressive) that they use in the pursuit of their ends. In so doing, it has suggested the way in which some of the questions which the Action frame of reference asks have been answered in existing organisational analyses. It is now necessary to move to the macro issue of the pattern of interaction and expected behaviour that arises between the participants.

REFERENCES

1. The terms 'attachment', 'involvement' and 'commitment' are used interchangeably to refer to the extent to which the present or prospective position of a member of an organisation in the dominant role-system is perceived to be satisfactory and the sense(s) in which it is judged. Thus a high instrumental attachment would indicate that the actor judges the organisation to be satisfactory in terms of the material rewards with which he is primarily concerned. Becker (1960) has suggested that commitment is measured by the extent to which an individual feels that

he has obtained 'valuables' during his stay in the organisation that would be lost if he left.

2. Thus Etzioni (1961) observes a 'strain' towards a congruence between the form of power exerted by the authorities and the involvement of the lower-level participants, while Argyris (1964) appears to suggest that men are necessarily motivated by a desire for self-actualisation at work.

3. Popitz found that his sample of German workers split in the following way between the different images of society: Type 1: 10%; Type 2: 25%; Type 3: 25%; Type 4: 10%; Type 5: 2%; Type 6: 1% (20% did not appear to have any image of society, while 7% were unclassifiable). These figures are taken from Alain Touraine, *La Conscience Ouvrière*, Éditions du Seuil, Paris: 1966, p. 182.

4. Within his structural-functionalist frame of reference, Selznick is committed to the view that the organisation itself may be thought to take such action. The cause of action is to be seen in the needs which the observer attributes to social systems. '. . . contemporary and variable behaviour', as he puts it, 'is related to a presumptively stable system of needs and mechanisms. . . . Observable organisational behaviour is deemed explained within this frame of reference when it may be interpreted (and the interpretation confirmed) as a response to specified needs' (1949, p. 252). For a further discussion of Selznick's work see Chapter Three.

5. Mechanic's analysis is somewhat trivial in parts—he hypothesises, for instance, that the 'attractiveness' of an individual is related to his power. He also fails to emphasise the use of predictability as a resource which Crozier (1964) has pointed out —see Chapter Nine.

6. Laing argues that schizophrenia may be seen as a (self-defeating) strategy in defence of the self. R. D. Laing, *The Divided Self*, Penguin, Harmondsworth, 1964.

7. Abegglen (1958) reports the existence of cliques (*batsu*) among Japanese managers which, because they are based on ascribed characteristics, may be of Dalton's parasitic type. Abegglen, however, seems to think that cliques are uniquely Japanese.

9

Patterns of Interaction

THE OVERALL set of expectations and meanings through which the members of organisations are able to act and to interpret the actions of others is a social construct. While they may find it politic to pay lip-service to the intentions of the founder or of past Great Men (especially in attempting to legitimate a course of action which is far removed from those intentions),the present participants continually shape and re-shape the pattern of expectation by means of their actions. For, as they act they validate, deny or create prevailing definitions of the situation. In doing so, they are influenced by the changing stock of knowledge in the wider social world, by their own particular interpretations of the situation, and by the form of their attachment to the existing system. The pattern of interaction that emerges is further shaped by the perceived ability of certain actors to impose a particular definition of the situation upon others, who may feel forced to accept (with varying degrees of enthusiasm) this view of the organisation and of their role in it.

To ask what is the role-system of an organisation is to freeze on-going interaction at one single moment in time. This is particularly important since rules of the organisational game frequently undergo discussion and planned changes. Nevertheless, as in other areas of social life, it is generally possible for an observer to make out a world taken-for-granted which is not frequently questioned by the participants and gives, therefore, a certain stability to their relationships. It is feasible then to ask how the present pattern of interaction has emerged historically and to consider the extent to which it represents the shared values of all or some or none of the contemporary participants. When this has been settled, the sources of stability and the potentialities for change in the existing structure become a little more apparent. This chapter is devoted to studies which, by asking questions of this nature, have illustrated the possibilities of an Action analysis of organisations.

The studies that are discussed in this chapter share a view of social life in organisations as the ongoing product of motivated human action. It is not maintained, however, that their authors have made full use of the potentialities of an action frame of reference or that, indeed, they are committed to the sort of theoretical scheme discussed in Chapter six.

Individualism or Group Action: the Origins of Patterns of Interaction

Tom Lupton's (1963) *On the Shop Floor* is concerned with explaining the conception of its own purposes which a group develops, the means which it uses in an attempt to impose its role-expectations upon others and the factors which influence the relative success of its strategies. In doing so, Lupton gives us a clear picture of the manner in which the realities of organisational life may be socially constructed. His book presents a comparison of the pattern of interaction in a garment workshop and an electrical components factory. In the former an individualistic ethic flourished among the workers, while in the latter a strong sense of group solidarity prevailed. Taking as his initial problem why workers should attempt to restrict production in certain situations but not in others, Lupton sets out to explain why different orientations arise in these two work settings and, more importantly, why management accepted in each case the behaviour that was associated with them.

At the Wye Garment Company, it was very much a case of the workers accepting *management's* definition of the situation. The production plan was based on the expectation that the individual worker would attempt to maximise her earnings. Thus an operative's earnings, within the piecework system, depended on her efforts, while the flow of materials in the production process was planned on the assumption of an adequate response to the monetary incentives that management offered. Lupton found that the workers did respond to incentives, worked at a relatively high speed and accepted management's view of what constituted a fair day's pay. Management was there, in the worker's opinion, to create the conditions which would allow hard work to produce the 'right' wages by rating each job properly and keeping the work flowing through. This view was generally supported by management. Even when it failed to keep to its role-obligations a worker would not take part in collective action to remedy the situation; indeed, Lupton observed no use of the union to enforce claims of any kind. The only controls over production that occurred were 'sweating' (sacrificing quality for speed when the rate was 'tight') and 'dead horse' (booking in dockets for work which was not yet completed: a wage rather than a production control). Yet these were individual practices and not sanctioned by the workgroup.

Since management was clearly prepared to accept this situation, the only problem that needs to be explained is why the workers should behave as they did. Lupton provides two sorts of answers for this, one relating to the structure of this particular enterprise and the other to more general extra-organisational factors. In the first place, the organisation of production made it very difficult for output norms to be developed. Workers were anchored to their separate benches and communications were, therefore, difficult to maintain. They worked in multi-skilled groups and very complicated rules would have had to be developed governing often as many as sixteen people with widely differing earnings. The wages system emphasised individual rewards, and the pre-designed line of work flow meant that each worker provided the next with her materials and thus governed her ability to maximise her earnings. However, while this system created the opportunity for competition and petty jealousies, it is dangerous to explain the absence of what Lupton calls 'the will to control' purely in terms of it. Instead, we must focus on the environmental factors which influenced the orientations of those concerned and explains why they reacted as they did to their organisational roles.

It is important to note, firstly, that the workers were almost entirely women who looked upon work as a means of providing a marginal income for their family and as a place for pleasant social intercourse. With their lack of interest in combining to control the conditions of their employment and with their allegiance to the company (because of their reluctance to leave their friends), they thus provide a very good example of Ingham's 'instrumental-expressive-positive' orientation. Unfortunately, as Cunnison (1966) has noted, Lupton pays relatively little attention to non-work factors and argues, with some justification, that women will tend to accept the prevailing customs of the industry in which they are employed. Thus he prefers an explanation of their individualist orientation in terms of the cyclical nature of the garment trade and of the remaining possibility of setting up one's own workshop with a little capital; both of these encouraged workers to 'look after number one' in all situations.

Jay's Electrical Components also had a piecework system, but here 'the fiddle' was a strongly held group norm and sanctions were exerted against deviants. Each worker was expected to work slowly when a task was being timed by the ratefixer and, when the rate was 'agreed', to put a ceiling on the bonuses he earned by saving time so as to safeguard against rate-cutting. Thus, nearly all workers paced themselves in a similar way, observed the 'unofficial' tea breaks and the customary late starts and early finishes. The 'fiddle' had developed, Lupton suggests, because of the sense of group solidarity encouraged by the systems of production and reward. Work was usually done in pairs with personal freedom to choose the other member and thus, unlike the situation at Wye's, the workgroup corresponded to a friendship group. Moreover, since co-operation in the productive process was limited to each pair and the foreman, no worker was in a position of dependence upon many others and little strain was put on their relations. The wages system encouraged each worker to take an interest in the 'allowed times' for any job since he might be asked to do it himself at some future time. Everybody, therefore, was always prepared to leave work to go to argue with the ratefixer, and group solidarity was strengthened by the consequent spread and exchange of information among workers.

The action of the workers has to be explained by a combination of their orientations to work, which included a desire to exercise a control over their situation (Ingham's instrumental-expressive-negative case), and the set of meanings which had developed within the organisation which put a premium on co-operation. This would not explain, however, why management should accept their definition of the situation.

An answer to this problem is provided by the relatively safe market in which the firm operated. With little price competition in the industry, and with wages a relatively small proportion of total costs, managers were far more concerned to maintain a steady rate of production than to limit the manner in which lower-level participants were working the system. Similarly, those directly concerned with dealing with workers perceived that they had more to gain by seeking a quiet life than by attempting to provide management with correct information and to ensure that work was completed in the quickest possible time. Since management could hardly admit the degree of flexibility in its position, officially discrepant role-obligations were mutually adjusted by a mechanism whereby management blamed production planners and ratefixers, rather than workers, for creating anomalies in workflow and job prices. Workers, in turn, blamed staff rather than line management when their expectations were not wholly satisfied, while the solidarity of each side was strengthened by its ability to blame an outgroup for all grievances.

While Lupton describes very fully the sources of stability in the role-systems of the two organisations, his analysis is somewhat limited by a tendency to concentrate on the character of the organisation itself as a source of orientations. Even when he does examine the environment, he is mainly concerned with its economic rather than its social make-up. Sheila Cunnison (1966) deals far more directly with the way the norms and expectations that people bring to their work impinge on their pattern of interaction within the organisation. It should be pointed out, however, that both Lupton and Cunnison seem to be committed to a rather more traditional view of the nature of sociological explanations than the view outlined here. Lupton, for instance, argues that 'social forces' are both separate from the orientations and purposes of the actors and in practice determine them. 'It seems to me', Lupton writes, '. . . that the most interesting task for the field investigator . . . is to map out what may be described as the field of social forces which operate to produce certain kinds of behaviour' (1963, p. 10). A concentration on the demands of social structures can easily miss the point that, while we are defined by society, we are co-definers of our social situation (cf. Berger, 1966).

In the course of her research on the social organisation of a waterproof garment workshop, Cunnison grew dissatisfied with the usual method of confining analysis of extra-organisational factors to a brief introductory chapter in a research report. The pattern of 'Militant Individualism' which was found could only be explained, she argued, by examining the inter-relatedness of work and non-work roles. 'This was not a system defined by the organised activity of work alone,' she suggests, 'rather it emerged from the congregation of a number of people each occupying a unique cluster of positions in different social systems. The social processes of the work situation were seen as the acting out of these positions' (Cunnison, 1966, p. 268).

While this is slowly changing, working in the garment industry still often implies membership of an occupational community in which managers and certain workers may share the same area of residence, religion and ties of kinship and friendship. Thus the wages system and the organisation of production reflects, and is interpreted in terms of, very complex systems of expectation. Since many-sided issues are nearly always raised in any dispute, workers cannot identify with one another and are always ready with charges of favouritism when one of their number does relatively well, especially when work is short.

Given this situation, grievances tend to be treated as specialised and individual affairs. Another important factor is the tradition of the industry that it is possible to set up small businesses with relatively little capital; this encourages workers to look out for themselves and to accept a definition of each other as potential entrepreneurs. Conflict between management and workers is thus confused, with patterns of authority in work relationships often counter-balanced by a completely different organisation of roles outside work. The individual relationship between a worker and the manager of the workshop becomes, therefore, of crucial importance, and the ability of one to influence the other derives, as often as not, from the statuses which they perceive themselves as holding in the wider community.

Much of Cunnison's argument bears a strong resemblance to Gouldner's discussion of an American gypsum mine (presented in Chapter Three). Here too, the pattern of interaction could not be understood except by locating it in the customs of a local community. Gouldner's work is also important, however, for the way in which it takes up the implications of something Lupton had noted, namely the ability of certain actors to impose their definitions of the situation upon others.

Rule-Compliance as Problematic

Gouldner (1954) pursues his argument in the form of a critique of Weber's theory of bureaucracy. He suggests that, if we are to understand the behaviour of people with reference to rules, it is first necessary to specify the typical ends which they pursue. Rules are not rational in themselves, but merely a means by which certain ends may be attained. Where there is no consensus among the actors, then the relative power of each group will determine the nature of the rule. Therefore consent ought never to be treated as given just because rules exist, for the attachment of the actors to the rules and hence the manner in which they carry them out (if at all) may vary. Gouldner goes on to suggest, somewhat misleadingly, that Weber overlooked the element of coercion in the legitimacy which people are prepared to give to rational-legal authority.[1]

Most important of all, however, is Gouldner's schema of the three bureaucratic forms which arise, in varying mixtures, in organisations and reflect different combinations of coercion and consent. 'Mock' bureaucracy describes rules which are imposed by actors external to the enterprise and which are evaded by the participants because they fail to serve their own ends. The most common reason that they offer is that the rules go against 'human nature'. Where rules serve the ends of most of the participants (although, perhaps, for different reasons), Gouldner speaks about 'Representative' bureaucracy. In this situation it is expected that the rules will be obeyed since everybody gains by compliance. Deviance from representative rules on the part of an individual is thus generally attributed to ignorance or to well-intentioned carelessness. Finally, 'Punishment-centred' bureaucracy is characterised by rules which serve the ends of only one group and are accepted by others only through expedience. Thus there is no moral commitment to such rules except on the part of their originators. These explain rule-evasion in terms of deliberate, wilful intent.

Gouldner gives a 'no-smoking' rule imposed by an insurance company and ignored by most members of the organisation as an example of mock bureaucracy. An instance of representative bureaucracy is the safety rule in the mine which was supported by both management and workers. A seniority system for worker promotion—which was imposed by the men on management—was a case of punishment-centred bureaucracy.

Where one type of bureaucracy or another predominates, Gouldner would suggest that the nature of the interaction of the participants becomes relatively predictable. However, although each type may be stable, this need not (and, in the case of punishment-centred bureaucracy, does not) imply a consensus of values.

The view that interaction within organisations often occurs without any value-consensus among the members but may take a form which is, to a certain extent, imposed by some of the participants, is supported by the organisation theory of Simon (1957), March and Simon (1958), and Cyert and March (1963 and 1964). The stated organisational objectives are seen to arise out of the particular compromise of interests which is tolerable to the different groups; once established, moreover, the goals pursued are not static but change in response to group pressure. 'We have argued', note Cyert and March, 'that most organisations most of the time exist and thrive with considerable latent conflict of goals. Except at the level of non-operational objectives, there is no internal consensus. The procedures for "resolving" such conflict do not reduce all goals to a common dimension or even make them obviously internally consistent' (1963, p. 117).

While this rightly suggests a continual state of flux, patterns of interaction are likely to become stabilised for two reasons. First, a 'controlling group' (Simon) or 'organisational coalition' (Cyert and March) set the conditions of membership, the goals towards which the participants are supposed to orient their behaviour, and the means that may legitimately be used to attain them. Secondly, equilibrium is more or less maintained by an 'inducement-contribution balance'. This idea, which is based on the work of Barnard (1938) suggests that the participants have to be offered inducements (e.g. moral or material rewards) in order to contribute to the organisation. When an individual perceives that his inducement is lower than the contribution which he is asked to make, he will, therefore, no longer participate. Since the contributions of one group are the source of the inducements that are offered to others, organisations survive (or, more precisely, interaction and its legitimating symbols continue in a relatively stable manner) to the extent that the contributions made provide sufficient inducements for the members to wish to continue to participate.

Limitations on the Rationality of Decision-Making Systems

The perspective on organisations which these theorists introduce is, however, consciously different from that used in the other work discussed in this chapter. This is made clear when March and Simon (1958) point out the special view of Man which they seek to employ. Scientific Management, they note, implicitly treats man as a passive instrument acted upon by external forces, while much sociological analysis is concerned with the orientations that men bring to organisations and the power relationships that develop among them. Instead of seeing Man as a 'recalcitrant tool' (cf. Selznick, 1948), their own view is of Man as a decision-maker and problem-solver. This is to be linked with an explicitly social psychological perspective concerned with the factors that impinge upon the individual decision-maker.[2] Thus their work takes up Simon's (1957) notion of Administrative Man and discusses the implication of the way in which he differs from the Economic Man of Classical economics. In particular, Administrative Man accepts the first satisfactory course of action: he 'satisfices' rather than maximises.

It is not a very long step from viewing Man as a decision-maker to viewing organisations as decision-making systems: this is the concern of the later works of Cyert and March (1963 and 1964). They are principally interested in the degree of rationality which decision-making systems can develop. Systems may have substantial elements of rationality in the sense of possessing an ordered set of preferences, the procedures for revealing the available alternative courses of action and the ability to choose between them in terms of the preferences. Rationality is limited, however, by the existence of many preference orders within an organisation, although the vagueness of the general goals pursued by the organisation and its sequential attention to goals (which masks their incompatibility) may permit a 'quasi-resolution of conflict'. There is no continual weighing of ends and means, instead the organisation merely attempts to avoid uncertainty by trying to make its environment more subject to prediction and control: this is called 'uncertainty avoidance'. The problems with which the organisation is immediately concerned, moreover, structure the range of alternatives considered. Just as Simon's administrative man 'satisfices' not maximises, so an organisation does not consider all its problems or weigh all the options: its 'search' for solutions is, therefore, 'problemistic'. Finally, certain areas are avoided or stressed as a result of previous experience. Thus methods which have been successful in the past will tend to be used in the future, instead of considering their present applicability ('organisational learning').

While Cyert and March go on to show how the process outlined here can be readily translated into a computer programme which, when used in simulation studies has approximated the actual decisions of organisations in regard to price, output, and so on, their approach tends to neglect, as Mouzelis (1967) points out, the specifically social characteristics of organisational interaction.[3] By concentrating on organisations as decision-making systems, one may too easily conclude that all that happens within them can be understood purely in terms of this system, and that meanings which derive from outside it are residual or random. This argument is taken up by Burns (1966), who has noted that there is 'a plurality of action systems' open to the actors, who may define their actions by means of their likely consequences for the political and status systems as well as (or instead of) the way in which they affect the work structure. Thus Cyert and March's 'Rationality Model' which implies 'that organisations exist as instruments for the attainment of valued future states, which are construed as goals' (Burns, 1966, p. 171), leaves out much that is of interest to the sociologist.[4]

This takes us back to some of the basic differences between a System and an Action approach. For Simon, March and Cyert are primarily interested in organisations from the point of view of the management of the system. Thus, as Krupp (1961) has noted, they stress the functions of conflict and examine the environment 'only through the mind of the decision-maker' (p. 143), in order to judge how it affects the problems of the organisation. On the other hand, it is possible to take up their insights about the different ways in which men define their situation and the limits on their rationality in order to examine the varied meanings systems and patterns of interaction that develop in organisations. Systems in themselves, therefore, only have problems from the perspective of the participants, and there are as many different problems as there are definitions of the situation and ends. This point is taken up in Scott *et al.*'s (1963) *Coal and Conflict*, which illustrates the process through which the role-system of an organisation is constructed and the varying attachments to it of the different actors.

Types of Conflict: the Maintenance of a Pattern of Interaction

The specialisation of modern industrial organisations, Scott *et al.* argue, has favoured the development of separate outlooks and perceived interests among different occupational categories such as managers, clerks and manual workers. However, within each of these categories may exist separate definitions of the situation deriving from experiences at work (e.g. immediate economic rewards, working conditions and security of employment) and in the local community (e.g. leisure patterns, family responsibilities and status which is accorded to the actor). Consciousness of these different situations can be reinforced by the culture which may develop among small face-to-face groups arising out of physical proximity at work. Because of these varied interests, conflict is to be regarded as typical of industry rather than as an occasional trouble-spot in an otherwise harmonic system. Finally, absenteeism, go-slows, minor disputes and strikes should not be regarded as different in kind, but merely different ways in which the same conflict manifests itself.

As they present their findings, it becomes clear how an analysis in terms merely of strikes would have given a misleading impression of the nature of interaction in the organisations studied.[5] Instead, taking the generalised end of all groups as the maximisation of rewards, they show how different actors have used, and have felt able to use, widely varied means in attempting to achieve their ends. Organised Conflict is used to refer to action which requires group solidarity, and is expressed in the use of established negotiating procedures or, where these fail to have the desired result, by strike action or other collective sanctions. The use of the official conciliation machinery which existed at the mines studied was not, therefore, an alternative to strike action: groups which went through official channels were also the most likely to use collective sanctions. Unorganised Conflict refers to individual means of expressing grievances, such as poor timekeeping, absenteeism and, ultimately, moving to another place of work, all of which might go unobserved in the more traditional institutional analyses of industrial relations.

Since Unorganised Conflict is far less likely to attain the actors' ends than Organised Conflict, Scott *et al.* go on to explain why the former occurred. Organised Conflict, they argue, requires a certain sense of group solidarity if it is to be carried through successfully. The rewards and status of groups at the bottom of the occupational and community status hierarchy are insufficient to generate the high morale necessary to make this possible. The low bargaining power of these groups also means that they will feel that the use of the official machinery or the threat of strike action will be unlikely to succeed. The result is a vicious circle in which the existing distribution of rewards and morale is continually reinforced by the relative success or failure of the strategies which different actors feel that they are able to use (see Figure 9.1 below).

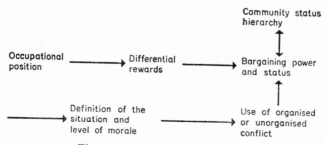

Figure 9.1: Scott's Vicious Circle

The importance of *Coal and Conflict* is twofold. First, it suggests the range of actions which actors can use to attain their ends—from the instrumental rationality of organised conflict to the affectivity of unorganised conflict. Secondly, it shows how the pattern of expectations that is built up by their interaction may favour certain participants far more than others. Nevertheless, the system that arose at the mines, while certain actors experienced it as more constraining than others, was not separate from and external to those who participated in it. It relied on certain definitions of the situation being maintained; if it were once to become clear that these were no longer valid (for instance, if a relatively unfavoured group managed to organise and to attain its ends) then the existing pattern could easily be toppled.

The Struggle for Powers of Discretion: Crozier's 'Neo-Rationalism'

The 'neo-rationalist method' which Michel Crozier uses in *The Bureaucratic Phenomenon* to explain the nature of social relationships in a clerical agency and a tobacco factory comes closest to expressing the view of organisations which has been suggested here and, in so doing, gives a relatively full picture of the strategies used by the actors and the rules of the game by means of which they interact.

If one accepts that the participants may bring different ends to their involvement in an organisation and come to define the situation in rather different ways, then the strategies which they use to protect their perceived interests become of great importance. In this respect, Crozier (1964) shows how each group attempts to preserve and enlarge its areas of discretion, in order to limit its dependence upon others, by making its behaviour more unpredictable. Thus the dependence of the production workers upon the maintenance workers in the tobacco monopoly was manipulated by the latter, who knew very well that only they could repair broken machines and thus prevent the production workers from losing money.

The use of such a conscious strategy is also suggested by Crozier's re-analysis of the source of the ritualistic rule-following of the bureaucrat. While Merton (1949) had suggested that a special type of training engendered a 'bureaucratic personality', Crozier argues that an emphasis on keeping to the letter of the law may be strategy which the bureaucrat uses to protect himself, for instance, against having to get dangerously involved in particular cases.[6] Equally, it is possible to maintain that foremen who avoid enforcing certain rules and workers who 'restrict' production are unconsciously acting to reduce the impersonality of their situation. But a far more convincing explanation is that they find that such actions serve to make their future behaviour more unpredictable and thus enlarge the area of their discretion.[7]

The ability to predict depends not only on the extent of the evasive action taken by others but also on the amount of information which is held about them: the use of information as a strategic resource comes out very clearly in Crozier's analysis of the clerical agency. The agency has a highly bureaucratised structure with a well-defined hierarchy and works in what appears to be a very impersonal manner. The amount of work going through the organisation at any time determines what its employees have to do and promotion depends on seniority rather than observed performance. What might appear on a wall-chart as a smooth system of communication and authority is, Crozier notes, the scene for a power struggle between the Head of a Division, his Section Chiefs and the supervisors below them. This is because the Head, without any staff experts to advise him, depends on the information provided for him by the Section Chiefs. However, each of these are running parallel, identical units and have to compete for scarce resources. Thus they tend to view each other as competitors and to bias the information they pass on in order to maximise the resources and personal favours which they can obtain. At the same time, the supervisors, since successful performance does not lead to promotion, are concerned (as in Lupton's electronics firm) only with having good relations with their workers and are uninterested in performing services or providing information for members of staff senior to themselves. The Division Head is then condemned to get only unreliable information and a multiplier effect occurs as he bases future decisions on false premises.

It is important to remember, however, the limitations of a purely strategic model. In the first place, many of the relationships that Crozier examines grew, as he himself argues, from the prevailing values of participants in the French bureaucratic system, which, in turn, reflected the stock of knowledge that characterises French society. Thus the actors' definition of the situation shaped the actions that they took and their interpretations of the actions of others. Their behaviour cannot be understood simply as the outcome of a rational weighing of ends and means for, within a different fabric of meanings, altogether different actions might have arisen. Secondly, the common symbols of legitimacy which these values produced were strengthened by a shared belief that the rival groups must not attempt to destroy each other, for ultimately they had to live together. Thirdly, a certain stability in group relations, which depended upon the actors sometimes foregoing the most effective means, was desired by all. The participants thus interacted within the limits of the rules of the game. This did not imply, however, that they all were equally attached to these rules or that they regarded them as given and not subject to change.

Interaction as a Game

In social life, as Crozier points out, people use strategies to attain their ends and are able to interact with one another because of common expectations of the likely behaviour of different actors. Even when they pursue purely sectional interests, they often feel constrained to pay lip-service to symbols which legitimate their behaviour as being in the general interest, while if they overstep the rules of expected behaviour, any gains that they make may be removed from them or regarded as illegitimate by others. It is hardly surprising, therefore, that the analogy between social interaction and a game should be highly suggestive. In order to illustrate its usefulness, we can look briefly at Norton Long's approach to community relations and Walton and McKersie's *Behavioural Theory of Labour Negotiations*. Long (1958) suggests that the local community may be viewed as an 'ecology of games'. A number of actors play several games which are concerned with different rewards, for instance status or power. While they tend to concentrate on one single game, the strategies which they develop seek to make use of the resources held by players of other games: thus a banker may seek to co-opt a newspaperman in order to help his own performance in a power game. At the same time, Long argues that the participants work within a set of shared expectations and a consensus about the prestige that should be given to different status-positions: all players play the social game and see it as the highest-level game of all.

Long's view, that conscious rationality is far more character-istic of the parts (the actors) than the whole (the community), is taken up by Walton and McKersie (1965), who view be-haviour as: 'a set of instrumental acts which can be more or less intelligently conceived and more or less expertly executed' (p. 2). They go on to examine the various strategies which are used in labour negotiations and to relate these to the ends pursued by the actors. Four types of collective bargaining relationship, they suggest, are associated with the ends and strategies available to different groups. 'Distributive' bargain-ing over the distribution of available resources arises where the ends of the parties are in conflict in a zero-sum game situation where a gain for one group is necessarily a loss for another; 'Integrative' bargaining occurs where both sides perceive that they may benefit from their interaction and thus should work together; 'Inter-organisational' bargaining is the attempt by members of one group to achieve unanimity within their own camp; while 'Attitudinal Structuring' arises when the tactic of the parties is to influence favourably the perceptions of them held by the other. Each involves a different sort of game with its own rules and standards of expected behaviour.

As applied to organisations, one can see distinct advantages in the game analogy. People do not usually seek to destroy their opponents but merely to gain certain symbolic advantages as in a game. They may often appear to agree about the nature of desirable rewards and the means that may legitimately be used to attain them. Much of their behaviour, too, may seem to the observer to have a ritualistic element, in that it follows certain repeated patterns which are not questioned by the participants.

There remain, nevertheless, important differences between games and social interaction. In the first place, as Shubik (1964) has pointed out, a game has a clear terminating date, while in the social world as a whole this is uncertain. Moreover, games have a fixed number of players and the participants are unusually well supplied with information; at the very least, they have a clear idea about those areas in which their knowledge is relatively good and those in which it is relatively bad or even absent. Further, as Cohen (1968) notes, in games the past interaction of the parties need not affect their subsequent performance (they both go back, as it were, to the centre of the field after one side scores). In social life, however, past victories may establish new situations in which the rules of the game itself become altered.[8]

The acceptance of rules in social life may, therefore, imply something quite different to the acceptance of rules in a game. In the former case, there need not be an implicit agreement that the rules should be equally fair to all the actors and, as a consequence, they may have different types of commitment to any existing set of rules. Again, the participants may be involved in interaction for varying reasons and differ, therefore, in how they conceive 'winning' or 'losing'. Finally, their strategies may be designed to overturn the rules of the game rather than to obtain a larger slice of the cake (as presently defined) by means of legitimate actions.

Summary and Conclusions

The theme that has underlain this discussion is that of the social world in a continuous process of definition and re-definition through the motivated interaction of men. In particular the following aspects of this interaction have been stressed:

1. The nature of the attachment by the actors to any existing norms is shaped by the orientations that they bring to the situation (especially taken-for-granted worldviews) and by their subsequent experience of the situation itself. The actor's definition of his condition is therefore an *emergent* characteristic which is continually reshaped by his experiences.

2. When this subjective view is expressed in action one may speak of the use of tactics or strategy. By so doing, we catch the purposive nature of social action. Most strategies seem to be defensive but this may be because action that is defined

as aggressive may not be acceptable in cultures where tradition and 'playing the game' are still quite important.

3. When subjective views become institutionalised, one may speak of the emergence of rules of the game towards which actors orient themselves. Which views become institutionalised depends upon several factors including:

   (a) The already existing world-taken-for-granted of the participants.

   (b) The ends they pursue and the degree of attachment to the existing pattern that this implies.

   (c) The strategies they perceive to be available to them and the resources they can call upon to attain their ends.

   (d) The actions in which they engage and their ability to convince others of the legitimacy of these acts.

4. Compliance with any institutionalised pattern is always problematic. The problem of legitimacy continually recurs and cannot be escaped; apparently stable definitions of situations are always threatened, sometimes by 'heroes, prophets or saviours', but more frequently by meanings which emerge in the course of everyday interaction.

5. Neither a purely strategic model (where the participants are prepared, if necessary, to destroy one another) nor the model of a game fully catch the complexity of social life. Men in organisations (as elsewhere) are both defined by, and define, social reality; social interaction is a process whose course is pre-defined yet one through which new definitions of reality emerge.

Taken with the previous chapter, the studies discussed here illustrate the contention that the action frame of reference is capable of grappling with the content of social life in organisations by means of its emphasis on the meaningful nature of human interaction. The final chapter of this study will take up some of the implications of the approach for research and methodology.

REFERENCES

1. Weber notes about rational-legal authority: 'This legality may be treated as legitimate in *either* of *two* ways: on the one hand, it may derive from a voluntary agreement of the interested parties

on the relevant terms. On the other hand, it may be *imposed* on the basis of what is held to be a legitimate authority over the relevant persons and a corresponding claim to their obedience' (Weber, 1964, p. 130, my italics).

2. 'Taking the viewpoint of the social psychologist,' March and Simon write, 'we are interested in what influences impinge upon the individual human being from the environment and how he responds to these influences' (1958, p. 2).

3. Mouzelis notes about this approach that: '. . . although the organisation is treated as a system, the specifically social aspects of the system are more or less neglected. It is only the aspects common to all sorts of self-controlled systems (thermostats, human bodies and what not) which are emphasised' (1967, p. 141).

4. For instance, Cyert and March's suggestion that decisions, especially those concerned with price, investment etc., are 'the primary output of organisations' (1964, p. 289), takes up a limited view which would not necessarily be acceptable to sociologists. I might equally argue that the primary output of organisations is the generation, confirmation or repudiation of images of the self. Neither view is, of course, the right one; each reveals a different sort of interest brought to bear on the analysis.

5. Up to the time of writing, there has been no *official* strike in the coal industry since nationalisation, shortly after the end of the Second World War. In my view, the relative lack of significance of official strike statistics (or, perhaps, the multiplicity of significances) casts grave doubts on attempts to use them to build complex social theories—see Kerr and Siegel (1954).

6. In a similar way, Weber (1964) has noted the bureaucrat's manipulation of the official secret in order to conceal his activities from unwelcome scrutiny.

7. Both the enforcement and the non-enforcement of rules may be meaningful tactical ploys in differently defined situations.

8. 'A team that scores a goal must agree to permit the other side to try to do the same *from a position of equal strength.* . . . But in war, if one side wins a battle it pursues its enemy from a position of strength; in collective bargaining, if workers succeed in winning some concession from managers they use this to strengthen their future bargaining position. Games, tournaments and ritual contests may resemble other conflict situations in *certain* respects; but they cannot be treated as models in which most forms of social conflict are simulated' (Cohen, 1968, p. 148 fn).

10

Conclusions

FROM THE point of view presented here, the study of organisations ought not to be regarded as an end in itself. While the substantive examples used to illustrate some of the possibilities of an Action approach have been drawn from analyses of organisations, the aim throughout has been to raise some of the central issues of sociological theory. Even if one is not primarily committed to Grand Theory or even to Sociology, some consideration of wider theoretical issues is inescapable if one is to present a coherent analysis of organisations. Indeed, the difficulty that there is in distinguishing formal or complex organisations from other types of social structure suggests the close link that exists between theories of organisations and theories of society. In this concluding chapter, it is proposed to clarify the nature of the contribution that it is hoped this work will make to a particular theoretical debate and to discuss some of the methodological problems associated with the application of an Action frame of reference to the study of organisations.

With the development of Sociology, certain writers became primarily concerned with setting against each other rival models of the 'dominant' features of social structures, maintaining that either consensus or coercion is more 'natural', or more to be expected. As it was realised that these models could not tackle one of these problems without suggesting an explanation of the other, less interest began to be shown in making *a priori* substantive judgments of this nature and more attention was paid to evaluating ways of perceiving social relationships which made fewer assumptions about their necessary content. One perspective—Structural-Functionalist, Transcendental (Horton 1964), Holistic (Cohen, 1968), or Systems—emphasised explanations of behaviour in terms of the interaction of systems attempting to satisfy their needs, and often made use of an organic analogy to explain the nature of the relationships between system-parts. The other—namely Action, Immanent or Atomistic—argued that attention should first be paid to the orientations of the participants who might be differentially attached to any aspect of social life and who themselves create, sustain and change the rules of the social game.

A large proportion of organisational analysis has been concerned to look for explanations in terms of the impersonal mechanisms through which Systems secure their stability. Beginning from the problems which threaten the security of organisations, and primarily concerned with the relative efficiency of certain processes and structures, it has used an implicitly Functionalist perspective. The emphasis on System problems in five leading schools of organisational analysis—namely Human Relations, Organisational Psychology, Socio-Technical Systems, Structural-Functionalism and Decision-Making Theory—is outlined in Figure 10.1 facing.

None of the approaches depicted in Figure 10.1—except Structural-Functionalism—derive from a sociological frame of reference. Thus Human Relations owes most to psychology, while Socio-Technical Systems mixes psychology with economics and Decision-Making Theory economics with cybernetics. Like the Action approach (and, indeed, Functionalism as well), none of these schools can offer a general theory of organisations. This is hardly a defect since it is difficult to imagine a theory of organisations which could be anything more than partial. Each perspective can contribute its own set of questions and its own method of answering them, and it is not expected that its conclusions will necessarily be interesting to those who are concerned with altogether different problems and who adopt an entirely different view of organisations. It is completely legitimate, for instance, for the chemist's view of a chair to differ from that of the philosopher or, indeed, from that of the man who is about to sit on it; it would be foolish to suggest that any view is better than any other or that each person ought necessarily to be interested in the conclusions of the others.

From a sociological perspective, a notable limitation of much organisational analysis is the lack of interest which has been shown, despite a commitment to an Open System in much of the work concerned, in the impingement of role-expectations arising in extra-organisational statuses upon the definition and performance of organisational roles. While Sociology begins by drawing attention to the multiple social statuses which are

Approach	Major Conceptual Tool	Orientation to Environment
Human Relations (Roethlisberger and Dickson, Mayo)	'Social Man' committed to his workgroup.	Organisations usually considered in a vacuum.
Organisational Psychology (Argyris, Likert)	A hierarchy of personality of needs. 'Self-actualisation' an important motivating factor.	Organisations as Open Systems—importation of personalities.
Socio-Technical Systems (Trist, Rice, Emery)	The impact of technology and market demands upon organisational form.	Open System—relation of environment to implementation of primary task of the organisation.
Structural-Functionalism (Selznick, Parsons)	The dynamic equilibrium of Systems which adjust to threats to their survival.	Open System—environment as a source of problems and of resources.
Decision-Making Theory (Cyert, March)	The language of a computer programme.	Open System—environment limits rationality of decision-making.

Choice of Major Problem	Approach
The satisfaction of the workgroup in order to attain managerial goals.	Human Relations
The degree of compatibility between the needs of the personality and of the system.	Organisational Psychology
The efficient performance of a primary task in relation to the demands of technology, the environment and the members.	Socio-Technical Systems
The nature of the interdependence of social systems.	Structural-Functionalism
The nature of the decision-making process in relation to the stability and growth of organisations.	Decision-Making Theory

Figure 10.1: Some Leading Approaches to the Study of Organisation

maintained by any one person, many organisation theorists have been satisfied to relate behaviour solely to organisational factors; although men are not viewed entirely as a black sheet, the only framework for analysis that has been used systematically is an assumed set of personality needs which are thought to mediate between structure and behaviour.[1] There has thus been a tendency, especially in Organisational Psychology and Socio-Technical Systems, to view certain work situations as inherently alienating and to explain away apparent job satis-faction as an incorrect reflection of Man's real needs and potentialities. Unfortunately, the subjective meanings of situations have also been missed by many sociologists, including those who make a great deal of the contribution that the study of organisations can make to the advancement of Sociology as a whole. Blau and Scott (1963), for instance, suggest that organisational analysis holds '. . . great promise for advancing systematic knowledge about the organisation of social life' (p. 14), but on the same page imply that the different reactions of workers to supervisory behaviour can be explained by the structural characteristics of the organisation.[2]

The paradox that arises in a commitment to a particular discipline coupled with an apparent failure to make use of its insights can be resolved when the contribution that many organisational analysts want to make to Sociology is stated a little more clearly. One might have imagined that an argument for the potentiality of the study of organisations would be supported by a consideration of the theoretical issues that it might be in a position to treat. Instead, the case that is made (as in Blau and Scott, 1963) is merely that, because of their clearly delineated formal structures, organisations are 'less complicated' to study than other aspects of society, and this essential methodological argument is taken to provide the theoretical significance of the field.[3]

This failure to come to grips with theoretical issues is due to the practice of carrying out organisational analysis within a theoretical framework which is assumed to have been already settled, rather than trying to use it to contribute to the evaluation of various perspectives none of which, at the present time at least, ought to be taken for granted.

Even the claimed major attraction of the study of organis-ations (their simplicity), only exists if generalisations which derive from 'objective' variables (i.e. solely from the observer's view of the characteristics of an organisation) are believed to be meaningful. Yet to consider organisations in this way ignores the nature of social life and excludes the very problems which provide the distinctive concerns of Sociology, i.e. the manner in which the social-world is socially constructed and sustained. If some organisational analysis does not, therefore, make the contribution to the advancement of Sociology that its mentors would wish, then this derives in large measure from their apparent lack of concern with the limitations of the orientations that constitute their analytical world-taken-for-granted, and from their inability to define, let alone to examine, the wider theoretical issues that the study of organisations might raise.

The Role of a Social Action Framework

While some of the more sophisticated functionalists are aware of the dangers of the organic analogy, many organisation theorists have had few qualms about considering the 'goals' of enterprises and observing the functions certain factors perform for these. In doing so, they have emphasised the unintended and impersonal nature of the processes through which organisations maintain themselves and adapt to their environment. This often implies a reification of organisations, in the sense that they are conceived as things which are separate from the definitions and purposes of their members, and creates difficulties when one attempts to assess the health, survival or maintenance of social as opposed to biological systems. It has also tended to direct attention to the consequences rather than causes of phenomena, while to the extent that it considers origins, its explanations tend to be teleological (i.e. by implying that the causes of a phenomenon are to be found in its consequences).

Both Nadel (1963) and Emmet (1958) have traced this tendency in sociological analysis. Nadel notes Leach's and Levi-Strauss's view of social structure as a model or explanatory construct developed in order to understand the patterning of social relations. As such it does not influence behaviour or have purposes. 'Yet', Nadel goes on, 'this logical distinction is often ignored. We find descriptions of social structure in wholly "realistic" terms as when Firth calls it "a reliable guide to action" . . . or when other scholars talk about a social structure "maintaining itself", exercising "pressure", or "resisting" the impact of change' (1963, p. 148). Similarly, Emmet argues the differences between the natural and social worlds. 'The anatomy of a society cannot be dissected in a way which is really comparable to the anatomy of a body', she points out. 'Moreover, the members of a society . . . have ideas and purposes of their own' (1958, p. 96), and this complicates the matter considerably.

The moral that each author draws from these arguments is rather different, although it perhaps reflects the differing aspects of the problem with which they are concerned. Nadel, while accepting the critique of reification, defines social structure, against Levi-Strauss, as 'the social reality itself, or an aspect of it, not the logic behind it' (1963, p. 150), while Emmet is exercised to suggest an alternative to a Functionalist frame of reference. 'We need', she maintains, 'to consider a social activity not only in functional terms, asking: "What does this activity effect . . . in some system?" . . . but also in purposive terms, asking: "What are these people trying to do?" ' (1958, p. 107). She recognises that what ultimately happens may not be what was originally intended, but argues that this, by itself, does not detract from the insights which such an approach can supply, providing that one uses 'purpose' to refer to consciously intended actions relating to specific ends. For, 'to try to estimate someone's intention, to ask "what is he at?", may be useful in predicting what he is likely to do' (p. 112).

The importance, which Emmet suggests, of coming to grips with the orientations of the actors has also been stressed in a critical commentary by Poggi (1965) on the current state of sociological analysis. Contemporary work, he argues, has been predominantly concerned with the way in which a System fits together and, in particular, the functions of the parts for the whole. He calls this an *intra-unit* problem. At the same time, the *extra-unit* problem of the relationship of one System to another and of the motivations which govern their interaction has received very little attention. As a consequence, the prevailing sociological theory is 'a theory of the *maintenance* of social systems and not of their *action*' (1965, p. 290). This reflects a learned incapacity for treating extra-unit problems which has resulted in a failure to ask questions concerning, 'the direction and content of social action . . .' (p. 284).

Now it might be argued against Poggi that it is misleading to suggest that analysis has only gone in one direction: 'to say that a room is half-full', as Cohen has put it, 'is not to deny that it is half-empty' (1968, p. 170). Again, Parsons in particular might claim that, by its concern with the services which each System plays for another, his theory has set about integrating intra- and extra-unit problems in the context of an input–output model.

While Poggi accepts that some attempts have been made to deal with extra-unit problems, he argues that this has often involved a form of reductionism which concentrates on the needs of Systems rather than the intended contents of social inter-action. Thus Parsons, by imputing needs and functions to the parts of the System, has de-emphasised consciously intended actions which are used to attain non-system ends. As such, his theory tends to be mechanistic: 'The outputs with which the theory works', Poggi suggests, 'are not unlike the secretions of glands in the organism; they are *necessary* results of the sub-system's functioning . . . not choices they make in the face of a certain range of action alternatives' (p. 291).

Poggi goes on to show how the intra-unit concerns of Political Sociologists have allowed them to offer an explanation of how a political system maintains itself but not why it is as it is. Even when such theorists do deal with the motivations of the actors, as in studies of voting behaviour, they tend to see them as the expression of deep-seated psychological needs, which sway individuals to support one candidate rather than another, and fail to locate political values in wider subject definitions of the situation. 'For all its accomplishments', he concludes, '[this tradition] has largely failed to give us a sociology of *policy*, to deal systematically and analytically with the *directions of action* actually pursued by its own units of discourse' (p. 287).

If we take seriously what Poggi and Emmet are saying, then it appears that an alternative to the prevailing Systems approach could usefully be developed. The aim of this work, within the context of existing empirical studies of organisations, has been to formulate and to examine the potential uses of such an alternative. Beginning from the subjectively meaningful nature of social life, it has been argued that explanations of social action must arise from the definitions of the situation and purposes of the actors. Organisations have been viewed as role-systems associated with particular types of meaning so that members are usually aware of the stated purpose of the founder, may seek to legitimate their actions by emphasis on this purpose and are concerned to discuss the rules and expectations which shape their behaviour. However, as these rules develop historically, they may come to represent at any one moment in time the values of all or some or, indeed, of none of the present actors. It thus becomes vitally important to understand the varying definitions of the situation held by the actors, the characteristic hierarchy of ends which they bring to the organisation and the nature of their attachment to the dominant role-system. It is then possible to come to grips with the subjective meaning attached to typical actions and to their intended and unintended consequences for the involvements of the actors, for their perceived place within the organisation, and for the stability of the common set of expectations within which they interact.

Seen in this light, social relations within organisations arise out of the interaction of the participants and may exhibit varying levels of consensus and conflict and of co-operation and coercion, according to the nature of the expectations and ends of the actors. Social change, either in the involvement of particular actors or in a prevailing set of expectations, occurs as the outcome of social action in which the members have different symbolic resources at their disposal and call upon a changing stock of knowledge within the wider society. The Action approach thus seeks to tackle both the 'micro' problem of the orientations and behaviour of particular actors and the 'macro' problem of the pattern of relations that is established by their interaction.

METHODOLOGICAL IMPLICATIONS

The Action approach, while it involves some meta-theoretical assumptions (discussed in Chapter Six), can most usefully be seen as a method of analysis rather than a theory. It offers a frame of reference from which can be derived a series of related questions about the nature of social life in any organisation. Only empirical studies can provide the answers to these questions but the material which they accumulate can be referred back to a consistent analytical structure.

All that has been said so far implies that the special role of the sociologist is to understand the subjective logic of social situations. Yet it is a characteristic of social life that individuals themselves interpret their reality. Is there anything to be gained by an observer re-stating these interpretations, especially since his inability, in Laing's terms, to experience the experience of another must involve an element of distortion of the individual's original perceptions?

The answer to this question is that the sociologist is concerned not with re-stating social meanings but with placing them in the context of the logic of an academic discipline. That is to say, he re-interprets the meanings of commonsense in terms of the meanings of Sociology. While normally one reflects very little on the taken-for-granted meanings associated with each act, the sociologist seeks to understand the nature and implications of the commonsense world. While the individual often believes that his actions are entirely unique to him as a person, the sociologist is concerned with interpreting the typical acts of typical individuals by the use of ideal-types which take account of subjective meaning. Sociology is thus specifically devoted to 'unmasking' (to use Berger's term) the assumptions upon which social life is based.

1. The Use of Concepts in Sociology

The concepts that sociologists use in description and explanation must to some extent be different from the terms of everyday language. The latter tend to have a wide range of meanings and, if they were used in academic discourse, might prevent discussion or replication of a particular work simply because colleagues might be troubled over the particular meaning implied by the vocabulary employed. Thus the argument that the jargon that sociologists use is unnecessary, despite its appeal, is rather weak. At the same time, the nature of social life implies that the concepts employed in Sociology should not be applied without taking into account the subjective meanings of those who are being observed. An example may help to make this last point a little clearer.

Let us suppose that prior to his study a sociologist defines 'authoritarian' supervision as behaviour in which the supervisor passes down instructions to subordinates but does not seek to understand their wishes; this may be distinguished from 'democratic' supervision, in which the views of subordinates are sought and decisions may not be taken unless there is some sort of group consensus. One can then try to detect patterns resembling these ideal-types in actual situations, and explanations can be offered in the form of correlations between 'authoritarian' or 'democratic' supervision and such 'objective' factors as type of technology, occupation and social class of those concerned, and length of experience in the organisation. Where few significant correlations are obtained (and this often happens), it is usually suggested that further research, which could take account of more variables, would go a long way towards resolving the problem.

The difficulty with work of this nature lies in the order of variables used rather than in their number. What is missing is any attempt to come to grips with the meaning of the situation to those involved in it. 'Authoritarian' supervision, as defined above, might be perceived by those who employ it or experience it in a different way than by the observer: for instance the supervisor might see it as the only means of enforcing his wishes on a recalcitrant or uninterested workgroup, while the workers might interpret it as an illegitimate attempt to limit their just rights. Or, in a society where traditional authority was predominant, both parties might regard such behaviour as a legitimate exercise of authority and would not think of questioning it. It would merely be the customary act of superiors and would not be interpreted as a strategy to obtain personal ends. On the other hand, 'democratic' supervision might not be a meaningful concept in such a society, while in industrial societies it might, in different contexts, be defined as either a tactic to be distrusted or the normal due of subordinates.

The point here is that where the meaning (and hence possibly the legitimacy) of an action differs, to impose one definition on it, without reference to the actors' views of what is going on, can seriously distort analysis. 'If men define situations as real', W. I. Thomas puts it, 'they are real in their consequences.'[4] Thus a typology of supervisory styles should derive from the various ways in which those concerned define the situation, rather than from the meanings which an observer, often ethnocentrically, sees in *behaviour*.[6] Given that social action is not the same in kind as the behaviour of physical objects, this is the only procedure which legitimately allows one to consider the origins or causes of social phenomena. Moreover, since social interaction has its origins in the meanings which people attach to the actions of others, and to the social and physical context in which these occur, both the dependent *and* independent variables which are used in analysis cannot be separated from their social meanings. Thus before a variable can be said to explain a certain action, it is necessary, as Cicourel (1964) has noted, to understand the rules which have been employed by the participants to 'make sense' of it. Even the most basic variables may not be as 'obvious' as they may seem: Cicourel cites a paper by Bennett Berger which fruitfully views chronological age as a cultural attribute.

To return to the original example, one would seek to construct several ideal-typical sets of meanings attached to the supervisor–supervised relationship. For instance, the empirical evidence might suggest a distinction between situations in which the relationship is perceived to involve the unwelcome (to the supervised) or necessary (to the supervisor) imposition of authority, or the provision of certain limited services which help both parties to obtain instrumental ends, or, finally, the expression of a moral bond which links together the members of an organisation. These differences in definition could then be related to the nature of attachment to the organisation of the participants, the type of authority which they regard as legitimate, and the types of resources, moral and physical, which they perceive to be available to them. When the definitions of a relationship change even where the original physical behaviour patterns remain, the relationship has in a very real sense changed. Gouldner gives a good example of this in the case of the gypsum mine.

When one moves to the 'macro' issues involved in a comparison of patterns of relationship in different organisations, the urgency of referring to the subjective meaning of interaction as well as to its objective consequences becomes even greater. To say, for instance, that what happens in contemporary

American prisons can be understood by their 'integrative' function for society (Scott, 1959) may not be very fruitful; to imply that this produces similarities with the social life of prisons in other societies or at different historical periods, is simply misleading.[6]

2. *The Measurement of Meanings*

If Sociology derives its data from the meanings which men attach to social life, it is by no means obvious how these meanings can be ascertained. Meanings are complex, as Karpik (1968) has noted in relation to work satisfaction,[7] and usually difficult for the actors to verbalise since they are often unconsciously adhered to. 'In the great majority of cases', points out Weber, the apostle of subjective meanings, 'actual action goes on in a state of inarticulate half-consciousness or actual unconsciousness of its subjective meaning' (1964, p. 111).

The problems involved in the empirical study of meanings, and a possible means of resolving them, have been most clearly stated in a recent work by Cicourel (1964). Cicourel agrees that the typifications and shared stock of knowledge through which social interaction proceeds are difficult to determine. They are the unstated conditions of social life and are rarely paid much attention to or questioned by those who use them, including the sociologist in his participation in the social world. It is thus easy, Cicourel argues, for the observer to assume that his subjects employ the same basic meaning-structures as his own. Therefore research instruments are constructed which take as non-problematic the way in which the respondents will perceive, say, job satisfaction (Turner and Lawrence, 1965) or promotion opportunities (Silverman, 1968). However, this is to make the assumption of 'a world taken for granted by both subject and experimenter' (Cicourel, 1964, p. 167) which may be far from the empirical reality. Moreover, such an approach directs attention away from the issues created by the character of social life. It is inappropriate and often misleading to look for relationships between variables defined in terms of the sociologist's world-taken-for-granted.[8]

Cicourel calls such an approach to research design 'measurement by fiat' because it imposes the observer's definitions on to a situation. It assumes a common culture in the standardised questions which it offers to respondents and in the assignment of importance to the answers. It may be more significant that a respondent has never thought about, say, the advantages of worker participation than that the forced response he gives to a question from a middle-class interviewer is of a particular nature. It may tell more about the meanings that black Americans use to interpret the political situation that the majority of them do not vote in presidential elections than that those who do tend to vote Democrat rather than Republican.[9] Yet all too frequently, studies seek to force respondents into categories which bear no relation to the subjective meanings of those concerned but, 'are deemed worthwhile because . . . [they] will scale or will provide for a test of significance' (Cicourel, p. 5).

While these factors do not rule out the use of questionnaires or interview schedules as research instruments, they do imply that they must 'be constructed in such a way that the structure of everyday life experience and conduct is reflected in them' (p. 120). In other words, they must be concerned with problems which are meaningful to the respondents and must use questions which are framed in terms which reflect their (but not necessarily the observer's) everyday meanings. All this is necessary in order to be sure that in constructing the questions the researcher does not completely determine the answers that he will get. For, as Cicourel puts it, 'We must be able to demonstrate a correspondence between the structure of social action (cultural meanings, etc.) . . . and the items intended as operational definitions thereof' (ibid.).

The most satisfactory way of measuring meaning, Cicourel suggests, is the laboratory study. These have been out of favour with many sociologists because they have tended to be used to demonstrate that people are shaped by psychological forces which compel them to act in a certain way. What is defined by the researcher as an encouraging statement or gesture is assumed to be perceived by the subjects in the same way and a response to the stimulus can, therefore, be predicted. However, it is nevertheless possible to treat the orientations and definitions of the situation held by the actors as important variables in themselves and to use laboratory conditions as a means of establishing their nature. Following Garfinkel (1967), Cicourel argues that the study of games may be particularly fruitful because the actors' expectations and routine definitions of the situation may be taken as given. When the researcher acts in a deviant manner, as when he fails to keep to the rules of a game, the subjects' world-taken-for-granted (or at least certain aspects of it) can be readily revealed.[10]

While Cicourel's general argument is convincing, it is not necessary to accept his view that the way ahead should be largely through laboratory studies. His arguments in favour of these mainly stem from the inadequacies of the other methods used in the social sciences. Yet, as he recognises, laboratory studies also have in-built deficiencies, notably the impact on the subjects' involvement in their roles of their knowledge that they are committed for only a relatively short period of time to the laboratory situation. It may well be possible, on the other hand, to reformulate the more traditional research instruments in order to come to terms, far more directly than in the past, with the expectations and purposes of the actors.

Some of the means by which this may be done Cicourel himself suggests. It is also useful, however, to note some of the techniques employed in the more worthwhile studies of organisations, the substantive content of which has been discussed in earlier chapters.

Dalton (1959), Goffman (1968) and Cunnison (1966) have used participant observation to great effect. By moving in and out of different situations and maintaining a series of contacts within the organisation, in their roles, respectively, of factory worker and officer concerned with the recreation of the inmates, Dalton and Goffman were able to demonstrate the nature of cliques in the social organisation and the patterns of adaptation to the dominant system of roles. Cunnison, by concentrating on the behaviour of garment workers when work was in short supply, was able to point out more clearly their ends and conceptions of legitimate actions. The parties, she found, were far more explicit about their social assumptions at times of great stress.[11]

Even interviewing may be useful, providing that the researcher retains no illusion about the necessary identity of a series of interview situations, since each interview, for the most trivial reasons, may be interpreted differently, even by respondents who share similar social assumptions, and the responses obtained may thereby risk being influenced by extraneous variables. Gouldner (1954), for instance, is able to come close to establishing the social expectations of his gypsum workers by exploring the complaints that they make in an interview about the behaviour or methods of superiors or subordinates. Another example is Crozier's (1964) report of the interesting insights that may be gained by confronting one group with the views expressed about them by other organisational members. Finally, Dahrendorf's (1968) suggestion that interviews can usefully be used as 'experiments in definition', in which the 'can' expectations which those concerned attribute to a social role are brought out, is clearly in line with the view of methodology (and of Sociology) which Cicourel implies.

It would be foolish to conclude this discussion with the implication that any one research method is inherently more satisfactory than any other. Questionnaires, interviews, participant-observation and laboratory studies all have their strength and limitations. Mills probably had something when he adopted as his slogan: 'Every man his own methodologist' (Mills, 1959). The fruitfulness of any method is structured by the degree of sophistication with which it is handled and its appropriateness to the task at hand.[12]

3. *The Relationship between Theory and Research*

Methods of social research provide ways of linking the development of theory to knowledge of the characteristics of the social world. The precise relationship between theory and research is, however, a matter of dispute among sociologists.

Glaser and Strauss (1968) offer a view of the research process which complements the analysis of organisations suggested in this book. They argue that the potentialities of research have been limited by a concentration on the testing and verification of theories. This fails to recognise the way in which research may be used to *generate* theory. Put very simply, their argument is that the *a priori* assumptions about the objective characteristics of social situations which are often made at any early stage of the research process (in the form of hypotheses and operational definitions) serve to mask important features of social reality. Research must instead be used to generate 'grounded' theories which, rather than forcing data into a preconceived 'objective' reality, would seek to mobilise, as an explanatory tool, the categories which the participants themselves use to order their experience. Two types of theory would emerge from such a step: first, 'grounded substantive theory' which would seek to explain the nature of social relations in one particular setting; secondly, 'grounded formal theory' which, based on a study of many settings, would seek to generalise about the recurrent characteristics of an aspect of social life.

Glaser and Strauss use their own research data to illustrate their approach. Involvement in the social life of a hospital revealed to them that the management of death was an important problem to the staff. From this knowledge, they generated a substantive theory to explain awareness of dying in a hospital context. A formal theory, on the other hand, would need to compare the various contexts in which death occurs. In much the same way, following the suggestions made in this book, one could move from substantive to formal theories of attachments, strategies and rules of the social game by ever broadening the scope of the study.

Concluding Remarks

I have tried to argue that there is a great deal of material in existing studies of organisations which can be mobilised to make a substantial contribution to Sociology; there is also a profusion of work which is not really relevant for sociological interpretations. My aim in adding one more voice to the prevailing din has been to suggest the elements of an analytic scheme into which much that is worthwhile may be fitted and which, more importantly, may prepare the way for an attack on the many substantive issues that remain. It is one thing to end, after a survey of the literature, with a demand for a more strictly sociological treatment of organisational behaviour; it is quite another to attempt to show how this could be carried out. In the emphasis of this work on the similarities of social processes (whether in 'formal' organisations or not), and through its presentation of a coherent theoretical framework, it is hoped to have gone some way towards doing just that.

REFERENCES

1. It is true that functionalists do offer an explanation of the orientations of organisational members in terms of an assumed 'central value system' of a society. However, this fails to pay proper attention to the way in which different experiences may create finite provinces of meaning which crucially affect interaction.

2. The full statement is as follows: 'Many factors beside supervisory practices affect the productivity of work groups. By selecting for study a large number of work groups, however, all recruited in the same way, engaged in similar tasks, using similar equipment, subject to the same rules, and working for the same rewards, the most important of these factors were probably held constant. Holding them constant made it possible to attribute the observed differences in productivity to contrasting patterns of supervision' (Blau and Scott, 1964, p. 14). No account appears to be taken in this list of the meanings which the participants attach to these variables and to the superior-subordinate relationship itself.

3. It is only fair to add that Blau and Scott go on to note that the formal structure by no means determines everything that happens in the organisation. Nevertheless, while they talk of the 'theoretical significance' of the study of organisations (e.g. p. 15), they give no hint of the theoretical issues that it might resolve.

4. Quoted by Schutz (1964), p. 348.

5. This is not to say that the observer cannot select certain aspects of these meanings upon which to concentrate in terms of the theoretical issue that he is most concerned to resolve. However, it is implied that these meanings provide him with his basic data.

6. Again it is possible that the meanings attached to cliques in Japanese management are altogether different from the way in which they are perceived in the West (compare Abegglen, 1958, with Burns and Stalker, 1961). In this case, too, it may be necessary to avoid a commonsense imposition of a category upon them.

7. See Chapter Three for a discussion of Karpik's arguments.

8. Thus, instead of assuming that familiar meanings will be used by the participants, unless there is evidence to the contrary, it is necessary for the observer to begin always by clarifying the social assumptions which underlie the action with which he is concerned. Hence Cicourel 'prefers to leave as problematic the ways in which social action is structured by the actors' stock of

knowledge, the kind of strategies they entertain . . . and the imputations or meanings they assign to objects and events in the social scene' (1964, p. 162).

9. *The Floating Voter and The Floating Vote*, a critical survey of voting studies by H. Daudt (1961), has come to this particular conclusion.

10. Garfinkel's view is expressed in the following two statements: 'Procedurally it is my preference to start with familiar scenes and ask what can be done to make trouble' (1967, p. 37); 'to produce disorganised interaction should tell us something about how the structures of everyday activities are ordinarily and routinely produced and maintained' (ibid., p. 38). The psychologist Osgood has also suggested a way in which meaning can be measured: the 'semantic differential'. Subjects are asked to give their impression of the meaning of words by indicating for several pairs of antonyms which description best fits the word in question.

11. The danger in proceeding in this way is that interactions at times of stress may not be typical. On the other hand, when all the parties are heavily committed to protecting their interests, their expectations and ends may become clearer. There are, of course, further difficulties with participant-observation. The researcher must decide the ethical and practical issue of whether it is appropriate for him to identify his true purposes (Goffman and Dalton do not provide such information, while Lupton (1963), for instance, does). Again, while the observer needs intimates within the organisation, those that are most ready to talk may be unrepresentative of all the membership groups.

12. Considerations of space have made this discussion of methodology rather more sketchy than I would have liked. For a fuller examination of these issues see my forthcoming paper: 'Methodology and the Problem of Meaning'.

Bibliography*

ABEGGLEN, JAMES C. (1958), *The Japanese Factory*, Glencoe, Ill.: Free Press.

ARENSBERG, CONRAD M. (1957), *Research in Industrial Human Relations: A Critical Appraisal*, New York: Harper.

ARGYRIS, CHRIS (1964), *Integrating the Individual and the Organisation*, New York: Wiley.

BAKKE, E. WIGHT (1966), *Bonds of Organisation: An Appraisal of Corporate Human Relations*, Hamden, Connecticut: Archon.

BANKS, J. (1964), 'The Structure of Industrial Enterprise in Industrial Society', *Sociol. R.* Mono., No. 8.

BARNARD, CHESTER I. (1938), *The Functions of the Executive*, Cambridge, Mass.: Harvard.

BATES, FREDERICK L. (1960), 'Institutions, Organisations and Communities', *Pacific Sociol. R.*, 3, No. 2, pp. 59–70.

BECKER, HOWARD S. (1960), 'Notes on the Concept of Commitment', *Amer. J. Sociol.*, 36, pp. 32–5.

BENDIX, REINHARD (1956), *Work and Authority in Industry*, New York: Wiley.

BENDIX, REINHARD (1959), 'Industrialisation, Ideologies and Social Structure', *Amer. Sociol. R.*, 24, No. 5, pp. 613–23.

BENNIS, WARREN G. (1966), *Changing Organisations, Essays on the Development and Evolution of Human Organisation*, New York: McGraw-Hill.

BERGER, PETER L. (1966), *Invitation to Sociology*, Harmondsworth: Penguin. (New York: Doubleday-Anchor, 1963.)

BERGER, PETER L. and LUCKMANN, THOMAS (1966), *The Social Construction of Reality: A Treatise in the Sociology of Knowledge*, New York: Doubleday.

BERGER, PETER L. and PULLBERG, STANLEY (1966), 'Reification and the Sociological Critique of Consciousness', *New Left Review*, 35, No. 1, pp. 56–71.

* Throughout this bibliography reference is made to the most recent available source of a paper rather than to its original place of publication.

233

BIDDLE, BRUCE J. (1964), 'Roles, Goals and Value Structures in Organisations', in W. W. Cooper *et al.* (eds.), *New Perspectives in Organisation Research*, New York: Wiley, pp. 150–72.

BLACK, MAX (ed.) (1961), *The Social Theories of Talcott Parsons*, New Jersey: Prentice-Hall.

BLAU, PETER M. (1955), *The Dynamics of Bureaucracy*, Chicago: University of Chicago Press.

BLAU, PETER M. and SCOTT, W. RICHARD (1963), *Formal Organisations: A Comparative Approach*, London: Routledge & Kegan Paul.

BLAUNER, ROBERT (1964), *Alienation and Freedom: The Factory Worker and His Industry*, Chicago: University of Chicago Press.

BLUMER, HERBERT (1962), a paper in Arnold M. Rose (ed.), *Human Behaviour and Social Processes*, op. cit., pp. 179–92.

BOTT, ELIZABETH (1964), *Family and Social Network*, London: Tavistock.

BOX, STEPHEN and COTGROVE (1966), 'Scientific Identity, Occupational Selection and Role Strain', *Brit. J. Sociol.*, 17, No. 1, pp. 20–8.

BREDEMEIER, HARRY C. (1955), 'The Methodology of Functionalism', *Amer. Sociol. R.*, 20, pp. 242–9.

BROOM, L. and SELZNICK, P. (1964), *Sociology*, New York: Harper & Row.

BROWN, J. A. C. (1964), *The Social Psychology of Industry*, Harmondsworth: Penguin.

BROWN, R. K. (1967), 'Research and Consultancy in Industrial Enterprises', *Sociology*, 1, pp. 33–60.

BURNS, TOM (1961), 'Micropolitics: Mechanisms of Institutional Change', *Admin. Sci. Q.*, 6, No. 3, pp. 257–81.

BURNS, TOM (1966), 'On the Plurality of Social Systems', in J. R. Lawrence (ed.), *Operational Research and The Social Sciences*, Oxford: Pergamon, pp. 165–77.

BURNS, TOM (1967), 'The Comparative Study of Organisations', Victor Vroom (ed.), *Methods of Organisational Research*, Pittsburg: University of Pittsburgh Press, pp. 118–70.

BURNS, TOM and STALKER, G. M. (1961), *The Management of Innovation*, London: Tavistock.

CAREY, A. (1967), 'The Hawthorne Studies: A Radical Criticism', *Amer. Sociol. R.*, 32, pp. 403–16.

CHINOY, ELY (1955), *Automobile Workers and the American Dream*, New York: Doubleday.

CICOUREL, AARON V. (1964), *Method and Measurement in Sociology*, New York: Free Press.

CLARK, PETER B. and WILSON, JAMES Q. (1961), 'Incentive Systems: A Theory of Organisations', *Admin. Sci. Q.*, 6, No. 2, pp. 129–66.

Coch, L. and French, J. R. P. (1952), 'Overcoming Resistance to Change', in C. E. Swanson et al., Readings in Social Psychology, New York: Holt.

Cohen, Percy S. (1968), Modern Social Theory, New York: Basic Books.

Coser, Lewis A. (1965), The Functions of Social Conflict, London: Routledge & Kegan Paul.

Crozier, Michel (1964), The Bureaucratic Phenomenon, Chicago: University of Chicago Press.

Cunnison, Sheila (1966), Wages and Work Allocation, London: Tavistock.

Cyert, R. M. and March, J. G. (1963), A Behavioural Theory of the Firm, New York: Wiley.

Cyert, R. M. and March, J. G. (1964), 'The Behavioural Theory of the Firm: A Behavioural–Science–Economics Amalgam', in W. W. Cooper et al. (eds.), op. cit., pp. 289–304.

Dahrendorf, Ralf (1958), 'Out of Utopia: Towards a Reorientation of Sociological Analysis', Amer. J. Sociol., 64, pp. 115–27.

Dahrendorf, Ralf (1968), Essays on the Theory of Society, London: Routledge & Kegan Paul.

Dalton, Melville (1959), Men Who Manage, New York: Wiley.

Daudt, H., The Floating Voter and the Floating Vote, Leyden, 1961.

Davis, F. (1968), Professional Socialisation as Subjective Experience, in H. S. Becker (ed.), Institutions and the Person, Chicago: Aldine.

Davis, Kingsley (1959), 'The Myth of Functional Analysis as a Special Method in Sociology and Anthropology', Amer. Social. R., 24, pp. 757–73.

Dawe, Alan (1969), book review, Sociology, 3, No. 1, pp. 115–17.

Demerath, N. J. and Peterson, Richard A. (eds.) (1967), System, Change and Conflict, New York: Free Press.

Dore, Ronald P. (1961), 'Function and Cause', Amer. Sociol. R., 26, pp. 843–53.

Dubin, Robert (1958), The World of Work, Englewood Cliffs, N.J.: Prentice-Hall.

Duncan, Hugh Dalziel (1968), Symbols in Society, New York: Oxford University Press.

Eisenstadt, S. N. (1965), Essays on Comparative Institutions, New York: Wiley.

Emery, F. E. and Trist, E. L. (1965), 'The Causal Texture of Organisational Environments', Human Relations, 18, pp. 21–32.

Emmet, Dorothy (1958), Function, Purpose and Powers, London: Macmillan.

Etzioni, Amitai (1960), 'Two Approaches to Organisational Analysis: A Critique and a Suggestion', Admin. Sci. Q., 5, pp. 257–78.

ETZIONI, AMITAI (1961a), *A Comparative Analysis of Complex Organisations*, New York: Free Press.

ETZIONI, AMITAI (ed.) (1961b), *Complex Organisations: A Sociological Reader*, New York: Holt.

FIRTH, RAYMOND (1964), *Essays on Social Organisation and Values*, London: University of London.

GARFINKEL, HAROLD (1967), *Studies in Ethnomethodology*, London: Prentice-Hall.

GLASER, BARNEY G. and STRAUSS, ANSELM L. (1968), *The Discovery of Grounded Theory*, London: Weidenfeld & Nicolson.

GOFFMAN, ERVING (1959), *The Presentation of Self in Everyday Life*, New York: Doubleday.

GOFFMAN, ERVING (1968), *Asylums*, Harmondsworth: Penguin.

GOLDTHORPE, JOHN H. (1964), 'Social Stratification in Industrial Society', *Sociol. R.* Mono., No. 8.

GOLDTHORPE, JOHN H. (1966a), 'Attitudes and Behaviour of Car-Assembly Workers: A Deviant Case and a Theoretical Critique', *Brit. J. Sociol.*, 17, pp. 227–44.

GOLDTHORPE, JOHN H. (1966b), *Factory Social Structures*, unpublished paper.

GOLDTHORPE, JOHN H. (1967), 'Reactionary Sociology', *New Statesman*, 15 September 1967.

GOULDNER, ALVIN W. (1954), *Patterns of Industrial Bureaucracy*, Glencoe, Ill.: Free Press.

GOULDNER, ALVIN W. (1957), 'Cosmopolitans and Locals', *Admin. Sci. Q.*, 2, pp. 281–306 and 444–80.

GOULDNER, ALVIN W. (1959), 'Organisational Analysis', in Robert K. Merton (ed.), *Sociology Today*, New York: Basic Books.

GOULDNER, ALVIN W. (1965), *Wildcat Strike*, New York: Harper.

GOULDNER, ALVIN W. (1967), 'Reciprocity and Autonomy in Functional Theory', in Demerath and Peterson (1967), op. cit.

GROSS, EDWARD (1969), 'The Definition of Organisational Goals', *Brit. J. Sociol.*, 20, pp. 277–94.

HAGE, JERALD (1965), 'An Axiomatic Theory of Organisations', *Admin. Sci. Q.*, 10, No. 3, pp. 289–320.

HAIRE, MAISON (ed.) (1959), *Modern Organisation Theory*, New York: Wiley.

HAWORTH, LAWRENCE (1959), 'Do Organisations Act?', *Ethics*, 70, pp. 59–63.

HEMPEL, CARL G. (1959), 'The Logic of Functional Analysis', in L. Gross (ed.), *Symposium on Sociological Theory*, New York: Harper & Row.

HICKSON, D. J. (1966), 'A Convergence in Organisation Theory', *Admin. Sci. Q.*, 11, pp. 224–37.

HOMANS, GEORGE C. (1950), *The Human Group*, New York: Harcourt Brace.

HOMANS, GEORGE C. (1954), 'Industrial Harmony as a Goal', in Arthur Kornhauser *et al.* (eds.) (1954), op. cit.

HOPPER, EARL (1965), 'Some Effects of Supervisory Style', *Brit. J. Sociol.*, 16, pp. 189–205.

HORTON, JOHN (1964), 'Alienation and Anomie', *Brit. J. Sociol.*, 15, pp. 283–300.

HUGHES, EVERETT C. (1958), *Men and Their Work*, Glencoe, Ill.: Free Press.

INGHAM, G. (1967), 'Organisational Size, Orientation to Work and Industrial Behaviour', *Sociology*, 1, pp. 239–58.

KAHN, ROBERT L. and GOULDING, ELISE (eds.) (1964), *Power and Conflict in Organisations*, London: Tavistock.

KARPIK, LUCIEN (1968), 'Expectations and Satisfaction in Work', *Human Relations*, 21, No. 4.

KATZ, D. and KAHN, R. (1966), *The Social Psychology of Organisations*, New York: Wiley.

KERR, CLARK *et al.* (1962), *Industrialism and Industrial Man*, London: Heinemann. (Cambridge: Harvard University Press, 1960.)

KERR, C. and SIEGEL, A. (1954), 'The Inter-Industry Propensity to Strike', in Kornhauser, A. (ed.), *Industrial Conflict*, New York: McGraw-Hill.

KRUPP, SHERMAN (1961), *Pattern in Organisation Analysis: A Critical Examination*, Philadelphia: Chilton.

KUHN, THOMAS S. (1962), *The Structure of Scientific Revolutions*, Chicago: University of Chicago.

LAING, RONALD D. (1967), *The Politics of Experience*, New York: Pantheon.

LANDSBERGER, H. (1958), *Hawthorne Revisited*, New York: Cornell University Press.

LANDSBERGER, H. (1961), 'Parsons Theory of Organisations', in Black (ed.) (1961), op. cit., pp. 214–49.

LAWRENCE, PAUL R. and LORSCH, JAY W. (1967), *Organisation and Environment: Managing Differentiation and Integration*, Boston: Harvard.

LIKERT, RENSIS (1959), 'A Motivational Approach to a Modified Theory of Organisation and Management', in Haire (ed.) (1959), op. cit., pp. 184–219.

LIKERT, RENSIS (1961), *New Patterns of Management*, New York: McGraw-Hill.

LIPSET, SEYMOUR M. (1960), *Political Man*, (New York: Doubleday-Anchor.)

LOCKWOOD, DAVID (1958), *The Blackcoated Worker*, London: Allen & Unwin.

LOCKWOOD, DAVID (1964), 'Social Integration and System Integration', in George K. Zollschan and Walter Hirsch (eds.), *Explorations in Social Change* (1964), London: Routledge.

LOCKWOOD, DAVID (1966), 'Sources of Variation in Working Class Worldview', *Sociol. R.*, 14, pp. 249–67.

LONG, NORTON E. (1958), 'The Local Community as an Ecology o Games', *Amer. J. Sociol.*, 64, No. 3, pp. 251–61.

LUPTON, TOM (1963), *On the Shop Floor*, Oxford: Pergamon.

McCARTHY, W. E. J. (1967), *The Role of Shop Stewards in British Industrial Relations* (Research Paper No. 1: Royal Commission on Trade Unions), London: H.M.S.O.

McGREGOR, DOUGLAS (1960), *The Human Side of Enterprise*, New York: McGraw-Hill.

McGREGOR, DOUGLAS (1966), *Leadership and Motivation*, Cambridge, Mass.: M.I.T. Press.

MARCH, JAMES G. (ed.) (1965), *Handbook of Organisations*, Chicago: McNally.

MARCH, JAMES G. and SIMON, HERBERT A. (1958), *Organisations*, New York: Wiley.

MASLOW, A. H. (1954), *Motivation and Personality*, New York: Harper.

MAYNTZ, RENATE (1964), 'The Study of Organisations', *Current Sociology*, Vol. 13.

MAYO, ELTON (1945), *The Social Problems of an Industrial Civilisation*, Boston: Harvard.

MECHANIC, D. (1962), 'Sources of Power of Lower Participants in Complex Organisations', *Admin. Sci. Q.*, 7, No. 3, pp. 349–64.

MERTON, ROBERT K. (1949), *Social Theory and Social Structure*, Glencoe, Ill.: Free Press.

MERTON, ROBERT K. (1957), 'The Role-Set: Problems in Sociological Theory', *Brit. J. Sociol.*, 8, pp. 106–20.

MERTON, ROBERT K. (1961), 'The Bureaucratic Personality', in Etzioni (1961b), op. cit.

MICHELS, R. (1949), *Political Parties*, Glencoe, Ill.: Free Press.

MILLER, E. J. and RICE, A. K. (1967), *Systems of Organisation: The Control of Task and Sentient Boundaries*, London: Tavistock.

MILLS, C. WRIGHT (1959), *The Sociological Imagination*, London: Oxford University Press.

MORSE, NANCY (1953), *Satisfaction in the White Collar Job*, University of Michigan.

MOUZELIS, NICOS P. (1967), *Organisation and Bureaucracy*, London: Routledge & Kegan Paul.

NADEL, S. F. (1963), *The Theory of Social Structure*, London: Cohen & West.

PARSONS, TALCOTT (1949), *The Structure of Social Action*, Glencoe, Ill.: Free Press.

PARSONS, TALCOTT (1951), *The Social System*, Glencoe, Ill.: Free Press.

PARSONS, TALCOTT (1961), 'Suggestions for a Sociological Approach to the Theory of Organisations', in Etzioni (1961b), op. cit.

PARSONS, TALCOTT (1964), 'A Sociological Approach to the Theory of Organisations', in his *Structure and Process in Modern Societies*, Glencoe, Ill.: Free Press.

PARSONS, TALCOTT (1965), 'An Outline of the Social System', in Parsons (ed.), *Theories of Society*, New York: Free Press, pp. 30–79.

PARSONS, TALCOTT (1967), 'A Paradigm for the Analysis of Social Systems and Change', in Demerath and Peterson, op. cit., pp. 189–212.

PERROW, CHARLES (1961), 'The Analysis of Goals in Complex Organisations', *Amer. Social. R.*, 26, No. 6, pp. 854–66.

POGGI, GIANFRANCO (1965), 'A Main Theme of Contemporary Sociological Analysis: Its Achievements and Limitations', *Brit. J. Sociol.*, 16, pp. 263–94.

POPITZ, HEINRICH et al. (1957), *Das Gesellschaftsbild des Arbeiters*, Tübingen: Mohr.

PRANDY, K. (1965), *Professional Employees*, London: Faber.

PRICE, JAMES L. (1968), *Organisational Effectiveness: An Inventory of Propositions*, Homewood, Ill.: Irwin.

REEVES, KYNASTON (1967), 'Constrained and Facilitated Behaviour', *Brit. J. Ind. Rels.*, 5, pp. 145–61.

REX, JOHN (1961), *Key Problems of Sociological Theory*, London: Routledge & Kegan Paul.

RICE, A. K. (1963), *The Enterprise and its Environment: A System Theory of Management Organisation*, London: Tavistock.

ROETHLISBERGER, FRITZ J. and DICKSON, WILLIAM J. (1939), *Management and the Worker*, Cambridge, Mass.: Harvard.

ROSE, ARNOLD M. (ed.) (1962), *Human Behavior and Social Processes: An Interactionist Approach*, Boston: Houghton Mifflin.

ROY, DONALD (1954), 'Efficiency and The Fix', *Amer. J. Sociol.*, 60, pp. 255–66.

SAYLES, LEONARD R. (1958), *Behavior of Industrial Work Groups*, New York: Wiley.

SCHEFF, THOMAS (1967), 'Towards a Sociological Model of Consensus', *Amer. Sociol. R.*, 32.

SCHEIN, EDGAR H. (1965), *Organisational Psychology*, Englewood Cliffs, N.J.: Prentice-Hall.

SCHNEIDER, EUGENE V. (1957), *Industrial Sociology*, New York: McGraw-Hill.

Schutz, Alfred (1964), *Collected Papers* (in two volumes, edited by Maurice Natanson), The Hague: Nijhoff.

Scott, Frances Gillespie (1959), 'Action Theory and Research in Social Organisation', *Amer. J. Sociol.*, 64, No. 4, pp. 386-95.

Scott, W. G. (1962), *Human Relations in Management*, Homewood, Ill.: Irwin.

Scott, W. H. *et al.* (1956), *Technical Change and Industrial Relations*, Liverpool: Liverpool University Press.

Scott, W. H. *et al.* (1963), *Coal and Conflict*, Liverpool: Liverpool University Press.

Selznick, Philip (1948), 'Foundations of the Theory of Organisations', *Amer. Sociol. R.*, 13, pp. 25-35.

Selznick, Philip (1949), *TVA and the Grass Roots*, Berkeley: California University Press.

Sheppard, H. L. (1954), 'Approaches to Conflict in American Industrial Sociology', *Brit. J. Sociol.*, 5, pp. 324-41.

Shubik, Martin (1964), 'Experimental Gaming and Some Aspects of Competitive Behavior', in W. W. Cooper *et al.* (eds.), op. cit., pp. 449-63.

Sills, David L. (1958), *The Volunteers*, Glencoe, Ill.: Free Press.

Silverman, David (1968a), 'Formal Organisations or Industrial Sociology: Towards a Social Action Analysis of Organisations', *Sociology*, 2, pp. 221-38.

Silverman, David (1968b), 'Clerical Ideologies: A Research Note', *Brit. J. Sociol.*, 19, pp. 326-33.

Simon, H. A. (1957), *Administrative Behaviour*, New York: Macmillan.

Simon, H. A. (1964), 'On the Concept of Organisational Goals', *Admin. Sci. Q.*, Vol. ix, pp. 1-22.

Stagner, Ross (ed.) (1967), *The Dimensions of Human Conflict*, Detroit: Wayne State University Press.

Stagner, Ross and Rosen, Hjalmar (1965), *The Psychology of Union–Management Relations*, London: Tavistock.

Stevens, Carl M. (1963), *Strategy and Collective Bargaining Negotiation*, New York: McGraw-Hill.

Stinchcombe, Arthur L. (1965), 'Social Structure and Organisations', in March (1965), op. cit., pp. 142-93.

Survey Research Center (1950), *Productivity, Supervision and Morale among Railroad Workers*, Human Relations Series 2, Report 3, Ann Arbor: University of Michigan Press.

Sykes, A. J. M. (1965), 'Some Differences in the Attitudes of Clerical and of Manual Workers', *Sociol. Review*, 13, pp. 297-310.

Taira, Koji (1964), 'The Labour Market in Japanese Development', *Brit. J. Ind. Rels.*, 2.

TANNENBAUM, ARNOLD S. (1966), *Social Psychology of the Work Organisation*, London: Tavistock.

TAYLOR, F. W. (1913), *The Principles of Scientific Management*, New York.

THOMPSON, JAMES D. (1967), *Organisations in Action*, New York: McGraw-Hill.

THOMPSON, JAMES D. and McEWEN, WILLIAM J. (1958), 'Organisational Goals and Environment: Goal-Setting as an Interaction Process', *Amer. Sociol. R.*, 23, No. 1, pp. 23–31.

TOURAINE, ALAIN (1964), 'Pour une Sociologie Actionnaliste', *Europ. J. Sociol.*, 5, No. 1, pp. 1–24.

TOURAINE, ALAIN et al. (1965), *Workers' Attitudes to Technical Change*, Paris: O.E.C.D.

TRIST, E. L. et al. (1963), *Organisational Choice*, London: Tavistock.

TURNER, ARTHUR N. and LAWRENCE, PAUL R. (1965), *Industrial Jobs and the Worker*, Boston: Harvard.

TURNER, H. A. et al. (1967), *Labour Relations in the Motor Industry*, London: Allen & Unwin.

UDY, STANLEY H. (1962), 'Administrative Rationality, Social Setting, and Organisational Development', *Amer. J. Sociol.*, 68, pp. 299–308.

UDY, STANLEY H. (1965), 'The Comparative Analysis of Organisations', in March (1965), op. cit., pp. 678–709.

VAN DEN BERGHE, PIERRE L. (1963), 'Dialectic and Functionalism: Toward a Theoretical Synthesis', *Amer. Sociol. R.*, 28, No. 5, pp. 695–705.

VON BERTALANFFY, LUDWIG (1967), 'General System Theory', in Demerath and Peterson (1967), op. cit., pp. 115–29.

VROOM, VICTOR H. (1964), *Work and Motivation*, New York: Wiley.

WAGNER, HELMUT R. (1964), 'Displacement of Scope: A Problem of the Relationship between Small-Scale and Large-Scale Sociological Theories', *Amer. J. Sociol.*, 69, No. 6, pp. 571–84.

WALKER, CHARLES J. and GUEST, ROBERT H. (1952), *The Man on the Assembly Line*, Cambridge, Mass.: Harvard.

WALTON, RICHARD E. and McKERSIE, ROBERT B. (1965), *A Behavioral Theory of Labor Negotiations: An Analysis of a Social Interaction System*, New York: McGraw-Hill.

WEBER, MAX (1964), *The Theory of Social and Economic Organisation*, New York: Free Press.

WHYTE, WILLIAM F. (1959), 'An Interaction Approach to the Theory of Organisations', in Haire (1959), op. cit., pp. 155–83.

WILENSKY, HAROLD (1957), see ARENSBERG (1957).

WISEMAN, H. (1967), *Political Systems: Some Sociological Approaches*, London: Routledge & Kegan Paul.

WOODWARD, JOAN (1958), *Management and Technology*, London: H.M.S.O.

WOODWARD, JOAN (1965), *Industrial Organisation: Theory and Practice*, London: Oxford University Press.

WRONG, DENNIS (1967), 'The Over-Socialised Conception of Man', in Demerath and Peterson, op. cit.

ZALEZNIK, A. *et al.* (1958), *The Motivation, Productivity and Satisfaction of Workers*, Boston: Harvard.

ZALEZNIK, A. and MOMENT, D. (1964), *The Dynamics of Interpersonal Behavior*, New York: Wiley.

Author Index

Subject Index

The Theory of Organisations

David Silverman

The comparative study of complex organisations (factories, hospitals, schools, and prisons, for instance) has a relatively short history. This book examines the development of organisation theory and reveals its links with two main types of sociological analysis and with the prescriptive concerns of earlier studies of business enterprises.

It shows how the systems model, which begins from the point of view of the organisation itself and goes on to consider its actions in response to system needs, has come to dominate contemporary work. It examines the uses and limitations of systems analysis and goes on to offer as an alternative an action frame of reference which draws on the work of Weber, Schutz, and Peter Berger.

All the main studies of organisations are summarized, but this book is much more than a review of the literature on the subject. Through sociological analysis of a substantive area an important and original argument is offered to the reader. No prescriptions for "efficient" or "happy" organisations are offered, but instead an analysis of what could be made intelligible about organisations as they are.

This is a text for students of sociological theory and industrial sociology. It will be of great value to students contemplating research in organisations or, indeed, for anyone interested in this significant field of contemporary debate amongst sociologists.